To Jon,

The

Radiant Warrior

Path

Peace & Wisdom

Jason Chan
with Jane Rogers, Ph.D.

Order this book online at www.trafford.com/07-1486
or email orders@trafford.com

Most Trafford titles are also available at major online book retailers.

© Copyright 2008 Jason Chan.

All rights reserved. No part of this publication may be reproduced, stored in a retrieval system, or transmitted, in any form or by any means, electronic, mechanical, photocopying, recording, or otherwise, without the written prior permission of the author.

Note for Librarians: A cataloguing record for this book is available from Library and Archives Canada at www.collectionscanada.ca/amicus/index-e.html

Printed in Victoria, BC, Canada.

ISBN: 978-1-4251-3748-9

We at Trafford believe that it is the responsibility of us all, as both individuals and corporations, to make choices that are environmentally and socially sound. You, in turn, are supporting this responsible conduct each time you purchase a Trafford book, or make use of our publishing services. To find out how you are helping, please visit www.trafford.com/responsiblepublishing.html

Our mission is to efficiently provide the world's finest, most comprehensive book publishing service, enabling every author to experience success. To find out how to publish your book, your way, and have it available worldwide, visit us online at www.trafford.com/10510

www.trafford.com

North America & international
toll-free: 1 888 232 4444 (USA & Canada)
phone: 250 383 6864 ♦ fax: 250 383 6804
email: info@trafford.com

The United Kingdom & Europe
phone: +44 (0)1865 722 113 ♦ local rate: 0845 230 9601
facsimile: +44 (0)1865 722 868 ♦ email: info.uk@trafford.com

10 9 8 7 6 5 4 3 2

Contents

Dedication

5   **Jason's Dream** . . . . .

Part I – The Path of Awakening
11   Chapter 1 - What is the Radiant Warrior Path?
23   Chapter 2 - Seven Stages on the Path
38   Chapter 3 - Awakening Through Stillness
57   Chapter 4 - Mastering Your Daily Life

Part II – The Path of Healing
76   Chapter 5 - Healing Your Physical Body
85   Chapter 6 - Transcending Your Disturbed Emotions
106   Chapter 7 - Understanding Relationships
119   Chapter 8 - Healing Relationships
138   Chapter 9 - The Spiritual Art of Forgiveness

Part III – The Path of Empowerment
150   Chapter 10 - Spiritual Empowerment and the Body
176   Chapter 11 - Cultivating Radiant Qualities
198   Chapter 12 - Manifesting Abundance

Part IV – The Path of Surrender
220   Chapter 13 - Developing Trust
229   Chapter 14 - Undoing Your Personality Self
241   Chapter 15 - Selflessly Serving Others

253   **Another Dream** . . . . .

Dedication

With heartfelt gratitude and humility, I dedicate *The Radiant Warrior Path* to all my students, past and present, whose courage, dedication and devotion to the path have been such an inspiration to me, and without whom this book could not have been written.

Jason Chan

Jason's dream…………..

Within the awesome heights of the Himalayas, the truth was revealed to a loving couple. The teachings came from the Radiant Kingdom. Their teacher was a Light Master named Zun-Ji who told them that purity of heart is the key to transcending all our self-imposed limitations in life. Zun-Ji then transmitted to them all the knowledge and skills they would need to assist human beings to heal themselves and the world. These teachings are a priceless gift to humanity.

In August 1998, I was leading an intense ten-day retreat at the Purelands Retreat Centre, close to the Samye Ling Tibetan Buddhist Monastery in Scotland. The energy was very pure and high, extremely potent. One night, after our evening group meditation, I was semi-asleep, lying in my room, gazing out of the window at a star-filled indigo sky. My whole body felt very relaxed, and my mind was still but alert. I then experienced a vivid psychic dream that I can still recall in great detail all these years later.

In my dream, I was a young Chinese man called Lee. Lee had come to London to study for a degree, but he had to pay his own way and so worked as a waiter in a Chinese restaurant. One evening a beautiful young American woman came into the restaurant on her own and ordered a meal. As soon as Lee saw her, he felt as though he had always known her and that he could see deep into her soul. Lee started talking to the young woman and discovered that her name was Jean, but there was no need to woo her, their deep attraction was mutual and instant.

Lee and Jean fell in love with each other and almost immediately started to plan a life together. They were both very interested in esoteric ideas and both wanted to understand the real meaning of life. Very soon they had agreed to save up enough money to travel to the Himalayas together in search of mystical teachings.

When they finally set out on their adventure, they knew in their hearts that something very significant was about to happen to them. On the seventh day of a guided trek in the Himalayas, they felt a strong pull to wander away from their group and very soon they could no longer see the group or their guide. They were alone together in the awesome mountains.

Lee and Jean kept following some strange internal guidance and eventually found themselves near the top of a peak. They no longer needed to talk to each other. They communicated all their thoughts to one another heart to heart and soul-to-soul. They camped out on that mountain for three days and nights, meditating together for much of the time. During these meditations, they experienced a series of major spiritual openings and gained many insights into the nature of human existence. They felt as though they had both grown up in just a few short days.

One early morning, they stood hand in hand waiting to watch the sun rise over the mountains, lost in the wonder of nature. Suddenly they felt a strange trembling under their feet. A few seconds later, a roaring sound seemed to come from the depths of Mother Earth herself. The trembling and the roaring became very intense. Lee and Jean looked up and saw an avalanche of ice rushing towards them. There was absolutely nowhere to run and they just knew at that moment that they were going to die. They simply smiled lovingly at each other, strangely without fear. They knew that they would be buried alive, but in that moment they felt nothing but tremendous love and peace. Then the ice overwhelmed them and they lost consciousness.

In the next part of my dream, I observed Lee feeling a pulsing in his heart, even though he no longer had a physical body. When Lee looked about him, he saw nothing but a brilliant brightness that felt incredibly soothing and yet energising at the same time. He wondered to himself 'Am I dead?' 'Have I gone to heaven?' The radiant light that surrounded him was so strong that it took him a while to adjust his vision, but after a few moments, he felt a tremendous warmth in his heart and sensed that Jean was standing next to him, even though she no longer had a very clear shape or form.

In his mind Lee asked Jean 'What on earth has happened, are we really dead or are we still alive?' Before Jean could reply, they both became aware of a very bright presence communicating to them without words the message 'There is no death. You have just travelled to the Radiant Kingdom. I am Zun-Ji, and if you would like to follow me I will show you around the kingdom.' Jean and Lee felt incredibly safe and loved in the presence of this being. They gladly followed him and soon found themselves looking down on a city of light with thousands of buildings shimmering all around them.

At the centre of this light city they came upon a vast temple of light. They asked Zun-Ji whether it was a place of worship. He replied 'Yes, but it is also a place where light-beings come to learn.' Lee said 'But surely this is heaven and no-one needs to learn anything in heaven?' In reply Zun-Ji explained that learning is infinite until each separated soul merges back into Source.

Then Jean turned to Zun-Ji and said, 'I feel as though I already know you, please can you tell us why we have come here?' Zun-Ji replied 'My dear Jean, I knew you before you were born as a human being. I knew you when you were a light-being in the Radiant Kingdom, and now you have returned to us. But you will not stay with us very long this time. You and Lee have volunteered to become my students for a while, so that you can learn the secrets of life from me, your appointed Teacher.

When I have taught you all that you need to know to become Radiant Warriors, you will go back to earth to assist in the awakening of that planet. You will love and support all your students there, as we in the Kingdom love and support you here. We will give you all the knowledge and skills that you will need to teach all those who are inspired to learn the Art of Radiant Warriorship. But you will still experience many challenges in the negativity and darkness of the physical world. What you have volunteered to do is not for the faint hearted!'

Lee and Jean were almost overwhelmed by the waves of love and peace radiating towards them from Zun-Ji, but insisted that they were ready to do whatever it took to train as Radiant Warriors.

Zun-Ji then said 'Before our teaching and learning can begin, you must both take a solemn vow to protect the purity of your heart's intention throughout all the trials, challenges and temptations that you will encounter as Radiant Warriors.'

Lee and Jean repeated after Zun-Ji 'We swear to keep our hearts pure and to uphold the integrity of the knowledge and power of our Radiant Warrior training at all times and through all temptations.'
Zun-Ji then led Lee and Jean into the Radiant Light Temple where they spent the next three years (in worldly time) learning the great mysteries of

life and practising how to anchor themselves in the Great Light so that they could continue to be guided by it when they returned to planet earth.

As part of their spiritual training Zun-Ji explained to Lee and Jean that although there seemed to be billions of separated minds on earth, there was really only one pure consciousness. But the vibrations on that planet were still so low that only a handful of very advanced individuals were able to connect to this pure consciousness for any length of time whilst still in their physical body.

Zun-Ji warned Lee and Jean that it was now urgent to assist as many human beings as possible to raise their vibrations and their consciousness. He explained that there was still so much suffering, wars, sickness and pain on planet earth because everyone's vibrations were still so low. Moreover, because human evolution had advanced to the point where everyone could be anihialated by a nuclear holocaust, it was imperative to implant true love and peace in everyone's hearts and minds to counter-balance the destructive forces of hate and aggression.

Although collectively humanity was trapped in darkness and felt totally helpless, more and more advanced human beings were praying for help to lift them out of this darkness. The light-beings of the Radiant Kingdom were responding to these calls for help and were training many light workers, including Lee and Jean, to go down to planet earth to guide others back to the light.

To Lee and Jean the three years of training seemed to pass by in a flash. As their intensive training drew to an end, Zun-Ji spent more and more time meditating with Lee and Jean to prepare them to return to earth. He explained to them that their physical bodies had been preserved in the ice of the avalanche and that all they had to do, when it was time for them to return, was to keep lowering their vibrations until their light bodies merged back into their old physical bodies.

On the day appointed for their return to earth, Lee and Jean thanked Zun-Ji from the depths of their hearts for all his teachings and guidance and promised to do everything in their power to give his teachings to anyone who was ready to receive them. Then Zun-Ji enveloped Lee and Jean in his radiant presence and held them there as he assisted them to lower their vibrations gently back down to a level compatible with physical existence.

In the final part of my dream, I witnessed Lee and Jean finding themselves back on the snow-covered mountain that they had left three years earlier. They both felt very cold and rather strange, but then they looked deeply into one another's eyes and remembered how and why they were there. They knew that they could now use the power of their minds to reactivate their physical bodies.

But before they took this final step, they took a silent vow together to spend the rest of their physical lives assisting all those human beings who were ready to commit themselves to raising their vibrations and to training their minds to hold only love, light and peace. They vowed to dedicate every moment of their remaining time on earth to assist the planet to begin to heal itself and to climb out of the darkness into the radiant light that was always its true destiny and its eternal Source.

Part I

The Path of Awakening

Chapter 1

What Is The Radiant Warrior Path?

A Radiant Warrior commits wholeheartedly to the highest levels of personal and spiritual healing and selfless service.

Our descent from heaven

Once upon a time, we were pure consciousness. We knew nothing about physical form. We were life itself and dwelt eternally in dynamic emptiness or the absolute. In the East they call this the Tao; in the Western world we call it God. This perfect wholeness existed before time and space began and we were all an integral part of this wholeness. But then we gradually sank down into physical consciousness and now we have to make an incredible effort to rise back up to the light again.

How did this happen? How did we separate from the light? We cannot actually remember, but it was as if a strange little idea arose in our one mind. 'What if?' This mad idea then manifested itself as a desire to experience something other than wholeness or totality. Of course, we do not remember making this crazy wish, but once this desire arose in our mind, perception began. We could perceive something happening. We became the observer of a vast ocean of space and light. We could actually watch this natural goodness extending infinitely.

But then another desire arose in our mind to become even more individualised and so our one mind began to separate itself from infinity. We began to descend out of pure oneness into duality and thus we began to embody, or individualise, infinite, unified consciousness. At first we embodied our individuality as beautiful light-beings or angels, but gradually as our separation from Source continued, our vibrations dropped lower and lower, and as we descended further from 'heaven,' fear set into our mind and we created heavier and heavier matter.

As our 'bodies' became grosser and we felt more and more separated from our Source, we began to feel so much fear that we just had to project it outwards and so we began to see more and more darkness around us and less and less light, until we lost contact with the light completely and found ourselves in an unconscious, dark state known as physical existence. Our bodies by this point had become so gross and heavy and our original life force was so dim, that our whole existence became dominated by fear, and out of this fear we began to experience hate instead of love.

Our collective consciousness now became dominated by fearful animal instincts, particularly the instinct to survive as a physical body. Our fearful need to survive as individual physical beings in turn created an instinctive need to attack all perceived external sources of threat and a powerful urge to reproduce ourselves in physical form through the sexual act.

Even today, billions of years after the big bang (mad idea) that created this physical universe, the great majority of human beings are still controlled by very powerful survival instincts that are associated with our base centre. The majority of the six billion people on planet earth are still struggling to make enough to feed themselves and their families. Many of us, at least when we are young, are still at the mercy of overwhelming sexual urges that dictate our fantasies and our behaviour. Most of us are still prepared to kill our enemy, particularly if that enemy directly threatens our life.

Even in the Western world, where we all have enough resources to meet our basic survival needs, most people are still caught up in making money and in making ends meet. Virtually everyone is thus still trapped in survival issues. Even millionaires are terrified about losing their millions and many rich individuals still lie, cheat and even steal from others in a vain attempt to enhance their sense of security. But when our consciousness becomes trapped in money issues like this, we all become up-tight and fearful.

We also tend to have a lot of repetitive negative thoughts that are associated with our unconscious sense of loss and separation from our Source, such as 'I am not good enough,' 'I am unworthy,' 'I do not have enough,' and from these deep negative thought patterns comes all our competitiveness, and even cruelty, as we fight each other viciously for scarce resources.

Returning to the light

Eventually, each and every one of us has to raise our consciousness from gross physical awareness to an awareness of the light. We all have to transcend our instinctive survival issues, including security issues, sexual desires and a deep sense of unworthiness, step-by-step. These issues are so powerful and instinctive that it can take us a long, long time to cultivate enough strength of mind to live with ease and grace in the world. But as well as learning to live fearlessly in this physical world, we also need to extend our consciousness upwards through our higher centres so that eventually the light that is our true existence can permeate through our whole being and extend out into the world around us.

Now you may well ask, 'If God is all powerful, why does He not just raise us all back to heaven?' The answer is that God always respects our free will and choice. Nobody pushed us out of heaven. We jumped. God did not create our physical forms, we ourselves lowered our vibrations down and down until we found ourselves lost in the darkness of physical existence, and so it is up to us to choose when to go back up to the light.

Human beings have evolved a long way since we all dwelt in dark dank caves, but it will take another quantum leap in human evolution for us to gear back into the light. This quantum leap could stop all wars and conflicts, all pollution and all starvation and it has to start with you. You have to be a pioneer on the Radiant Warrior Path. It will take you great courage and persistence to return to the light, because you are so used to the darkness that you are afraid to leave it, but every effort counts and the rewards for perseverance are beyond your wildest dreams.

Ultimately your goal is to return to pure consciousness. Here you are above the battleground of physical consciousness. Your lower mind is completely still and quiet and in this pure space of infinite creativity you can heal all your pain.

As you merge back into this pure consciousness, you will ultimately realise that we are all one with everything. We are the trees, the oceans, the sun the moon and the stars. Everything is us and we are everything. The world of duality dissolves and we become one vast space of wholeness or oneness.

This is total joining and in this space there is no 'you' and no 'them.' You know that everyone is you and from this knowingness you cannot hurt a living soul.

This is the Path of the Radiant Warrior. First we descended into fearful, physical consciousness and now we have to rise up again, step by painful step, until we open ourselves up to infinity and reach back to the Tao itself. Following this path home to your true self is not an optional journey. Sooner or later you have to take it, as does every other human being on the planet.

All the paths and all the journeys that we ever take, ultimately lead us back home to liberation and fulfilment. However, even though the spiritual path is universal and inevitable, there will come a specific moment in time when you will say 'I am ready.' If you fail to do this, you will not begin to search for the answers to life, and you will stay sleeping and experiencing endless nightmares.

Conscious spiritual awakening is the beginning of your new, purposeful life. Once you begin to awake, you will understand that you have a real purpose to fulfil this lifetime, as well as some limitations to overcome. How to overcome these limitations and how to cultivate the core inner qualities needed to become a Radiant Spiritual Warrior, who bravely continues down the path of return, overcoming all obstacles on the way, are the key themes of this book.

As you allow your true nature to unfold, you will commit yourself to your spiritual path, with all your heart, mind, body and spirit. You will vow to overcome all your limitations in order to reach your highest potential this lifetime. From the outset you should know that your own liberation will not only bring peace, joy and abundance to you personally, it will also bring these eternal gifts to your family, your loved ones, your friends and, eventually, to the whole world.

What is the Radiant Warrior Path?

The Radiant Warrior Path is a revolutionary spiritual path, or training programme, for the 21st century. It is a way of true peace and healing that synthesises spiritual wisdom, energy work and psychotherapeutic insights. It combines tried and tested spiritual practices including meditation, a modern Western understanding of the individual's mind and emotions and an emphasis on energy work such as tai chi, chi kung and yoga. Overall, this path is intended to be a unique journey to personal and spiritual radiance. It aims to bring forth a new form of consciousness that can be called 'enlightened living.'

This path is both deeply spiritual and highly practical. On the one hand, it has been designed to re-awaken our spirit or soul, so that we may once again experience true love and grace in its most natural state (heaven). On the other hand, it focuses on bringing this heavenly state of being down into our physical world and out into our everyday lives or worldly human existence (earth).

Traditionally, genuine spiritual seekers would give up the world and retire to a lonely cave or mountaintop in order to seek enlightenment. But this spiritual path is not one that appeals to many seekers in our modern world. If you are a mother of two small children, abandoning them for a mountaintop is just not practical, or even ethical. If you are running a small business and several people depend on you for their livelihood, saying 'Sorry, I'm off to find a cave in the Himalayas, the business is closed as of today' may not sound like a practical or ethical option to you either.

In any case, whether or not retiring to a remote cave would suit you personally, the hyperactive, stressed out, materialistic, violent, scary world in which we now live desperately needs shining examples of Radiant Spiritual Warriors, whom we can actually see, hear and touch. Our world urgently requires totally accessible spiritual leaders, who can clearly demonstrate how to live successfully in the world, whilst transcending all its limitations and entrapments. Radiant Warrior training is intended to produce such leaders.

At the core of this path of spiritual growth and development is the transformation of the fearful personality-self into a fearless Radiant Warrior, who is committed to the highest levels of personal and spiritual healing and selfless service. The ultimate aim of a Radiant Warrior however has nothing to do with this world. The Radiant Warrior's supreme goal is to return to wholeness, or oneness with life itself (the Tao).

If you choose to follow this path, you will be asked to transform your consciousness (through the training and development of your mind), your physical and energetic bodies and your emotions. A world of new opportunities will open up to you, to enable you to reach your highest potential. You will be guided to fulfil your deepest dreams this lifetime, by learning how to remove all your self-imposed blocks to complete fulfilment and lasting happiness. On the very practical level, including your work, income and close relationships, this path will give you a set of specific tools and simple practices that will enable you deal calmly, and optimistically, with all the challenging situations that you may encounter in your daily life.

When you have a difficult decision to make, you will learn how to listen to your inner wisdom and higher guidance. When you come face to face with your fears and doubts, you will acquire tools for calming your mind, and healing the darkness with the light. When you long to connect to the source of your being, you will be shown how to make this connection. Step-by-step, you will be guided to move out of separation and darkness and to return to wholeness and unity with all that is.

As you become more and more proficient in using the tools for personal and spiritual growth that are at the heart of this transformational path, you will experience increasing levels of peace and radiance. Eventually your calm, radiant presence will extend to everyone whom you encounter. You will become a shining light to guide others out of the darkness.

The importance of practice

Whatever you practise you eventually become. A great pianist will undoubtedly have practised playing the piano for up to eight hours a day for many, many years before his playing becomes effortless. Someone with a serious drinking problem practises drinking several hours a day for years before turning into a full-blown alcoholic. In our modern society, we all have a tendency to deny responsibility for our lives. If we are poor, we say

'It's the government's fault.' If we are sick we say 'It's a nasty bug' or ' It's a genetic weakness.' If we are miserable we blame our parents, or dark winter nights.

Very few people say to themselves when they are suffering, 'What have I been practising that has created this unhappiness?' 'How have my beliefs, thoughts or actions led me to this very uncomfortable place?' Similarly, if we meet someone who is really successful and fulfilled in life, we may have a tendency to say to ourselves 'What a lucky bastard!' rather than to wonder what this person has been practising that has led to their success.

Believing that we are the victims of circumstances, or oppressive forces beyond our control, may seem temporarily comforting, as it appears to let us off the hook. If we are not responsible for our fate, we do not need to feel guilty about our failures. However, in the long run, blaming others, or external circumstances, for our suffering means that we have no way out. We have to wait for a change in government, or a change in our partner, before we will have any chance of happiness or fulfilment.

If, on the other hand, we begin to accept that we are the masters of our own fate, and that our happiness is primarily determined not by external circumstances, but by our inner state of mind, then we have all the means at our disposal to improve our chances of leading a life full of joy, abundance, peace, love, and anything else that we may truly desire.

The fact that we are the masters of our own fate, and that our innermost thoughts and beliefs determine our external circumstances, does not mean, however, that chanting a few positive affirmations will immediately transform our lives. The Radiant Warrior Path is not New Age magic, nor is it based on wishful thinking. This book will not tell you that your guardian angel is just waiting for you to ask, before he/she finds you a parking space, or guides you to pick six winning lottery numbers. Radiant Warriorship is not about seeking instant fixes for all of our problems.

No one can change themselves overnight from a normal, fearful human being into a spiritual master of life. You actually need great spiritual discipline to transform your personality-self from a fearful, chronic worrier into a fearless Radiant Warrior. You need fantastic willpower to develop radiant inner qualities such as loving kindness, compassion, inner joy, generosity, bravery, trust and selflessness. All these qualities are already in you, but they remain only potential until you can express them.

Developing spiritual discipline

Discipline may sound like a rather old fashioned virtue, but all spiritual seekers need strong self-discipline on the spiritual path if they are going to overcome all their well-established unhelpful habits. Otherwise, their self-sabotaging habits and unskilful actions will just keep coming back to haunt them. If you are not consciously awakening, you will unconsciously hurt yourself over an over again. You will also violate other people in an endless cycle of defence and attack, persecution and victim-hood. When you are not living consciously, your mind is blurred, and you are trapped in a karmic web of cause and effect and karmic relationships. You will need great willpower and persistence to get yourself out of these traps.

Spiritual discipline is about becoming unwavering in overcoming all worldly temptations. Ego self-cherishment is very strong, particularly amongst Westerners, who are so used to having the right to pursue individual happiness.

Both compassion and determination are necessary to overcome self-cherishing. In other words, you will need to adopt both a yin and a yang approach to your spiritual awakening. If you are always too pampered and too comfortable, you will simply perpetuate your weaknesses, and, in the bigger picture, you are not being kind to yourself by opting for a cushy life. On the other hand, if you constantly beat yourself up for being an imperfect spiritual seeker, you will simply become a beaten up miserable individual, rather than an awakened spiritual warrior.

Developing self-discipline and willpower will enable you to look at all your unskilful actions and to say 'No, I am not going to behave in this unskilful way.' Discipline is not just about meditating every day whether you feel like it or not. It is also about wanting to project your anger at someone and stopping yourself. It is about resisting negative gossip, and refusing to blame others when things go wrong in your life.

We all have a strong tendency to cover ourselves up with a protective coating, or layer of armour, in order to hide form our inner darkness. Without discipline, without exerting our higher will over our rampant ego, we cannot bring all our shadows up to the light to reveal our true nature. Being positive for a few minutes every now and then is easy, but it takes real discipline to overcome the moodiness of our mind and all our negative habits.

However, please understand that you do not need to search out hardships in order to develop spiritual discipline. Life will always bring you lessons, sometimes gently, sometimes quite forcefully. At these times, sticking to your practice through thick and thin takes great will power, but you also need to be loving and compassionate towards yourself. The trick is to find a perfect balance between being kind to yourself, and giving yourself a loving kick-start whenever you slip back into your habitual, negative patterns.

To begin with, transforming your habitual thoughts, feelings and actions from negative to positive, and from self-centred to selfless, may seem like very hard work, and even an impossible task at times. But please remember, that as well as being extremely challenging, the path of the Radiant Warrior is also strewn with so much fun and joy, and with so many instants of amazing love and light that eventually you will not even be able to count your numerous blessings.

Choosing one path

There are now thousands of different paths and skilful means designed to aid you to transform yourself, but this can be a trap as well as an opportunity. You must eventually choose one path and stick to it through thick and thin, or you may be in danger of becoming a spiritual junkie. You may go from one transformational course to the next, seeking the magic mantra or formula that will make everything all right. You go to a 'Find Your Soul Mate' weekend in January, a 'Connect to Your Guardian Angel' workshop in February and an 'Introduction to Tantric Sex' evening in March, but at the end of April, you are back where you started, lonely, unfulfilled and still searching for happiness.

To begin with, all spiritual seekers wander around like this, looking for someone, or something, to guide them to the Promised Land, but at some point we all have to choose a path that makes our heart sing and then stick to that path through thick and thin. If you truly master just one path, or practice, you will have mastered all of them. Your chosen path may be far from easy at times, but I strongly recommend that you resist abandoning it to start again with a new, and initially more exciting, practice. All true spiritual paths will challenge your personality-self to the utmost. You need to be brave and determined and stick to one practice. Let it unfold. Let it work for you.

If I could only give you one piece of advice this lifetime it would be 'Give priority to your one path and your internal growth day in day out, or when you die, you will have great regrets.' When you die and ask yourself 'What have I achieved this lifetime?' I can assure you, you will not answer 'My house was very big' or 'I had a lot of educational qualifications.' You cannot take your house, or your certificates, with you when you die, but you will take with you all your internal qualities, whether positive or negative. Whatever you master this lifetime will be yours to keep eternally. Therefore, you should never give up trying your utmost to transcend your personal limitations and negativity. Every single effort counts.

Following a map

You do not have to understand your true nature, or the meaning of life in order to begin your transformational journey, just as you do not need to know how a car works, to drive it from A to B. Learning any new skill is never easy to begin with, and your path may seem hard at times, because you have unwittingly invested so much time and energy into your suffering. Like mountain climbing, the Radiant Warrior Path can sometimes be so scary, that you may seriously doubt your ability to go another step further.

You may also feel, at times, as though you are totally lost, and do not know which way to turn. This is why it is so helpful to have a guide, or a roadmap, to follow, a guide that has been written by someone who has already gone down the path you need to tread, someone who has experienced all the ups and downs of the path, and who now knows the easiest way to get from A to Z.

This book is designed as a road map for you, a map that can take you from the very beginning of your spiritual journey to your final destination. Of course, following a map can sometimes be much more difficult than following a personal guide, and a spiritual guide book is no substitute for having direct contact with a genuine spiritual teacher, but I am confident that this book can point you in the right direction, and continue to inspire, support and reassure you as progress on your unique, essential journey back to your true self.

Exercises

Noticing what you are practising

Sit quietly and contemplate your daily life over the last six months. What have you been practising? What have you spent most of your time doing? Have you been giving priority to your personal and spiritual growth and development, or have you been too busy with your career or your family life? What have you achieved in the past six months? What would you like to achieve in the next six months? What would you need to practise on a very regular basis to make your dreams come true?

Making a commitment to your spiritual awakening

If you would like to give more time and effort to becoming a Radiant Spiritual Warrior, make a commitment to yourself today to find an extra 20 minutes to half an hour each day for your spiritual practice.

Be very specific about this commitment. What will you practise, for example, tai chi, yoga or meditation? What time of day will you do this practice? Where will you do it?

Remember, 'What you practise you become.' If you practise being a couch potato in front of the TV every night, this is what you will become. If you seriously devote just a relatively small amount of time *every day* to practising tai chi, chi kung, yoga, or meditation, one day you will become a master of your chosen art!

Jane's Story: Part 1

Before I met Jason and discovered my true path this lifetime, my life already looked pretty good – on the surface. I was a Senior Lecturer at a major British university. I had published several well-received academic books and was very popular with my students. I had a beautiful home, plenty of good friends, and enjoyed almost perfect health. Compared to the vast majority of human beings on this planet, I was truly blessed. Yet deep down I was still dissatisfied with my life. At the time, I believed this was because I was so unlucky in love. I was always searching for 'Mr Right' but finding one 'Mr Wrong' after another. My heart had been broken so many times that I had almost decided that love was too painful and I was better off without it.

Moreover, even after several years of psychotherapy I still felt that there must be something more to life than the life I was living. I did not like the world I saw around me and I certainly did not love God. In fact I could not bring myself to believe in a God at all. How could any supreme being have made such a mess of creating a world? How could a loving God have created a world in which the Holocaust could happen? It just did not make any sense to me, and so I defined myself as an atheist and could see absolutely no point to human existence, given that we were all just born to die.

This belief system was very uncomfortable and fearful, but I got used to it. It did not occur to me that there could be another way. So I just did my best to make the most of my day-to-day existence. I tried to be a good, kind person and I learned to take pleasure in the little things in life. For example, I really enjoyed going to classical concerts and contemporary plays. Basically however I knew something was wrong, something was lacking. The problem was I did not even know what I was looking for. But deep below the surface of my life, my trapped soul was longing to break free and, unbeknown to my personality-self, was already searching for the light.

Chapter 2

Seven Stages on The Path

A wise person who glimpses the truth determines to follow a path towards it. A foolish person glimpsing the truth soon forgets all about it.

Before we begin to set out on the Radiant Warrior Path together, let us take a brief overview of the way we will go, from the very beginning of our journey, to our final destination.

To help us follow our lengthy route from the start, we have divided our journey into seven stages. In real life of course, these stages will overlap and at times you may take a by-way, or go right back to the beginning of a previous stage, before finding your forward again. But in this short introductory guide, we will assume that, however long it takes, and however many times we deviate from our path, all genuine spiritual seekers will eventually go from stage one to stage seven, although maybe not in this lifetime.

As you read through these seven stages, you might like to consider where you are in relation to your own spiritual journey. By the way, if you have already reached Stage Seven, 'Divine Integration: At one with the Tao,' you really do not need to read this book! If, on the other hand, you are some way off this ultimate spiritual goal, I hope and pray that this guide will assist you to progress further.

Stage One: A burning desire

Life is beautiful, if you really understand it, if you truly know it. Have you ever asked the question 'What is life?' Have you ever wondered, 'Where do I come from?' 'Where am I going?' 'Do I live only to die?' 'What is this world all about and what is my purpose for being here?' Everyone in the world will ask these sorts of questions at some point in their lives. Sometimes these deep questions will just spring up in our minds, but many people push them aside. Some people, being of a very practical nature, dismiss these questions as being impractical and fanciful. Others will think about them briefly, but then just bury them again, and get on with their day-to-day lives. But, at this very moment, many people are reaching a point in their lives where they have a burning desire to know the truth about their existence, and, if you are reading this, you are probably one of them.

The first stage of the Radiant Warrior Path is this burning desire to know the truth. Without this desire, there will be no spiritual journey. Just like anything else, you must really want to know the truth about your existence in order to take some kind of action to find it. A desire to know the truth has to well up from deep within your loving heart.

This love of the truth is actually much, much deeper than the love you feel for your parents, your children or your partner. This love in your heart is very deep and, at times, well hidden. But this love always wants to know. It wants to know the secret of life. When you experience this burning desire to know, a sense of frustration will rise up in you. At this first stage of your spiritual journey, you will have a strong sense that something of fundamental importance is missing from your life, and so you will begin to search for that something, and thus begins the second stage of your spiritual journey.

Stage Two: The dynamic search

The second stage of your journey is called the dynamic search, the search for the meaning of existence, or the meaning of life. At this stage in their journey, a lot of people will begin to buy spiritual or New Age books. Many people will go to Mind Body and Spirit exhibitions, or festivals. They will also begin to make new friends, who share the same burning desire to search for the truth.

Once you begin your search, you will find, sometimes to your amazement, that there is so much out there of potential interest to you. You may find spiritual teachers or gurus, psychic healers, many different meditation methods and techniques, various types of personal development courses and workshops, and all kinds of teachings from different cultures ancient and modern: Native American rituals, Hindu chanting, Tibetan Buddhism, Taoist tantric practices, to name but a few.

We live in exciting spiritual times, and all these courses, teachings and practices can be fascinating. Your spiritual search may even seem like a drug. You will just love it, and you will discover so many things completely out of the ordinary. Meditation, for example, is very rarely featured on television, so it can seem very different and stimulating. You will be offered so much. You will be offered instant healing, instant transformation and even instant enlightenment.

This exciting search may last for just a few months, or for many years. Some people may become workshop junkies. Others may become New Age travellers. They will leave their jobs, pack their bags, and go off to join an Ashram in India or a trek in Tibet. Some individuals keep searching all around the world for many years, until they have seen it all and experienced it all, or until they begin to realise intuitively that 'It's not out there.' 'The truth is not out there.'

If you have already become disillusioned in your search for the ultimate enlightening experience, the perfect enlightening guru, Congratulations! If you realise that your true path is not out there in the external world, you have already reached a certain level of spiritual maturity and insight. In your external search, you will not find the truth, but you may begin to see more clearly what is not true. As you begin to turn your attention from searching the external world to examining your own heart and mind, you will reach the third stage on your journey, although, in real life, stages two and three often overlap.

Stage Three: Initial understanding

Now, through all your searching, you have gained a little understanding. This understanding may be intellectual, but as well as that, you have an intuitive sense that you are now on a path, or journey, inwards into your own heart and mind. After your dynamic search in the external world of personal growth and spirituality, you realise that nothing out there can do it for you. So, you begin to come back into yourself from your external search, even though you may still cling on to the hope that something, or someone, out there will rescue you; that some spiritual experience in a workshop, ashram or temple will lift you so high, that you will know the truth, and your search will be over.

Now it is certainly true that if you pursue your spiritual path for some time, you will experience spiritual or psychic 'highs,' or 'peak' experiences. But no experience lasts. No matter how hard you try to hang on to them, or to recreate them, these spiritual highs will just slip through your fingers. As you mature into your path, you will come to recognise that all these peak experiences are actually unrepeatable. As you continue to grow, your experiences will change and your perception will alter.

You will also realise that your path is unique and very personal. Sometimes you may be able to share your experiences with a group of like-minded seekers, but nobody will ever have exactly the same experiences as you. You have to understand and accept that your path is unique. Different people on the same spiritual path always have completely different experiences.

Once you begin to realise that the truth lies within you, you will begin to turn your attention inwards and will naturally be drawn to meditation, contemplation or more meditative forms of prayer. As you go deeper and deeper inside your own mind and heart, you will begin to see clearly for the first time your busy, confused mind. You will also discover that inside your mind there are a lot of different voices. Some of them may seem to be kind, but others will sound very loud, aggressive and attacking.

Quite often when you first look within, you will find two conflicting voices inside your mind. One is a peaceful voice that is very much on your side; the other is very loud and persuasive. This loud voice will urge you, for example, to watch TV or to go out shopping, rather than spend some quiet time meditating on your own. At this stage, you will probably have a lot of resistance to just sitting quietly for a while each day. This very loud, strong voice inside yourself will see meditation as a real threat and try to convince you that you cannot do it.

If you persist in looking inward at this stage, you will also find lots of confused emotions or turbulence. A lot of people, at this point on their path, find it almost impossible to sit quietly for any length of time. They need constant stimulation from the outside. They need to listen to music, or watch TV or read a newspaper. This is the first major obstacle on your internal journey, your over-busy, over-active mind. But if you persist in sitting quietly for just a little time each day, say ten minutes only to start with, you will begin to gain some basic level of discipline or mastery over your undisciplined mind. This is very good progress.

After you feel comfortable sitting still for ten minutes a day, you can extend it to 20 minutes a day, and eventually to 30 minutes or even an hour. How long will it take you to discipline your mind sufficiently to enable you to feel momentarily at peace with yourself? How long will it take before you can sit still with a calm, peaceful mind for up to an hour at a time? As long as it takes!

Once you have achieved some level of internal peace through regular meditation or contemplation practice, you are ready to begin the fourth stage of the Radiant Warrior Path, during which you learn to bring your spiritual practice and awareness into your everyday life.

Stage Four: Cultivating mindfulness in your daily life

During the fourth stage of the Radiant Warrior Path, your primary focus is to bring constant mindfulness into your daily life and all your routine activities. At this stage in your spiritual development, you can no longer split your life into two; times when you are being spiritual, for example when you are on a spiritual retreat, and the rest of your life when you are working, looking after your family and undertaking daily chores such as shopping or cooking.

The mindfulness that you must cultivate at this stage is not just about your actions and the results of your actions, it is also about your thoughts and intentions. This is very, very challenging for most people, because our thoughts come and go so quickly, and because the personality-self tries its best to hide its true intentions from our conscious mind.

However, at this stage in your journey, you will not make further progress unless you stop denying responsibility for all your thoughts and actions. You can no longer say 'I did not mean to do it' when your thoughts or actions harm someone else. You can no longer pretend that you did not realise what you were doing. You begin to grow up spiritually, at this point on your path. You cannot be like a child anymore, who hits out at their brother or sister and then says 'It wasn't me. I didn't do anything wrong, they started it.'

At this stage in your journey, you also have to take responsibility for healing your relationships. You can no longer blame your father, or mother, or ex-partner, for all your current unhappiness. You can no longer think to yourself 'I would be perfectly happy if only my partner would …..' Instead of continuing to blame others for making you unhappy, angry or fearful, you actually begin to thank those who push your buttons, on the grounds that they are assisting you to be conscious of all your hidden fears and darkness.

As you bravely take responsibility for all your negative thoughts and feelings, some of which have been stored in your sub-conscious for a very long time, you will also begin to free all your loved ones. You will begin to find that you are less needy or clingy and that you start to judge others less harshly.

As you focus on taking responsibility for all your thoughts and feelings, you will probably notice that your physical vitality, or lack of it, strongly influences your mood and your responses to the world around you. This close link between your physical well-being and your emotional and mental state is one reason why I recommend a balanced approach to spiritual development. It is usually not enough just to read spiritual texts and practise meditation or prayer. You also need to incorporate some form of holistic exercise into your daily spiritual practice, to strengthen your body, calm your mind and create an inner strength and confidence to see you through all the ups and downs of the path.

This is why I strongly recommend that you choose some type of mindful, wholesome exercise that you will love, such as tai chi, chi kung, yoga, aikido or five rhythms dancing. You can then use daily mindful, holistic exercise to bring balance and vitality back into your physical system. Regular exercise of this kind will definitely enhance your levels of mindfulness, particularly if you always bring your mind into your physical practice.

Although cultivating mindfulness is crucial at this stage on the path, it is not enough, on its own, to transform your personality-self from a chronic worrier into a Radiant Spiritual Warrior. As well as being mindful throughout your day, you will also need to practise bringing your loving intention into everything that you think and do.

Every single effort counts. Every time you remember to do something with loving intention, it will bring you back to your true self, because underneath all the layers of your personality, you are love itself. The truth or love heals everything and brings every aspect of your life, including the most mundane daily activities, back into wholeness and perfect harmony. This is why combining being mindful with bringing your loving intention into everything you say and do is so important.

Gradually, as you become more and more mindful throughout your waking hours, you will be ready to embark on the fifth stage of your journey, the stage of healing into wholeness.

Stage Five: Healing into wholeness

Before you can gain genuine spiritual insight and power, you have to heal yourself; all your junk, your shadows, all your fears, guilt, jealousies, all your attack thoughts and all your unkind or hurtful intentions. These shadows are in all of us, whether or not we are fully conscious of them. Do not be too hard on yourself, as you begin to see all your shadows.

Every human being on this planet has a dark side. At this moment, there are six billion of us on this planet and we all need healing, every single one of us. We not only need to heal our emotions and our physical bodies, we also have to heal our deep down subconscious layers, wherein we all store a load of dark shadows and fears based on separation and ignorance. So the healing path is crucially important.

The true healing path consists of letting go and non-attachment. This letting go of all your accumulated layers of defences, all your suppressed fears and shadows, will eventually bring love and harmony back to you. This healing will go deep into your subconscious psyche to restore love and light into both your conscious, and your subconscious states of being. As you continue to heal yourself, by bringing all your subconscious shadows up into the light where they can be observed and then transformed, you will find that life is beautiful. Life is always beautiful, but so many people find life dark and difficult, because they have not yet healed themselves deeply enough.

As you unfold spiritually, you will inevitably go through a healing process and possibly even experience a healing crisis. You should welcome such a crisis rather than fear it, because it has to happen to you sooner or later. Whilst you are going through this healing phase, you should be very kind and gentle with yourself. Sometimes you may feel tremendous anger or fear. You may even feel a little insane, or crazy, at times, and you may have to seek medical assistance, but on no account during this stage of your awakening should you abandon your spiritual practice, or your spiritual friends.

Your family and old friends will probably not understand what is happening to you, and they may become very afraid for you, or angry with you. But your spiritual friends will reinforce your truth. Do not despair if your healing journey takes some time, maybe several months or, more likely, several years. All your past wounds are locked away inside you. You need bravery, understanding, spiritual discipline and persistence to unlock and release them. However dark this process may seem at times, always gear yourself into the sunlight. Always remember that the sun is still shining on you, however much it appears to be covered by thick dark clouds.

Please do not be discouraged if the healing process seems endless at times. If you really find it too much to handle, you can always pray for the process to slow down to a pace that you can handle. Also, keep reminding yourself that we are never given more pain than we can bear on our spiritual journey, even though we may be challenged to our limits at times. The more you heal yourself, the more you will come to recognise that each time you release another layer of suppressed pain, joy will just flood through your heart. Every time you release some pain or difficulties from your subconscious state, you will feel like you are in heaven. Heaven will just open up for you.

During this healing stage of your journey, you may tell yourself at some point 'It is too hard. I can't take any more. I want to quit.' But, once you reach a certain point on this healing journey, you will realise that you cannot quit. You cannot go back to your old, unconscious way of living, even if it seems like a tempting option at times, because your soul, or spirit, is getting stronger and stronger. Your soul desperately wants you to awake and will not let you go back to being unconscious again.

Gradually, as you heal more and more of your dark shadows, the light in you will shine more strongly and brightly, and your fears will begin to subside and become subtler. That's great! The hardest part of your healing journey is now behind you. Now you have become so familiar with your shadows and your fears that they begin to lose their power to hurt, or to scare you. You will still have your moments of fear or anger, but these moments will no longer trap or imprison you for eons of time. These moments will be like passing clouds in a clear blue sky.

You still cannot say 'I am never angry. I am never fearful or doubtful,' that would be spiritual arrogance, and insane self-denial. There is no such thing as a completely trouble free life in this physical world of duality. However, the more you heal yourself, the less you will be troubled by your shadows. The more you have direct experiences of divine light or love, the less you will let your shadows take hold of you.

At this stage in your healing journey you will begin to feel free, and this sense of freedom is so real to you, that you want it more and more, even though you do not yet experience it at all times. Peace and freedom go together, and you begin to want this dynamic peace more than all the external things that you used to crave. You long to experience this dynamic peace all of the time, The really good news is that after you have bravely gone through the stage of healing your dark side, you will eventually emerge into the sunlight, and experience the sixth stage on the path, the stage of miraculous living.

Stage Six: Miraculous living

All spiritual seekers who diligently and bravely continue to follow their path will eventually emerge from a period of meticulously practising mindfulness and healing into a time of miraculous living. This stage on the path is a lot of fun. Miraculously, you will experience so much joy and love that you will scarcely believe it. In this stage you will test the truth. You will play with life, and become very creative and artistic. You will be an inspired individual, full of light.

You will love all of humankind. You will really see the beauty in being human. When you look at men and women, you will not focus on the differences anymore. You will simply see the wonders of manifestation. Seemingly, we are all separate and separated, but now suddenly you will see the unity, as well as the infinite variety, of all manifested life. At this stage in your path, you will even be able to look beyond human personalities and see the soul within. You will become a witness to the truth at work.

What will you want to do with your life in this stage? Internally, you will just want to connect more and more to your God, your wholeness, your divinity, or the Tao. Externally, you will want to express your inner light. You will just love to extend divine joy and beauty out into the world around you. This beauty is like a bubbling spring of pure, sparkling water rising up from the earth and pouring through you. This beautiful energy constantly fills your whole body.

Every day when you awake, you will like to focus on a project through which you can express your infinite creativity. You will no longer have to labour, or suffer, to make a living. You will just naturally want to create beauty, peace and love all around you. You will feel drawn to express your childlike innocence and joy. When you join up with spiritual friends, you will create together like angels. When you are dealing with business matters, you will be effortlessly innovative and successful, because you will no longer be held back by endless fears or doubts within you.

When you finally reach this stage on the path, you will become a walking miracle. Everyone you meet, even if they are not on their spiritual path, or spiritually awake, will sense some secrets in you.

This stage is so beautiful, that words simply cannot fully describe it. On the one hand, you are no longer really in this physical world of separation and suffering, but on the other hand, you will still go through a maturing process or path. You will still learn to deepen your understanding of humanity. You may still have some healing to do of the more subtle layers of your internal darkness, but you will go through this healing with great confidence, inner joy and faith. You will begin to know the truth and to integrate all the wisdom you acquired on the previous stages of your path. You will at last begin to integrate the oneness of life within you, until you ultimately reach the final seventh stage of your journey.

Stage Seven: Divine integration: one with the Tao

You do not have to become an enlightened master, or saint, to become one with the Tao. In reality you are already oneness itself. However, you won't be consciously aware of this oneness, unless you remove all your obstacles, or shadows, that hide the light within. Until you have removed all these internal obstacles to the truth, your Radiant Warriorship will remain just a potential. But eventually divine light will shine through you without any impediment.

It is almost impossible to write about this final stage of your journey. Whenever human beings try to describe the truth we misinterpret it. So, the wise master, in both ancient and modern times, always says; 'Look, you cannot really describe the truth. Every time you try to name it, or pin it down, you always miss the point. The Tao is not this. It is not that. The Tao is not here. It is not there. But the Tao is everywhere. It is this and also that. The Tao is so simple. God is. Love is. Truth is.'

Do not take the following description of the seventh stage of your spiritual journey too literally. The only way to know the Tao is to experience it fully for yourself and to surrender completely into it. But I can tell you that it is like a vast space full of infinite potential. Just as our sky embraces everything, the Tao embraces everything. It is the mother of all things. Without it, nothing has its being. The Tao is never absent from anyone, or any event. It is not in time or space, but it embraces both time and space. Everything that manifests exists because of it.

Individually, you will experience the Tao as your true potential. You will discover that here there is no fear, no beginning and no end, and you will know the meaning of eternity. Everything is one immeasurable, unified vastness or greatness. When you dwell in this vastness, you will not see other people as separate from you. Now you will see everyone as a part of you. You will love everyone indiscriminately.

At this stage you will not even see yourself as 'me' as such. You will only experience 'I AM' that includes you and every other being in the past, present and future. You will know that you can never actually create anything new. It was there already in the Tao that holds everything within it eternally. Every manifestation comes from this vastness that cannot really be named. It just is: The Tao, God, life itself. Nothing to do, nowhere to go, no one to be. You have merged back into the Tao. You have returned home, and your long, long spiritual journey is finally over.

Exercises

Where are you looking for love and happiness?

Looking back over the last 5 to 10 years of your life, think about how much time and effort you spent looking for love, approval or the solution to all your problems in the external world. Did you find it? Did it last?

How much time and effort did you spend going within to find what you are seeking for?

If you have begun to look within for the meaning of life, what have you discovered?

Feeling what it is like to live miraculously

Would you like to feel what it would be like to live miraculously? If you would, please sit in a comfortable position with your spine upright. Relax for a few moments and bring your awareness to your breath. Now imagine that your day-to-day life is filled with laughter, joy and sincerity, with true friendship and no enemies, with exciting, fulfilling projects that fulfil your deepest desires.

Close your eyes and fully visualise this life in your mind. Let joyful images pour through you. Let uplifting emotions inspire you. Imagine you are creating your ideal career, or service to the world, with like-minded colleagues / business partners.

The joy of this vision will fill up your heart, and you may even feel tears well up in your eyes. Feel the true passion of life. Tell yourself that miraculous living is very much like being in heaven whilst still living on planet earth. Tell yourself that miraculous living is your birthright and really commit to following your chosen path until your dream comes true.

Jane's Story: Part 2

Looking back, I can now see clearly that my own conscious awakening began at the end of one terrible day in 1997, the day my best and oldest friend got married. My best friend and I had been single together forever and there she was marrying some guy I hardly knew, looking blissfully happy and expecting me to be happy for her too. All through the wedding ceremony and the reception I could feel this horrible knot growing and growing in the pit of my stomach.

But it wasn't until I finally got back to my own empty house late that night that I found myself collapsed on my kitchen floor wailing my heart out. I didn't exactly want to die, but the sense of despair and personal failure I felt was overwhelming. From this place of utter hopelessness I found myself crying out 'God, if you are out there, which I doubt, please help me. I just cannot do this on my own anymore. I have tried the best I can to make my life work using my own initiative and it's a mess. I am so lonely and miserable. I give up. You take over!'

A few months later a friend took me along to an evening talk by Jason Chan. The flyer for his talk said 'This evening will transform you life forever' and I remember thinking to myself 'that's a pretty grand claim, I'm sure it won't transform *my* life!' Jason's talk was intriguing, although a lot of what he said went straight over my head. I do remember thinking that he had really nice energy, but I remained rather sceptical, and nothing dramatic seemed to happen to me.

Then, just a few weeks later I went to present a paper at an academic conference in Lincoln. During a break from the conference, some friends persuaded me to go with them to look around Lincoln Cathedral. I went along for want of anything better to do, even though churches were not 'my thing.' Once inside the cathedral, I wandered off from my friends and found myself in an alcove with an image of Christ hanging on the wall lit up by a candle.

Suddenly I found myself on my knees crying and praying with all my heart 'Oh God, oh Christ forgive me, please forgive me.' In my heart I knew that I had turned my back on God for a long, long time and now I yearned to return home. My heart felt as though it would break with the pain of my 'betrayal' but at the same time I felt uplifted, comforted and loved by an incredible presence that I could not begin to describe or understand.

After about half an hour my crying subsided and I eventually wandered back to the conference centre in a daze. At the time I really could not understand or explain what on earth had happened to me, but I now know that my soul had begun to awake. A little spark of light deep inside of me had been re-kindled by my meeting Jason Chan, and I had begun my long journey home at last.

Chapter 3

Awakening Through Stillness

If you truly want to transform yourself into a Radiant Warrior, being still on a daily basis is a must.

The true purpose of meditation

Unless you take time to go within, you will have no chance of finding lasting happiness and no real opportunity to serve others effectively. I promise you that if you sit still without any distractions for just ten minutes a day, every day for a month, your life will begin to transform miraculously. But one day of sitting still will not help; daily meditation has to become a firm habit.

We make so many mistakes in our lives by not being still. All worldly wisdom is geared into action, and yet how often do so-called intelligent human beings act in supremely unintelligent ways? Think of world leaders, they and their advisers are some of the most intelligent and highly educated people on the planet and still they seem to make such a mess of things. Some practically minded people may ask, 'How can you live without acting?' But the true sage thinks differently, he/she knows that all harmonious events emerge from great stillness.

The stillness of the mind that you can eventually reach through meditation cannot be over-stated. You can experience everything that you could ever truly desire in meditation: peace, loving kindness, inner joy, unconditional love, clarity of mind. The more you dip into the divine peace that is available in a truly meditative state, the more you will unfold into the radiance that is your natural state of being.

During deep meditation, your mind should become open like a clear sky. Meditation is not contemplation. In a deep meditative state, your mind just opens and you do not think. Thinking is mankind's biggest problem.

Whenever we look at something, we think about it, we conceptualise it, we judge it to be good or bad. But when you think about something, you do not know it. When you are in a natural sate of being you just 'know.' This is quite different from thinking. Even the greatest philosophers, or thinkers, do not know. But the quiet mind, dwelling in its true natural state, always knows itself. Meditation is returning to this natural state of knowing.

Because we do not know ourselves, we do not know one another, so we think about one another, we imagine one another and make each other up. You may tell yourself that the world is a dangerous place, that your ex-partner is a mean guy, or that all women are money-grabbers, or you may tell yourself that everyone you meet is an angel. None of it is true. It is all your imagination. Do not believe any of your descriptions, or perceptions, about other people, or the world in which you think you live. None of them are accurate.

We calculate and speculate, but we do not know. Individuals who cram their brains full of information are not wiser than others, they are just stuffed full of meaningless junk. The natural 'empty' mind, on the other hand, is a wish-fulfilling jewel, the most precious gift in the universe. But most people do not know about this state of being, and so most people suffer. Go to a hospital and look at the faces distorted by pain and fear. Is this God's creation? Give God a break!

Meditation is the most powerful and effective tool for coming back to know our natural state of being 'in love.' When you are in this universal, or divine love, you will not think about harming anyone. When you are fearful, you cannot love or be loved, and you suffer for it, but when your mind is completely open and at peace, love just naturally pours though it.

In time, the love that you experience whilst you are meditating will begin to permeate your daily life. Once you experience the beauty of your soul during meditation, you will want to hook onto this experience. Once you begin to give less power to your egotistical personality-self, you can more and more merge with your spirit or soul. Eventually, you will go back into your natural state of being, your state of wholeness before you were conditioned, and then you will realise that you have created all your own negative thought patterns and have turned them into your own living hell or nightmare existence.

From this place of wholeness or transcendent wisdom, you become purified and spiritualised and you start to transform. As your connection with the divine becomes stronger and stronger, you will experience heaven. One day you will realise that you never really left your heavenly home, and you will understand the true meaning of eternity. You will realise that, whilst a part of your mind is dreaming this physical life, you are still living in eternity, and that your true consciousness does not experience time or space.

Genuine meditation is thus a journey inward to the light, or a return to love. How long does this journey take? As long as it takes! This is what time is for, to enable you to take this journey home to your natural state of being. When you get a glimpse of eternity, what will you do with it? You will understand that you are simply a manifestation of life itself. Once you gain this understanding, all you will want to do will be to extend the beauty, the love and the glory of life out into your physical existence and the world around you. This wonderful state is available to anyone who takes up a meditative path and sticks to it with great sincerity, earnestness and discipline until their spiritual journey reaches its natural conclusion.

Wanting to meditate

Meditation is more concerned with heaven than earth. It connects you to your soul, and your soul exists beyond your thinking mind. So, you will not begin to meditate until you are ready to connect to your soul.

The spiritual path is a seeking for wholeness, a natural state of being beyond illusionary conditioning. We think we can understand life through thinking, but whilst thinking plays a part on our spiritual journey, it will not take us very far by itself. Reading spiritual books is not enough. Acquiring spiritual wisdom second hand will not work. You have to experience life for yourself. You have to figure out your true nature for yourself. No one, not even Christ or Buddha, can do this for you.

In order to contact higher or universal consciousness, you have to train your mind to be still. How do you know you are ready to be still? When you want to do it, when you know that you need to look within for the answers to life. No one can force you to take up the life-transforming practice of sitting still on a daily basis. You can buy hundreds of books and meditation CDs, but none of these can make you practise.

You have to develop your own motivation to meditate, and like any good habit, you have to stick at it for a while, before it becomes engrained. You are the only person who can discipline yourself to develop the habit of sitting still every day. You just have to exert your will over the part of your mind that resists this practice very strongly. Remember how, as a small child, you used to resist cleaning your teeth twice a day? Now you do this without even thinking about it and, eventually, you will meditate every single day, without having to struggle with resistance in your mind.

At first, everyone has some resistance to just sitting still, because we all have so much fear just below the surface of our over-active minds. But, if you do not develop this fundamental spiritual practice, you will continue to live a fearful life. You will simply go on drowning yourself in an endless stream of useless activities, so that you do not have to face your inner fears and demons. If you wish to become a true Radiant Warrior, you cannot keep worshiping idols. You cannot worship worldly things, which means that you can no longer give priority to gaining a better car, the perfect house or the perfect lover.

If you are seeking the truth you have to give all worldly possessions away, not in the sense of living in total poverty and isolation on a mountaintop, but in the sense of losing your strong attachment to these temporary, external phenomena. You have to change your priorities in life from seeking external pleasures and physical satisfaction, to searching for the truth within. All the pleasures of the earth are just temporary. As a Radiant Warrior, you are seeking the eternal. You are aiming to find heaven before you drop dead.

The world's agenda is completely opposite to a spiritual agenda. The world believes in death, but for those on the spiritual path there is no death. The world likes to rush, but on the spiritual path, you need to slow right down to find peace within. The world wants more and more possessions. The spiritual seeker begins to see that possessions are a form of imprisonment.

The world divides everyone into friends and enemies. The Radiant Warrior aims to see all human beings as brothers and sisters.

The personality-self doubts the existence of God, but deep in your mind and heart, you continue to yearn for God. Out of this yearning, you will begin to seek. You will begin to ask 'Who am I?' 'What am I doing here?' Don't stop until you find the answers. Your personality-self will tell you that you are mad, or stupid, to give priority to sitting 'doing nothing' everyday, but you will still persist, because your heart is seeking answers.

Everyone wants to experience true love, but most people never do. Everyone wants to live in joy, but most people can't. We feel imprisoned because we are slaves to engrained patterns and habits of negative thinking and feeling. Meditation enables you to change these deep-seated habits. In meditation, you can watch your moodiness and your ever-changing thoughts and feelings. Then, as you go deeper, you will begin to discover the unchanging qualities of your true nature underneath your moodiness. You will begin to see that on one level you are always changing and uncertain, but underneath all this lies certainty. This is what you truly want. This alone will bring you lasting happiness and fulfilment.

Learning to still your mind

The first stage in meditation is learning to still your busy mind and calm your turbulent emotions, but you cannot force your mind to be quiet. This is impossible, because if you try to force your mind into stillness, you will simply be creating another conflict inside your mind, and this is not peace. Many Westerners are convinced that they cannot meditate, because they know how busy their minds are, and they know that they cannot just sit still and have no thoughts.

It is true that meditation very rarely comes easily to Westerners, because they have all been so well trained to think non-stop. From the age of three to eighteen or even twenty-one, most of us are immersed in an education system that rewards us for our thinking and problem solving skills and punishes us for daydreaming in class. In America, there are even classes for pregnant women who want to stimulate their unborn child to think, whilst it is still in the womb!

So, most of us find it almost impossible to sit still and stop our ever-thinking brain. The answer, at first, is to just sit still in any case and observe your mind being busy, without getting completely lost in your train of thought. If you just sit and observe your mind, you will notice that it is full of involuntary junk. To start with, your task is to just sit for several minutes at a time and watch this junk impassively.

The busy mind is full of involuntary thoughts that come and go without your consent. Your mind is constantly jumping around from the past to the future. It never stops fantasising and running around like crazy. This is normal, and discovering how busy and even agitated your mind is when you try to meditate, is also quite normal. All you have to do, as you sit there, is to maintain an awareness that your mind is busy, and then focus on gently bringing your mind back to the present moment whenever it rushes off to the past or the future. In meditation, you have to bring your mind back to the present moment thousands and thousands of times, until you reach the stage where you can actually stop your undisciplined mind from thinking for a while.

Since it is nearly impossible for a beginner to settle their hyperactive mind, you will at first need to find something really interesting to distract you from all its meaningless chatter. Very few people, including experienced meditators, can hold divine consciousness for any length of time. Prolonged periods of meditation, particularly for beginners, can therefore become dull and unskilful. Your aim is to stay conscious throughout your meditation, and simply to acknowledge your impatience.

Helpful meditative techniques

At first, you will probably need to adopt a range of techniques in order to achieve some temporary stillness of mind. For example, if you do not adopt the right posture for meditation, you will have no energy, and your meditations will be very flat. There is no point in being still like a stagnant pond. You are aiming to be still like a calm sea, that looks as smooth as glass, but is powered by mighty energy just beneath its surface.

To empower yourself through meditation, your spine needs to be straight and strong. If you are a beginner, using a meditation stool may help you to strengthen your spine. You can also do holistic exercise, such as yoga or chi kung, to strengthen your three base centres and your spine. When your three lower centres and your lower back and abdomen are strong, your upper body can be very relaxed. Your goal is for your lower body to be strong like a mountain and your upper body to be flexible like a tree bending in the wind.

It can take months, or even years, to adopt the correct meditation posture, but every effort counts. Occasionally, you should check your meditation posture in a mirror, because most of us are not aware of how we curve our spine, even when we think that we are sitting upright. If your body becomes painful, do not keep sitting in exactly the same position throughout your meditation.

If you find that sitting on the floor is too uncomfortable for you, you can use cushions to support your body, or sit up against a wall until your back becomes stronger. Alternatively, you may find it comfortable to sit on the edge of a chair. If you are sitting in a classic meditation posture and you develop pins and needles in your legs (a very common problem for beginners) you can gently stretch one or both your legs out in front of you, but do this slowly and gently, so that you do not disturb your mind too much.

Sometimes you may find that your body sways automatically, and you may even feel as though something deep inside you is shaking your physical body. This is the chi moving you and re-aligning your physical system. If this happens to you when you are in meditation, just let your body move without paying too much attention to it.

As you sit still, you can bring something beautiful into your mind as a meditative object. For example, you might like to think of someone you love, or once loved, or picture your favourite place, a place that makes your heart sing with joy. As well as focussing your mind on something beautiful, or full of love, you should also learn to bring your attention to your breath. As you gently do this, your breath will naturally soften and lengthen and you will feel more alive, as you connect to your life force.

Silently repeating a mantra is another classic technique for training the mind during meditation. You can use a classic Buddhist mantra such as 'Om Mani Padme Hum,' or simply 'Om,' or you can keep repeating English words such as 'I am Love' 'I am Peace' or even just 'I Am.' Keep reminding yourself that 'one thought can over-ride a thousand thoughts' and bring your mind gently back to your mantra, whenever you notice that it has run away.

At first, you may think that sitting still is making your mind go crazy, and that the more you try to calm your mind, the more your thoughts rush in on you. But if you persevere through this frustrating phase, you will eventually notice a difference. Your thoughts will not distract you quite so much, and you will be able to sit still for a little longer before the urge to move overwhelms you. This is a very good sign that you are making real progress.

Do not say to yourself 'I just cannot sit still and do nothing.' Even the most hyperactive person can sit still for ten minutes a day, and after a while you should find that you can sit still for longer and even begin to look forward to it. Your heart will rejoice whenever you sit still and attempt to calm your mind, even though a part of your mind may still be telling you that you are simply wasting your time.

Overcoming sleepiness and flatness

After the busyness of your thinking mind, sleepiness is the other major obstacle you will need to overcome in your meditations. When you meditate, your lower mind interprets the quietness you experience as boring. It wants to push this peace away by going to sleep. Even very experienced meditators sometimes go through a stage when they feel sleepy during their meditations. This indicates that your mind is trying to run away.

Your personality-self does not want to know the truth about who you really are. Your intellectual mind never wants to know the truth, and, when it is threatened by the truth, it will run away by going to sleep. When you feel your mind running away like this in meditation, it is very helpful to use breathing exercises such as chi kung to increase your energy and pull your consciousness upwards. You will need a lot of energy to sustain your concentration during meditation. To produce this energy at will, it is really helpful to develop your internal vitality through practices such as tai chi, chi kung and yoga, otherwise meditation can become very flat and boring.

Some people can meditate for years and still be as flat as a pancake energetically! Some individuals can apparently meditate for hours on end, but they have no life in them. They are actually using meditation to blank out and as a defence mechanism against their pain, rather than training their mind to rise above that pain. You cannot get enlightened by doing this type of meditation. The stillness you seek in meditation is not a passive, drowsy, blank type of peace. The sky at night looks very peaceful, but it is full of activity.

Whenever you meditate, you are aiming to achieve a state of spaciousness, not 'spaced outness.' Blankness is not creative. People who are flat energetically are not peaceful. They are stuck. You are seeking a calm mind, not a lifeless one. Remember that a stagnant pond is not calm, but rotten. The apparent stillness, lies on top of rotting material just underneath the surface of the water. The calm sea, on the other hand, is genuinely peaceful because it has so much natural energy and movement within it. Similarly, in meditation there is physical inaction, but action is already there, without you moving a finger.

Meditative stillness is dynamic not dull. True peace is juicy with potential. When you can get in touch with this energised inner peace, you can transcend all your personal problems and become truly creative. The great masters tell us that stillness is more favourable than action, because when you still your busy mind, and reconnect with universal consciousness, the universe will act for you. The ancient masters called this 'effortless accomplishment,' and, as a Radiant Warrior in training, this is what you are aiming for.

To transcend the obstacles that block your path to genuine meditation, particularly the busyness and then the sleepiness of your mind, will take many years of effort. Some people give up meditation, because they are not prepared to put all this effort into it. But as a would-be Radiant Warrior, you have to learn to command your mind, so that it can serve your spirit.

When your mind is too busy, you must command it to be quiet. When your mind is sleepy or dull, you have to wake yourself up. But you do not have to do this through willpower alone. Ancient spiritual tools, such as mantras, mudras (hand positions) and breathing techniques, are still available to us today, and by finding the tools that feel right for us and using them diligently, we can all overcome the busyness and sleepiness of our lower mind to find the dynamic peace that lies deep within.

Experiencing spiritual highs

At some point, most people who meditate on a regular basis will experience tremendous light, peace and love, or even religious ecstasy. For example, you may see the face of Christ or Buddha. You may feel the presence of great angels. You may hear messages that seem to come directly to you from God. None of these experiences will last.

If you go on a spiritual retreat, or meditate with very experienced meditators or masters, you will almost certainly have some amazing spiritual experiences. You may even think that you have become enlightened. It is actually very easy for an advanced meditation master to facilitate spiritual openings and 'high' spiritual experiences in a retreat setting. But when you return home and resume meditating by yourself, you will probably be very disappointed to find that these experiences have disappeared, and, try as you might, you cannot get them back.

What should you do when your spiritual highs disappear? You should simply let them go. You have to learn not to strive to re-create them. Meditation is the art of relinquishing all attachments, but, at the same time, its effects are cumulative. If you meditate for any length of time, you will come to see that your progress always goes in cycles. As you mature into your practice, you will gladly accept a period when you appear to go down into the valley, as you know that this is the prelude to going up to the spiritual mountaintop again. Challenges on the path should therefore always be welcomed as giving your practice more focus.

The more you dip into divine peace, the more you will unfold, but you cannot strive egotistically to achieve a blissful meditative state. Meditation is a subtle art. The more you surrender, and stop striving with your intellect to achieve a beautiful, natural state of being, the more it is just there. On the other hand, surrendering is not passive. You need to work on your breath, your posture and your energy flow during meditation, in order to raise your consciousness and connect to the light.

At first, when you begin to experience divine states of peace and joy, you will put more and more effort into your meditation in a vain attempt to re-create these beautiful experiences, but at this stage you are creating a split in your mind. Once your blissful meditation is over, you will come straight back to being an ordinary, neurotic person who seeks to avoid pain and grasp pleasure.

Your daily life will still reveal to you all your neuroses, your victim-consciousness, your bitchiness, aggressiveness or laziness. So, if you are determined to become a Radiant Warrior, you cannot just sit quietly and run away from your life. You cannot bliss out for one hour a day, or for two weeks a year, and think that you have solved all your problems. You will just have to come back and face the same problems in your daily life, over an over again.

Nevertheless, the direct experiences of spiritual presence that you can reach during meditation are a crucial part of the awakening path. Once you experience an inner connection to life, you will gain a sense of well-being that has nothing to do with external circumstances, and nothing to do with sensual pleasure or comfort. Once you see the light, you will know that there is so much more to life than physical pleasure or success and this knowing will inspire you to keep seeking for the truth through all the ups and downs of your spiritual journey.

The desire for the truth is built into every one of us. The truth is that you are one with life, but knowledge of this truth transcends the human mind. It is an eternal part of the knowing mind that is beyond physical existence. In deep meditation, you realise that you never separated from life or God and that, in this eternal reality, there is no fear and no desire.

The human mind is never certain, this is why we have to merge back into the natural state of mind that guides every moment and transcends time and space. The real 'you' lives in eternity. You are life itself. Once you have transcended duality, your physical life will become a liberating and joyful journey rather than a prison. Your physical existence will take on a new meaning. First, you will become a fearless Radiant Warrior, then, ultimately you will become a pure manifestation of life itself.

Opening your heart to divine romance

Most people in our society yearn for romantic love to fill the gap they feel deep inside themselves, but romantic love does not last and, at some point in any relationship, you will inevitably find that you are still yearning. As you advance in your meditation, you will discover a desire that is stimulated deep within by God or life itself. When you try to fill this deep desire by finding something on the outside of you, for example a 'soul mate,' you make a big mistake. No one can ever fill this gap inside of you. In the West, we believe so strongly in romantic love and finding the right person who is waiting for us, but this type of human love can never fill the gap deep inside us. Romantic love is always painful, because there are no perfect human beings out there.

Because of the pain we have all accumulated through relationships, we tend to close our hearts to protect us from further hurt. But would-be Radiant Warriors need to risk going through the pain of fully opening their hearts. Meditation is not just about sitting quietly and doing nothing, we need to open up our hearts and minds fully to the divine.

Divine romance is ultimately an empty space, a no-thing-ness full of potential. However, beginners will find that their meditations will be much richer and more fruitful, if they learn to connect up to a divine figure who represents this pure sensation inside the heart. For example you might like to focus on Christ, Buddha, Krishna or Kuan Yin, while you meditate. The crucial point is that this divine figure has to resonate in your own heart in order to be of incredible assistance to you on your spiritual journey.

Devotion to a divine figure can become a means to help you to transcend your self-importance. Asking 'What is in this for me?' is a major obstacle to liberation. Having an inner connection to the divine is far more important than anything you do or achieve in the outside world. First things first, cultivate your connection to God or the divine first and foremost. Give priority every day to your meditation and your prayers. Everything else can wait. There are so many temptations in this physical existence to lure your mind into seeking pleasure on the outside, and you must gradually build up enough inner strength to avoid all of them.

Even if you think you have advanced to the stage on your spiritual path where you are selflessly serving mankind, if you forget your own internal connection to God you can still get lost again. There is nothing greater in life than your connection to the divine, to God, to the Tao. This physical world of duality will always tempt you and try to suck you into its temporary pleasures, but your inner connection to the divine is the key to lasting joy and fulfilment.

Many people in our world are devoted to a deity in a superstitious way. They go to their church or temple to pray to their deity for personal favours. 'Oh Buddha, please heal my painful hip.' 'Oh Christ, please keep my marriage from failing.' But true devotion is neither self-centred nor superstitious. Spiritual masters know that true devotion to a divine figure such as Christ or Buddha has tremendous power in it.

If you cannot find devotion and dedication on the spiritual path, you will get lost. Devotion connects you to something greater than your little, separated self. Devotion and dedication can give your meditations focus and purpose. Your physical life is meaningless without purpose. When individuals have no connection to anything greater than themselves, they base everything on their own self-importance and they inevitably suffer.

Devotion to a divine figure will help you to open your heart when you meditate. Later, as you mature on your path, you can also practise opening your heart throughout your daily life. Each time you fill your heart with appreciation, love and joy, your heart will open. Deep inside your heart lies innocence, and this innocence has tremendous power in it. It really can move mountains.

If you meditate with an open heart, you will gain tremendous strength. Eventually, your pure heart and clear mind will become one, then your mind will fulfil your heart's desire. On the other hand, if your heart remains fearful, your mind will still be fearful. Insecure people can be very selfish.

They think they are so important, but, without a connection to the divine, they are no more than a speck of dust.

Devotion to something greater than you will also help you to transcend your suffering and loneliness. When you surrender to a higher power, your self-importance will begin to disappear and you will see your personality-self as quite insignificant. You will naturally stop taking life so personally, and therefore suffer less. You will come to know your true self as unconditional love that cannot be snuffed out by external circumstances. By contrast, if you continue to seek love on the outside of you, you will become bitter and disappointed sooner or later. You should therefore go within and pray to the divine 'Fill my being with love.' Or you may like to choose a great spiritual master, with whom you feel some connection, and pray 'Oh Christ, Oh Buddha, Oh Mohammed fill my being with love!'

Love always seeks to express itself through you, as love in action. When your heart is filled with fear, you will hate the world and at that moment you are the Anti-Christ. When your heart is filled with divine love, you are the Christ and in that natural state, you will perform selfless actions, just as he did. This is why your awakening is so important to the whole of humanity. This is why giving priority every day to your own quiet times of meditation, prayer and contemplation is quite the opposite of self-indulgence, or selfishness. Through constant devotion to the path of meditation, or self-awareness, you can awake. When your heart is fully open and you are fully awake, you are simply 'love in action.' You do not have to think about doing the right thing. Love simply extends itself through you and this love heals the whole world.

The fruits of stillness

Peace, calmness, self-healing, self-empowerment, health, wealth, happiness, harmonious relationships, wisdom, love and miracles are just some of the fruits of meditation.

All genuine spiritual disciplines train practitioners to gear their minds into stillness. The strength and power of a completely still and peaceful mind is amazing. As you still your mind through daily meditation, your body begins to heal and replenish itself. Your metabolic and hormonal systems will become more balanced and harmonised. Your heart rate will slow down and your automatic nervous system will be strengthened. Everything in your system settles down, your whole being becomes calm, and then repairs itself naturally. A sense of aliveness will rise up in you, and your consciousness will expand. Eventually, if you keep quietening your mind on a daily basis, you will find your true purpose in life. This is guaranteed.

Once you have calmed your mind, you will see more clearly, develop greater wisdom and find true love and joy within the stillness. Can all this come about just from sitting still? Ultimately yes, without a doubt, and it costs nothing except a small amount of your time and some mental discipline. When you finally reap the fully ripened fruits of daily meditation practice, you will be one of the happiest people on the planet. You will be radiant, and you will embody the art of radiant living. You will need and want less and less from this physical world, and sometimes you may even have an awesome glimpse of what lies beyond our physical existence.

Sitting still on a daily basis brings almost immediate benefits into your life, but you should also keep reminding yourself of the true purpose of meditation. The ultimate goal of meditation is not to feel calmer, or to cope better with the ups and downs of your life. It is to know yourself, to discover the true self that lies hidden underneath your artificial personality-self.

We live in a very strange, uncomfortable world, because we cannot really know each other until we awake. We look around and see a world full of threatening strangers, and then, in the name of defending ourselves from external threats, we are always poised to attack. But when you awake and know the true nature of your mind, you will know the others too. You will know that we are all fundamentally the same.

When you finally dwell only in love and peace, you will lay down all your weapons. You will no longer gossip about others, or stab someone behind their back. If you are not in love, you just cannot help yourself attacking others. But when, through meditation, you return to your natural state of dwelling in love and peace, you will want only to extend this love and peace out to everyone you meet. You will become a beautiful ripple of peace in the world, and each time you meet someone, you will naturally surround them with love and light.

As more and more individuals take the time and effort to still their minds on a daily basis, the whole world will benefit. As we each transcend our fearful, pain-filled personality-selves to become fearless Radiant Warriors, our beloved planet earth will breathe a sigh of relief, the wars and violence that currently rage all around us will eventually begin to subside, and a New Age of Enlightenment will inevitably dawn on earth.

Exercises

Committing to sitting still on a daily basis

If you do not yet meditate on a daily basis, make a commitment to yourself now to sit still for just ten or fifteen minutes a day for the next thirty days come what may.

Think of a time of day when taking 10 minutes out of your busy schedule would be convenient for you, a time when you would not be disturbed by your family, colleagues or friends. Now say to yourself 'OK I am ready to do this every day for the next month without fail.'

It is far better to begin by meditating for a short time daily, than to attempt longer periods of meditation and end up only meditating occasionally.

You may like to keep a journal for the next thirty days in which you note down any experiences you have during and after your meditations.

Improving your meditation technique

If you already meditate daily, take some time to observe your meditative technique. Is your spine straight and are your energy centres open?

If you notice that your meditations are rather flat, and your mind rather sleepy or dull, explore various options for energising yourself, such as doing some chi kung before you meditate.

If you notice that your mind still tends to wander all over the place when you meditate, experiment with using a mantra in order to train your mind to focus on just one thought.

Keep using these new techniques for at least a month and notice any improvements to your meditation and/or your daily life.

Lengthening your meditations

If you are confident in your chosen meditation practice and its results, Congratulations! But if you want to make further progress on your chosen path, make a commitment now to lengthening your daily meditation, or meditating more frequently for the next thirty days. Then mindfully observe any results that occur.

Jane's Story: Part 3

I remember when I was at Liverpool University in the early 1970s, some friends tried to persuade me to be initiated into Transcendental Meditation (after all, the Beatles were meditating so it must be good!) but I was incensed to discover that you had to pay a significant sum of money to receive your own secret mantra and decided that the whole thing was a con. Nearly thirty years later, another friend kept asking me to go with her to a meditation weekend run by an Australian psychotherapist and his partner, but I kept telling her that meditation was definitely not for me. She did not give up and after about two years of nagging, I finally agreed to go for just one day.

To my absolute astonishment I loved it. The teacher was so charismatic, and told me that meditation would help me to find the love that I had always been seeking (at the time I thought he meant I would meet my perfect 'soul mate'!). When I got home I found that I could not sit still and meditate for more than about ten minutes. My mind just raced and I longed to get up and do something interesting instead, but the weekend workshops with my new teachers were something else, and I began to look forward to them with surprising intensity, even though nothing much happened to me when we actually meditated.

Several years later, my mind was beginning to be just a little bit calmer when I sat on my meditation cushion and sometimes, when I was meditating in a group with my teachers, I would feel so happy and alive, but I still did not believe in God and I still did not think that life was truly meaningful. Then I signed up for a two week Christmas and New Year retreat with Jason Chan because I thought that learning a bit of tai chi might be good for my heath!

It was during this retreat that I had a major spiritual awakening. As we all meditated together, light and love just poured through me, and by the end of the retreat I knew that God was real and felt that God was in direct communication with me. My higher charkas were fully open and I was so joyful that I wondered whether I had died and gone to heaven. My years of meditating with my first teachers had undoubtedly prepared me for this dramatic spiritual opening, and I am profoundly grateful to them for their patience and wisdom as they gently guided me through the early stages of learning to still my mind. But nothing could have prepared me for the sudden opening of my consciousness that happened when I first meditated with Jason Chan. It was both a divine blessing and a horrible shock to my system that took many, many months to integrate and ground through my rather weak energetic and physical bodies. None of that mattered, however, all that mattered was that I had tasted the divine, and my whole life now took on a profound new meaning and purpose.

Chapter 4

Mastering Your Daily Life

You have to become the master of your own life. All other spiritual training will be pointless, if you do not take responsibility for your life.

Are you ready to take responsibility for your life?

The majority of people living on earth today are still not ready to take full responsibility for themselves and their lives. They would rather continue to play victim than to acknowledge the power of their minds. Radiant Warriors on the other hand, commit themselves wholeheartedly to the belief that they are the masters of their own lives. They accept that they create their own reality as long as perception lasts, and that, if they want their world to change, they have to change their own mind first.

You are so good at acting a role; you are so good at being your particular personality with your habitual emotions and thoughts that you have completely forgotten that you can un-act yourself. Everybody is doing the best they know how to be happy, but the majority of people just do not know how to get out of their own imprisonment. They suffer because they do not know any better. They do not see any alternative. There is always a choice: to stay asleep dreaming endless nightmares, or to wake up. But most people do not want to awake. They want to stay in illusion.

There is a big hook to our ignorant, or illusive, state of existence. It is an illusion that we all enjoy. We are all enthralled by the drama of living in the physical world, even the suffering that it causes us. We enjoy playing victim and persecutor. If you do not believe me, notice your reactions when someone shares a really juicy bit of gossip with you. Many of us do not want to escape from our dream world just yet, because in the enlightened state of being there is no drama, no ups and downs, no highs and lows.

From the perspective of the personality, the enlightened state is actually horribly boring. In the enlightened state there is no past or future. Your personality-self is not at all interested in this eternal now, because there is no room in it for imagination or fantasies of a better future. To live completely in the now seems so boring, that it scares you to death! Your personality-self just does not want to wake up, but pain is a perfect stimulus to awake. When none of your worldly dreams has brought you lasting happiness, and when you have suffered enough, you will decide to begin the awakening journey.

To an enlightened soul, the eternal now is very rich. Life becomes a spontaneous happening, a blissful moment-to-moment flow. However, because your personality-self really does not want to awake, you have to use all your skilful means to overcome your resistance to opening the prison door into the great unknown. You have to keep practising living in the dynamic emptiness of now, until you have achieved full mastery of your mind.

Everything is a manifestation of our minds

Out of six billion human beings, only a few thousand can control their minds; for everyone else their minds, thoughts and feelings, control them. Your mind is the most powerful agent in the whole universe. Everything in this world, from breathtakingly beautiful art to devastating wars, is a manifestation of people's minds. The world is nothing in itself. Your mind gives it all the meaning it has. If you do not learn how to control your mind, it will create chaos. It will cause you and those around you illness, pain and suffering. However, the power of your mind can also assist you to heal. Your mind can heal physical symptoms, even severe ones such as cancerous growths, and your mind can also heal deep-seated emotional wounds and scars.

It is not easy to change your mind, because you always justify your negative judgements and beliefs, and blame the world around you for your pain and suffering. However, if you are serious about becoming a Radiant Warrior and saving the world, changing your own mind is essential. In order to do this you will need a lot of practice. There is no other way to transform your life. If you do not train and discipline your mind to serve you, it will work against you and the whole of humanity. On the other hand, if you are prepared to learn how your mind works, you can train it to work for you. Otherwise you will go through the same negative patterns and emotions forever.

Every time you wake up in the morning you see a world of duality. You experience yourself as the subject and everything outside of you becomes 'object.' This is what you see every time you open your eyes: 'me' and the bed, 'me' and the bathroom, 'me' and other people travelling on the bus into work. You truly believe this is reality, because you have become so used to it. However, according to many great spiritual teachings, you are living in illusion. Your senses are deceiving you.

You think you are so smart, but you are just living in your own fantasy world. Your mind is in control of you, rather than the other way around. Your mind is in permanent turmoil and conflict and you swing from one crazy thought to the next. If someone does not agree with you, you see them as your enemy. If your loved one does not live up to your fantasy of them, you hate them. You make all this up. All your perceived problems happen in your mind first, then you project them out into the world around you and truly believe you are the victim of external circumstances.

Whenever you put your faith in anything that you believe is on the outside of you, you will be disappointed. Everything on the outside of you comes and goes. Nothing is permanent or unchanging and nothing can save you from yourself. But the good news is, you can still train your mind so that one day you can escape from your self-inflicted prison or illusory existence. All you need is a meditation mat, a cushion and some will power. This costs nothing.

Your mind is very stubborn

As a would-be Radiant Warrior, you need to understand, right from the word go, that your mind can be very stubborn. Even when you realise that it is not serving you, your mind strongly resists change, because your personality-self is so afraid of awakening. It prefers to stay in a familiar place, however painful that is. So, you have to persist, with great determination and discipline, to overcome the negative patterns inside your own mind.

If you think of your mind as a computer, you have to change both your hard drive and your software. You have to brainwash yourself on a daily basis. Your brain is full of viruses, so you need to install an anti-virus programme. You need to sit still, at least once a day, and imagine that you are sitting all alone on a beautiful mountaintop with a golden sun pouring its light down on you. From here, you can watch your hatred and negativity rising up and let it dissolve into the light. We all know that fear and hatred are not good for us, but most people do not know how to de-programme themselves by linking up to the light and allowing healing to happen naturally.

For the majority of people, body and mind cannot be separated. You have bodily habits, emotional habits and mental habits and you are imprisoned in all of them. Even though you often do not like your habitual emotions, mental attitudes, and frail, painful body, they are all you know. So you are trapped forever in this mindset, unless you begin to observe the workings of your own mind. When the mind does not know itself anymore, it is ignorant or delusional and you suffer. Even the most highly educated genius is still ignorant in this sense. This is what the Buddhists term 'ignorant mind.' The other state of mind is what Buddhists call luminosity, or enlightenment.

When your mind is illuminated, you are 'Buddha.' Buddha means awakened one or perfected one. When your mind is trapped in ignorance, you are in prison and there appears to be no way out. You suffer because you are not free. You are like a bird in a cage. You cannot soar like an eagle, even though this is your true nature. When your mind is ignorant, or separate from its source, you will always find fear or insecurity in your system, and loneliness will follow you wherever you go. The ignorant mind is full of pain, conflict, and fear. It is always judging, seeking and blaming.

Observing your mind is a must

You cannot just wake up one morning and decide to take control of your mind. Your thoughts will just keep popping up from nowhere into your conscious awareness and there is no technique you can perfect to stop this natural process. But you can learn to observe your mind. On the spiritual path one thing is an absolute requirement, the observation of your mind.

When you first stop and begin to observe your mind, you will find that it is full of conflict and does not make sense. Most people split off their mind from their heart, and then act in ways that conflict with their heart's desire. For example, deep in their heart they long to be a musician, but they train to be an accountant. They long to live in New York, but they actually live in Birmingham. Nearly everybody on earth has a conflicted mind and then constantly changes it. One minute they love someone so much and the next minute they hate them. The undisciplined mind just keeps oscillating like this.

Without developing an awakening agent or observer within, your mind will keep switching back and forth, and everything and everyone will continue to push your buttons. It is so painful to live like this. Most people just about cope, but this normal way of living is so fearful and full of angst. We all desperately need to find some inner peace, because we all experience this world as a very scary, warlike place to be. Unless you find a way to calm your mind, fear, doubt, jealousies, insecurities and desires will keep your mind in permanent conflict.

The greatest guru is life itself. What if you know all the theory of enlightenment and then your loved ones really push your buttons? The whole world is in pain. We all share our fearful thoughts and feelings in what can be called collective consciousness. Our thoughts do not just belong to us alone. Philosophy does not help us to escape this pain. An intellectual understanding that this physical world of duality is just an illusion does not help. If you do not change your mind, you will suffer over and over again in a perpetual cycle of ignorance, and the only way out is to awake.

Awakening from the dream

The awakening process is very strenuous. If you want to awake this lifetime, this goal will eventually demand your complete attention 24/7. Awakening means that you see all illusions more clearly, but your mind has to be trained to do this. You have to use both your mind and your heart to awake. When you reach a point of deep meditation, you will transcend duality, or the dream of your isolated, physical existence, and experience great love and bliss, but this alone will not transform your life. You have to become awake in your dream, and begin to dream your daily life with conscious awareness. You cannot just be awake in light and bliss.

At first, the gap between your worldly personality and your divinity may seem as wide as an ocean. But once you have had a glimpse of heaven, once you have experienced the peace, joy and light that is deep within you, you will strive to bridge that gap however long it takes.

You will still get irritated. You will still get tired, and then you will not be able to sustain divine love, but you can, and must, develop a warrior spirit to bridge this gap. At first, your daily life may seem particularly dull and problematic, compared to the glimpse you have had of heaven during a deep meditation. Moreover, as you increasingly experience divine joy, you will also experience your shadows much more vividly. As you become more compassionate, you will also have to face your own cruelty and you will inevitably see all your darkness more clearly as it comes up to the surface of your awareness. All this is certainly a challenge, but it will really help if you can also see it as a fascinating voyage of discovery.

In order to go back to your natural state of being, you first have to become mindful about all those aspects of your life in which you feel trapped or negative. In other words, for the truth to reveal itself to you, you need to become aware of everything that is not the truth. The further you go along the path, the more you will tread on thin ice and the more you will need to become conscious about all aspects of yourself.

Cultivating mindfulness

The first step in mastering the art of conscious living, is to develop mindfulness of all aspects of your life. For most people life is just a blur, but as a Radiant Warrior, you choose to learn from all your experiences and use them to lead you back to the truth. How conscious are you of your thoughts, speech and behaviour? How conscious are you when you are hurting someone you love? How conscious are you when you stuff yourself with a whole packet of chocolate biscuits or watch rubbish on television?

It is essential to differentiate between normal thinking and being conscious. Most people go from being asleep to being awake every 24 hours, but not to being conscious. If you are not conscious, you are sleepwalking through life. For the great majority of individuals, being awake during the daytime is still a form of sleeping, and usually these unconscious people are living out a nightmare. Their lives can be very painful, depending on how many strong desires and emotions they experience. 'Sleeping' people often shout at you. They can become very violent, and may even kill you. They simply do not know what they are doing. But when you become conscious, it is self-denial to say ' I didn't mean it.' It is a lie to say ' I was drunk. I did not know what I was doing.'

Developing mindfulness enables you to begin the process of awakening to your true, unchanging nature. When you live a mindful life, you are not watching yourself all the time, but you do begin to train yourself to know what you are doing. Once you train your mind in this way, you can begin to control your behaviour; your drinking, eating, sexual desires, your shopping habits, your interactions with others.

When you live life consciously, you live a full life; otherwise your life will drift by in a blur. Once you are living consciously, you can learn your lessons very fast. To become more conscious, all you have to do is to train yourself to be an observer. Once you get in touch with the part of you that is observing your life, you can examine where your thoughts come from and look at your motives and intentions behind your speech and actions.

When you live consciously, you begin to understand what you are doing. You achieve this by observing how your mind interprets your experiences, and gives its own meaning to them. When someone shouts at you, what does your mind tell you that this means? When you see a snake or a spider, what does your mind tell you about them, does it tell you to feel fear?

You should aim to become like a scientist exploring your own mind. You can only gain wisdom by being intensely interested in your life. This takes courage, because as you begin to observe yourself, you will witness thoughts and actions that seem very aggressive, unkind or unskilful. However, if you are not willing to observe yourself, including all your unskilful areas, you will continue to live a deluded existence and you will fail to learn your lessons this lifetime.

Examining your life

Some areas of your life are working well, others are not. If you examine your life on a daily basis, you will know where you are making progress and where you are still trapped in illusion. If you find that even though you have been on your spiritual path for quite some time, you are still fearful about money issues, or you still fight with your partner, your daughter, your son, your mother or your mother-in law, or you still lust after a fit, young body, please do not beat yourself up. Just look deeply into these areas of your life with compassion and understanding.

If you experience any pain or fear in your life, then you still need to put effort into awakening and into cultivating mindfulness. You still need to become more conscious of your negative thought patterns that will pop up over and over again in your daily life. We are all very stubborn in some areas of our minds. For example, you may have a strong habit of thinking or feeling that you are not good enough or unlovable, or you may habitually believe that other people are untrustworthy and always let you down. Stuck thought patterns such as these may protect you from having to take full responsibility for yourself and the world around you, but they also block the light in you and hide your true greatness.

If, each and every day, you commit to becoming more aware of these unhelpful thought patterns and to sending love and compassion to them, you can actually heal yourself with kindness and love. True love has a miraculous, healing power within it that can heal all your deep-seated unworthiness, once you become conscious enough to be aware of all your own destructive beliefs and mind patterns. Negative thought patterns are never a call for more punishment and guilt. They are always a cry for love.

Cultivating inner peace moment to moment

As a Radiant Warrior, you need to stay very alert and vigilant. You have to train your mind to stop worrying or fantasising about the past and the future. If you train your mind to stay in the present moment, you will find yourself becoming very sharp and alert. This is true living. Eventually, you should be able to maintain a calm and peaceful presence under all circumstances.

Daily life gives you a wonderful opportunity to practise this. For example, if you are late for a meeting and you are stuck in traffic, you can observe your reactions, and then train yourself to focus on inner peace. If a colleague begins to irritate you at work, you can tell yourself what a great opportunity this is to develop the capacity to stay calm under trying conditions. This training is literally a matter of life and death. It will determine whether you lead a life full of happiness, or one full of misery. It will even determine whether or not you die a good death.

By training yourself to remain calm in response to small daily challenges or irritants, you will eventually be able to focus on peace, light and love throughout much greater challenges. When we are tired, sick or in a bad mood, we all automatically think negatively about our situation and our loved ones. You therefore need to put a lot of effort into avoiding falling into these moods and even greater effort into not digging a bigger hole once you have fallen into one. Intellectually understanding how all this works is not mastery. Intellectually understanding that nothing on the outside of us can disturb our mind unless we let it, is a good starting point, but sustaining this understanding through the ups and downs of daily life is a very different matter.

Involuntary negative patterns are habitual. You have many years, if not lifetimes, of unconsciously falling into your bad moods at the drop of a hat. So you will need to stay very aware and alert to catch yourself over and over again. Each time you fall into a bad mood and hate those around you, you have a golden opportunity to own your own projections, to go deep into the hurt underneath your anger or hate and then to heal that wounded, fearful part of yourself with unconditional love and compassion.

Noticing your intentions

If you strive to be fully mindful in all that you do, you will never have a dull moment. As well as being mindful about your behaviour, you will also benefit greatly from truthfully examining your attitudes, your thoughts, your intentions and your speech. For example, have you ever noticed the impact of your intention when you say something? Gossiping is one of human beings' most popular pastimes, but, somewhere deep inside you, do not feel right when you gossip about someone. Gossip is often two people trying to glorify themselves through someone else's misfortune or inadequacies, whereas in a meaningful conversation, two people feed each other with positive energy. Sometimes gossip comes from self-hatred, so, please be brave and examine what lies behind your tendency to gossip.

The more you practise and develop your inner wisdom, the greater the power your words will hold. Therefore, as you mature spiritually, you should be more and more careful what you say to others, as you will have a stronger and stronger impact on them. Even your innermost thoughts have an impact on the world around you. Every time you think you hate someone, you influence the collective thought form. Every time you think loving thoughts, you help to heal our planet.

Mindfulness practice is very straightforward. You simply keep utilising all your experiences in life to get to know your own mind, until you go back to the truth, or until the truth is revealed to you. Going on holiday will not help. Making loads of money will not help. Experiences by themselves will never assist you to grow spiritually. You can only learn from your experiences in life if you are truly prepared to observe or examine them.

Experiences by themselves have no real meaning and will never bring you lasting happiness. If you sit by a one million pound swimming pool day after day, in perfect sunshine, you will not feel great for long. Eventually you will start to feel bored and restless. Even intense sexual pleasure becomes less exciting after a while. All you will end up with, eventually, are empty memories. But if you observe intently how you interpret these experiences, you will inevitably grow spiritually.

Everyone around you will contribute to your lessons to facilitate your growth. Even if you do not want to learn from life, people who press your buttons will still appear right in front of you. You cannot avoid this, so you might as well commit to seeing consciously what is going on and learning from it. People who irritate you keep you alert. In fact, if you really want to learn about yourself and grow quickly, I suggest you spend time with people who really annoy you!

Your daily life can teach you so much. Your relationships, your work, your worries about health, sex and money are all part of your physical existence, and learning to master all these areas of your life is essential. Saying 'I am a spiritual person, I am not going to engage with such worldly issues' will not work. If you ignore the world around you, you are just like an ostrich sticking its head in the sand.

Giving priority to your spiritual practice

When you are awakening, everyday there are lessons to learn and a purpose to fulfil, so, if you are wise, you will not waste a moment. Your goal is to be conscious every moment of your life. Until you take complete responsibility for every aspect of your life, many so called 'spiritual experiences' can be just self-deception. You still will not be able to make any sense of your life and true happiness will continue to elude you.

Occasionally, when you are in deep meditation or on a spiritual retreat, you may have blissful glimpses of your own divinity, to remind you of your true potential, but you will still have to return to your daily life and continue to work on yourself. You will still need to face all your personal desires and aversions, all your negative thought patterns, ancient hatreds and vengeances. If you do not heal these this lifetime, they will still be with you after you die. How you live your daily life is so much more important than once in a blue moon experiences of enlightenment. What will win out when you die, a few blissful, but unrepeatable, spiritual experiences or your daily habits and daily mindset?

In order to stabilise your spiritual light, you should give priority to your spiritual awakening on a daily basis. You should do your very best each day to nurture your flickering inner light and protect it. Never allow your enthusiasm for your one path to be dampened. Rekindle the desire for liberation deep within your heart over and over again. Use all skilful means to keep bringing your heart back to this one goal.

Please do not be tempted to go back to your old way of life, or old ways of thinking, or you will find yourself at a dead end. If you do not honour your soul's purpose, you will not only waste away your own life, but you will also cut off help to all those souls who are waiting for your assistance to awake. On the other hand, if you follow your intuition to fulfil God's purpose for you, despite your ego's strong resistance, everything you need to accomplish will be accomplished for you. You cannot even begin to imagine the richness of following your spiritual purpose; in comparison to this, worldly pleasures are literally nothing.

It is self-deception to use the busyness of our daily lives as an excuse to forget our spiritual path. Daily life will continue to challenge your spiritual ideals, but eventually, rather than separating your life into pigeonholes, you will realise that everything in your life is your spiritual practice. Unfortunately, it is not possible to be spiritual just one day a week, or one hour a day and reach the ultimate spiritual goal of full liberation or awakening.

The journey home to your true self takes total commitment. Eventually, you should be able to extend your meditative state of inner peace into 16 hours a day. You should be able hold your inner connection to the divine, whatever you are doing, and whatever is happening around you. Your plane is about to crash and you can still hold your inner light. A nuclear bomb is about to be dropped on your home and your mind and heart are at peace. Congratulations, you have graduated as a Radiant Warrior!

Connecting to God all day long

Your key goal is to live your whole life with one purpose. Do not forget about God when you go to work, or out to a party. Once you have established a connection with the divine through deep prayer, or meditation, commit to bringing this connection into every aspect of your daily life. For example, when you are working, you can still keep taking regular short breaks to reconnect to the divine. Whilst everyone else is having a tea break, take a 'spirit break.' Don't merge back into an unconscious state of living, even when you are behaving like a normal human being on the surface. Only when you become a true master, is there no effort involved in bringing the divine into your daily life.

It is wonderful to start each and every day by connecting to the divine. When you wake up each morning, you can begin with a short prayer of surrender to God or higher consciousness in which you ask, 'Where would you have me go today? 'Whom would you have me meet? 'What would you have me do or say? I say to myself every day 'I may miss all my appointments on earth, but I will not miss my appointment with God.'

It is so important to pray to God at the beginning of your day, because, without this vertical connection, you are nothing and can achieve nothing of any lasting value. Every morning, ask to be granted a day filled with peace and love. Every evening, review how much love and peace you have manifested in your day. Each night before you go to sleep, ask a higher intelligence, 'What lesson did I need to learn today? What is it that I need to know?' Finally, at the end of every day, give all your desires and all your pain back to the divine and surrender yourself to divine protection as you fall to sleep.

Observing all your negative judgements

As you go through your day, practise observing your ego mind judging and criticising yourself, others and the world around you. If you observe yourself each day, you will notice that your mind is always judging. Each time you notice yourself being critical, you can remind yourself 'This is a lack of love.' 'Why do I not love myself just now?' Please do not be tempted to judge your ever-judging mind, or you will just be going round in circles. Simply learn to observe all your thoughts with great interest and compassion. Look at the results of your constant judgements, and ask yourself whether they bring you peace or joy.

It will be also be helpful if you can see the funny side of your judging mind and have a good laugh at it. 'That woman is so overweight she is a disgrace.' 'That man's shoes are filthy.' 'I am such a bad person to care what people look like.' If you keep practising observing your rambling thoughts like this, you should begin to see how crazy most of your thoughts are. You may also notice that when your mind is very fast and busy, you see a busy world. When your mind is more peaceful, the world will equally reflect this back to you.

As you practise noticing your judgemental thoughts on a daily basis, observe what happens when your ego insists on being right about something, and ask yourself 'Do I want to be right or do I want to be happy?' Notice when you really want to win an argument with someone, and observe how that feels to you. Are you at peace? Are you in love?

Without judgement, everything is beautiful. This does not mean that you do not notice when others are doing something that may cause you or others harm so that you may take action to protect yourself and/or other people. It simply means that you do not judge someone as unworthy, however they are behaving. If someone is acting in a way that is dangerous, please take every step to minimise that danger to everyone concerned. Learning not to judge others has nothing to do with passively sitting in harms way! Being non-judgemental is a state of mind. You can disarm a potential mugger without judging him as a 'bad' person.

As you begin to notice just how much your mind judges yourself and others, please do not try to fix your mind, simply observe it, and then commit each day to learning a lesson that will help you to return to love and peace. You may find daily affirmations helpful, such as ' Today I am returning to love.' 'I choose peace instead of this.' 'I choose to be happy rather than right.' Every time you notice that you are irritated or agitated, pause, breathe, and do your best to return to love or peace.

The art of emptying your mind should also be practised on a daily basis. Every night you fill your mind up with the content of your dreams, so every morning you need to empty your mind again. Then, every evening before you go to sleep, you need to delete all the negative thoughts and emotions that you have accumulated during your day. Each time you have a negative thought, you can pause and delete it. Whenever you notice that you are thinking rubbish, or feeling a negative emotion, you can say to yourself 'Delete' and offer it all back to the universe.

You are always free to cancel your negativity, moment by moment. If, at the end of the day, some negativity is still left in your system, you can simply 'empty your waste-bin.' By giving everything back to the universe in this way, you allow it to digest your rubbish for you. Alternatively, you may like to imagine your dark thoughts and feelings being shone away by a very bright shower of divine light.

If you continue to be afraid of your negativity, you will give it power, and you will remain trapped indefinitely. This is why it is so important to learn how to delete or cancel it. If you practise deleting all your negative thoughts on a daily basis, in no time there will be no junk left in your system—no viruses, no 'spam.' Emptiness is associated with opening and awakening. The more you learn to empty your mind, the more you will find a connection to the eternal and absolute truth.

If you want to achieve great things on earth, you should learn the art of emptying yourself and releasing all your pre-set expectations. When your mind is not empty, you trap yourself inside your human games and emotions. True power lies in peace and dynamic emptiness. As you empty yourself, the source of all things manifest will constantly refill you. This source is eternal and un-programmed, and ultimately it will assist you to know once again your true self and your natural state of being.

Exercises

Becoming mindful of your unskilful thoughts and behaviour

Take 20 minutes or so to reflect on what areas of your life are working well and where you are not doing so well.

Explore your skilfulness and un-skilfulness in relation to three core areas of your life: money, health and relationships, **or** take one area in your life that is not working so well.

Now contemplate on what skills you would need to acquire to transform that area of your life.

At the end of your contemplation make a solemn vow to do something as soon as possible to improve your skilfulness in one aspect of your behaviour.

Please remember throughout this exercise that your goal is to become more mindful about just how you create your own reality. If you beat yourself up as you notice those areas of your life where you may be unskilful, you will just end up bruised and battered, so please examine yourself with unconditional love and acceptance.

Making a daily appointment with God

Take a moment now to think about the times in your day when it would be possible for you to take a 'spirit break' and write down in your diary a time each morning and afternoon when you will stop for just five or ten minutes to reconnect to the divine. Commit to taking these spirit breaks for at least thirty days and observe the impact this has on your life and your state of mind

Reflecting on your negative judgements

Take a minute or two now to remember a recent occasion when you judged someone very negatively. Pray for help to see the situation differently and then sit still and gently contemplate your negative judgement, without in any way judging yourself as you do so. Your goal is simply to allow yourself to see the situation in a different light.

Perhaps you will see the funny side of your judgement, or perhaps you will realise how your negative judgement affected your own peace of mind. Whatever you thought at the time about the person you judged negatively, please remember that you can always change your mind.

You might even want to close your contemplation by giving thanks to the person you judged negatively for giving you such a wonderful opportunity to reflect on your own judging mind!

Jane's Story: Part 4

Looking back on my awakening journey, I am so grateful that I had a major spiritual opening when I first meditated with Jason, even though the aftermath of that opening was incredibly hard to handle. Connecting to the light is amazing and, when it first happened to me, I felt so special and so spiritual, and that initial opening certainly inspired me to keep going, even when the path became very steep and challenging.

But now I can see that after this amazing spiritual high, nothing much had changed. I was the same old personality-self and even worse, my personality-self was now claiming the light as her own special achievement. Thankfully, Jason Chan is a wise spiritual guide who does not allow his students' egos to over-inflate as the light begins to empower them.

For a long time after my first opening I just wanted to repeat some of the amazing experiences I had had on retreat. But eventually I not only realised that this was impossible, since each meditation is quite unique, but I also began to see that if I was serious about spiritual awakening I could no longer just go on spiritual retreats and workshops to get high and then go back to my ordinary day-to-day life without giving any thought to my spiritual path.

Under Jason's guidance, I have slowly learnt to become more mindful in my daily life and I have begun to examine my day-to-day thoughts and my intentions as honestly as I can. Very often I have not liked what I have observed. I have discovered, for example, that I can feel violently jealous just because two close friends stay up talking after I have gone to bed. I have also noted how much I like to see others, even close friends as less spiritual than myself.

I have watched myself resentfully buying Christmas gifts for friends solely because it was expected of me, and listening only half-heartedly to the problems of other close friends who had turned to me for comfort. When I first began to practise noticing my intentions like this, I tended to beat myself up for being so selfish and egotistical, but more recently I am much more likely just to laugh at the tricks my ego-self gets up to, and then to remind myself that I still have an infinitely long way to go before I turn into a Bodhisattva!

Meditating seemed very hard to me at first, because my mind was so busy and over-active, but learning to be mindful in my daily life has proved to be an even more challenging spiritual discipline. Even now, after so many years of practise, I still love to turn on the TV, watch rubbish and become mindless for several hours on end. Even now, after watching others mindfully blessing their food before eating it so many times, I still find myself mindlessly gobbling my food without a thought, as though I were starving. Even now, after years of observing my judgemental lower mind I find myself enjoying a moment of gossiping negatively about a friend or acquaintance without stopping to think 'What on earth are you doing?'

Being mindful 24/7 is still way beyond me, but bit by bit and painfully slowly, I think that I am becoming just a little more aware of the tricks of my ego and the habitual workings of my lower mind. More and more, I do catch myself projecting my inner pain by getting angry with someone, or by blaming someone for their 'unacceptable' behaviour, and each time I bring these projections back and take responsibility for all my own negative thoughts and feelings, I know that I am taking another very small but essential step back to the truth.

Part II

The Path of Healing

Chapter 5

Healing Your Physical Body

To awake you have to master your body. You cannot be a Radiant Warrior with a stomach ulcer.

Sickness is a state of mind

'Why do people get sick, age and die?' is a 6 billion dollar question. But don't ask a doctor for the answer. Doctors tend to die at a younger age than the rest of us. Most doctors still know virtually nothing about the mind and its role in creating ill health. You have to look deep within your own mind for the answer.

Great masters understand that there is only mind, and that the cure for all sickness lies within it. When your mind finally merges back with the universal mind, or divine consciousness, you will laugh at sickness. You will know it is not real. When you can totally merge back with love, you will not be ill and sick. When you are spirit, you transcend duality and you are healed. This is why the greatest spiritual masters can raise the dead. They have totally merged back into love itself. They are forever free and have all forces at their command.

Most of us actually want to be sick, although we may not realise this on a conscious level. If, in some layer of your being, you are attached to being ill and sick, no one can heal you, however skilful they are. This is the power of the mind. If you really wanted to be healed, you would change your mind and you would be healed.

No one likes to accept the fact that we make ourselves sick. This is not part of our education or culture, and so it is very hard to convince people to change their minds about the fundamental cause of all sickness. But nothing will ever happen to you without your mind's consent, either consciously or unconsciously. As yet this is not accepted wisdom in our culture. If you tell someone that they want to be ill and sick, you will probably really annoy them. If you tell a parent that their child has chosen to be seriously ill, they will probably become extremely angry with you.

Why do we all suffer so much physical pain and sickness? Because fear, guilt and anger are inbuilt into our physical existence. If you are not awake, everything is fearful and what you call happiness, or a good time, is just a gap between your pain and suffering. Fear and lack of forgiveness create disease in all of us.

Sickness is anger taken out on the body. If you are angry for any length of time, particularly if you bury this anger so that you do not have to feel it consciously, you will eventually experience physical pain. If you are constantly bombarding your system with worry or anger, sooner or later you will notice physical symptoms. Doctors very rarely address this, and in any case doctors cannot change your mind for you, you have to do it yourself. The key formula for healing the root of your physical problems is to go deep into the emotional pain that lies behind them.

To heal, forgive and let go

Forgiveness and letting go are key aspects of the healing process, because forgiveness will restore love into your system and love can heal any problem, however great it appears to be. Forgiveness will enable you to see the body for what it really is, a teaching aid to be gladly set aside when your learning is complete. Healing always involves the grace of God, and so you need to surrender to this, higher power, but the ego never wants to do this.

The ego does not want to know that it has always been so wrong. The ego therefore does not want to be healed. This is why you have to rise above your ego's agenda in order to heal your mind. You have to be prepared to feel your emotional pain in order to release it from your mind. You will need to bring the light to your pain in order to heal it. The more light you bring into your mind the less you will be sick, so please, never miss an opportunity to connect to light, love and peace for the sake of your sanity and your physical health. Please keep searching through thick and thin for true love and peace. When your mind is healed, your body will follow automatically, because your body is simply a manifestation of your mind.

Fear and anger make us sick

We now spend billions of pounds and dollars each year looking for cures for cancer, but very little research has yet been done into the role the mind and our emotions play in causing diseases such as this. Fear and hatred that are held in your system will cause stuck energy, and eventually this energetic block may manifest in your physical system as a physical weakness or an imbalance such as a cancerous growth.

A cancer growth, in energy terms, is a localised, destructive energy force; a block of negative energy that forms into a mass. Cancer reflects our dark side, our shadows and our long held hatreds. Physical sickness can also be caused by a lack of energy that causes a hole, or lack of vitality, in your energetic body. Lack of love can create holes like this in your energetic body that will eventually manifest as debilitation in your physical system. Moreover, when you do not live in love, your heart tightens up and eventually you may even suffer a heart attack.

We are still at the kindergarten level in terms of understanding energy patterns and how they influence our physical bodies and minds. Even some great spiritual masters still get sick. But you need to do your very best to look after all levels of your consciousness, including your physical body.

Self-realisation on its own is not enough. 'I am enlightened.' So what? Your body will still get sick and die. People used to think that self-realisation or enlightenment was the end point, but self-realisation is only the first step towards enabling you to function as God intends you to, in accord with divine or universal law. Self-realisation will not automatically fill up a hole in your energy system or dissolve an energetic block. True healing has to include the elimination of all fear and hatred from your system.

Looking after your physical body

Only about 5 to 50 people in the world have ever been able to just think about healing an illness for it to disappear. In theory the mind can completely control the physical. Jesus Christ was not the first, nor the last, great spiritual master who could raise the dead, but this is an extremely rare phenomenon. Since we are nowhere near that level of spiritual or energetic mastery, it is simply wishful thinking to say 'I will change my mind and my sickness will instantly disappear.' Whenever you are sick or 'under the weather' it would be most helpful to consider healthy changes to your diet and your physical routines. You should really look after yourself physically when you are feeling below par.

As a Radiant Warrior you understand that you are not just a body, but this does not mean that you deny having a body when you are trapped in one. You understand that the ultimate cause of all illness lies in the mind, but you are also sensible enough to accept that you are not yet enlightened enough to cure yourself simply by changing your mind. While you still believe so strongly in your physical existence, you need to look after your body as best you can. For example, if you are lacking in energy you may need to take a holiday in the sunshine. If you become very physically weak and debilitated, you may need to change your diet and eat nourishing foods that you would not normally eat.

Healing into wholeness is not an easy path. When you are in great physical or emotional pain, death may even seem more tempting than life. But please accept that as long as you are going through time and space, you have lessons to learn. If you want to improve your health, please learn to love and learn to clear your mind. You should also do your best to heal and strengthen your energetic body and to look after your physical body with daily wholesome exercise and fresh food and water.

The point of healing yourself is not primarily to have a strong and healthy body. The real goal of all healing practices is to heal your mind, because you will take this with you when you leave your body. But it is far harder to be a diligent and effective spiritual practitioner when your body is very weak or in pain. A strong healthy body is a great tool for spiritual awakening and this is the primary reason why you should do everything in your power to heal any physical weaknesses or chronic health problems that you may have.

Looking deeply into your sickness

What should you do if, despite following a regime of meditation, a good diet and regular wholesome exercise, you get sick? First, do your best to give thanks to your physical illness. Reverse your usual mindset and give thanks to any illness on the grounds that it is trying to tell you something important about yourself. Then ask your sickness: 'What would you have me know?' Ask your pain or sickness, 'What lesson would you have me learn?' Really try to get to know your sickness or physical pain.

Whether you also go to see a doctor or healer, or take prescribed drugs or herbal remedies, is entirely up to you. If you believe that pills can set you free, they will undoubtedly help you. If you believe spiritual healing will assist you, do it. But, if you do not find the true cause of your sickness, it will persist. Do your best not to fear your illness, as this will give power to it. As much as possible, do not be fearful, although it is nearly impossible to go through sickness with no fear, because fear made you sick in the first place.

Sickness is never accidental. Two people can do exactly the same things and one will get sick and the other won't. There is no luck involved in who gets sick and who doesn't. Eventually your intuition can assist you to prevent an illness manifesting in your physical body, as long as you have a pre-warning. Your auric field and chakras can tell you that you are about to get ill. If you learn to listen to your charkas, your meridians, your state of mind and your disturbed emotions, you can actually prevent the manifestation of illness in your physical body. But like any other skill, this can take some time and practice to develop.

If you can find the cause of your sickness you can find the solution. This is a scientific fact. Scientists could not cure infections such as cholera until they understood what caused them. The science of the future will understand that in order to heal ourselves, we need to know our whole state of being.

If you can become aware of sickness in your etheric body and cure it at this level, it will not manifest itself in your physical body. Scientists do not have a machine to do this yet, but we can use our own intuition and psychic sensitivity. We are all sensitive machines. Your auric field gets sick before sickness manifests in your physical body and you can learn to sense this with a clear mind and intuition. For example, if you sense that you are running out of love and light, you can stop and give yourself as much light and love as you can, by directing them into your energy field.

Disturbed emotions are a major cause of physical ill health, so you have to be brave and transform all your negative emotions. Moodiness weakens your auric field and bombards your physical system with negativity. But you have to be disciplined to catch yourself going into a bad mood and change your mind. You will have to practise diligently for many years to change your habitual mindset from negative to positive. Once you begin to shift from being a constant worrier to being a Radiant Warrior, your physical health will undoubtedly improve. But to heal yourself at the deepest level, you will need to bring all your well-hidden fears and guilt up into the light where they can be released.

Anyone who has a physical body will experience illness and physical pain to some degree. We inherited our bodies from mother earth billions of years ago and our bodies are made up of heavy gross materials. Angels do not get sick, but we do, because our vibrations are too low and unbalanced. Every time you raise your vibrations through wholesome exercise or meditation; every time you transform your negative emotions into positive ones, you heal yourself to some degree and the whole of mankind will heal alongside of you.

Radiant Warriors who practise energy healing on themselves and others are healing pioneers. The science of energy healing is the medical model of the future, and one day everyone will understand the crucial link between the state of our minds and the state of our physical health. Until that time, you need to keep learning all that you can about the amazing connections between our state of mind, our energy levels and our physical health or sickness.

Please do not reject the undoubted benefits that modern medicine has to offer, particularly when you are very sick, but at the same time do your very best to look at the deeper causes of any illness that you experience and thus become your own healer. Once you have some mastery in self-healing you can, if you wish, assist others to heal their own physical, emotional, and mental problems and thus extend your radiant health and skills out into the world around you.

Exercise

Finding the deeper cause of your health problems

Take a few minutes to review your physical health and note any particular long-term health problems that you may have, or any acute conditions that tend to recur in your life.

Sit quietly and gently focus your mind on one particular health problem. Pray for help in understanding how this physical problem may be linked to an energetic or emotional imbalance, a negative thought in your mind or a trauma from your past – this lifetime or even a previous lifetime.

Do not be disappointed if the deeper cause of your physical problem does not immediately spring into your conscious mind. If you sincerely wish to understand the deeper meaning of any physical problem in your life the answer will be given to you, but you may not yet be ready to know the truth.

It can sometimes take a long time and a lot of brave soul searching before we are ready to face our responsibility for our own ill health. But every effort counts and even a little willingness to see the truth will, sooner or later, produce amazing insights.

Jane's Story: Part 5

I am a very healthy person, but like every other human being on this planet, I sometimes get sick. As far as physical illness is concerned, I am still not very good at working out the true cause of my tooth ache, my cold or my cough, but with the assistance of a very good spiritual friend who is also a wonderful spiritual healer, I have had one or two amazing insights into the process of releasing past traumas through the physical body. For example whilst suffering from a really deep and persistent cough during our one month long summer retreat, I asked my friend for a healing.

During that healing, I felt as though I was a child living perhaps two hundred years ago. I saw myself as that child lying on what appeared to be the floor of a large, dank prison cell full of people and I was coughing and coughing. After this healing, I had an insight that in this past life I had died in that prison, and it was this long forgotten trauma that I was now releasing through a bad cough this lifetime. A few years ago I would have dismissed such a story as fanciful, but now I am not so sure. What I do know is that after this healing the cough quickly improved and my rather fearful and depressed mood lifted almost instantly.

Nine months later, on a retreat in Wales I developed another troubling cough, but this time I had the insight that I was releasing the trauma of having had a dangerous and prolonged bout of Whooping Cough when I was only three year old this lifetime.

Whenever I have a bad headache or a cough I still choose to take painkillers or cough medicine but I am also now more and more aware that all my physical symptoms are simply the manifestation of pain within my mind. I am coming to accept that true healing always takes place within my mind rather than my body. I am also learning to be thankful for any physical sickness on the grounds that my body is just helping me to release fear and darkness from my mind.

I vividly remember getting food poisoning in Thailand and vomiting violently for what felt like an eternity. One brave spiritual friend who supported me through my ordeal kept saying to me 'I know you feel dreadful, but every time you vomit your energy just gets clearer and brighter!' So who knows exactly what this episode released in my mind, but after it was all over I prayed 'Thank you for assisting me to release some more of my deep down 'stuff' but in future could the whole process be a little gentler please?'

Chapter 6

Transcending Your Disturbed Emotions

Before you can reach the truth, you have to cut through all your inner pain, anger, fear, hatred and darkness.

Becoming aware of your suppressed pain

Most people distract themselves from their inner suffering by keeping very busy. We now live in a manically busy society. When people are not working at a frantic pace, they watch TV, read or daydream about sex, their next holiday, buying a new car, etc. However, if you observe your mind while you do all this, you will notice that the underlying fear, pain and upset are all still there. Your mind is trying to avoid pain by a moment of escape. This is why you spend so much time either fantasising about something pleasurable that you want to happen in the future, or remembering a happy moment from your past. Most people constantly seek to escape the present moment in order to avoid really feeling their underlying pain.

As a Radiant Warrior, you should not attempt to escape your underlying, fearful thought patterns. Your goal is to understand and ultimately to transcend, these negative patterns. So, first you need to accumulate some insights into these involuntary thought patterns in your mind.

In true meditation you can no longer deny the pain and fear in your mind, because when you sit still for a while all this painful stuff will be revealed to you. This means that sometimes you may feel that spiritual practice is making your problems worse rather than better. When you begin to meditate on a regular basis, you may well experience even more agitation, or conscious distress, than you did before you started to meditate. If this happens to you, Congratulations! You are beginning to see your crazy mind clearly for the first time.

If, as you train yourself to be still on a daily basis, you stay aware of your pain as it rises up to the surface of your consciousness, and if you can reach your clear quiet centre, you will be able to go through all your suffering and come out the other side. A Radiant Warrior cannot just say ' I am spiritual, so I know that all suffering is an illusion.' You need to cultivate courage and bravery, so that you can sit quietly, and allow all your pain and fear to come up to be observed and healed with true compassion.

No one consciously seeks pain, but pain is an inevitable part of our physical existence, and you will have to heal all the pain stored inside you by shedding light on it, before you can graduate as a genuine Radiant Warrior. All your pain has to come up from your subconscious. Please do not be tempted to suppress this pain, or run away from it by spacing out during your meditations, or by filling every moment of your daily life with constant distractions. Your awareness of your subconscious pain and fear is one of the fruits of meditation. When discomfort arises in meditation, or in your daily life, do your best to welcome it on the grounds that once you are aware of your suffering and how you create it in your mind, you can transcend it.

Clearing your stormy emotions through deep meditation

When you bring a problem into a transcendent meditative state, the problem will disappear. Just as the sky is big enough to clear after the worst storm, so your true mind is vast enough to clear your stormiest emotions. As you progress along the healing path to awakening, it is so important to take a keen interest in all your thoughts, feelings and actions.

All your life happens inside you first. The personality-self seeks to become indifferent or even unconscious during meditation, because it does not want you to know yourself. But the more you train your mind to reach and then stay in a transcendent state of dynamic emptiness, the more you will clear yourself and the more you will transform. Once you transcend all your pain, you will become sheer potential. Everything you wish for will happen. This is the power of the spirit.

When you first start out on the Radiant Warrior Path, many clouds will obscure the true, clear nature of your mind. When these clouds surround you, you will not be able to see the sun and you will say, 'There is no light.'

But gradually, as you heal yourself and remove the clouds, the light will reappear. Another analogy for healing your mind is the polishing of a mirror. When a mirror is clear and shiny, it will reflect the light. Or you can compare your mind to a muddy pond. When your mind is disturbed by all your choppy thoughts and emotions, it will be muddy and opaque, like a pond stirred up by stormy weather, but as you heal yourself, the mud will settle and the clear pond will again reflect the light.

Once you have cleared some of the junk out of your mind, and achieved a certain level of stillness of mind during your meditations, you will become aware of your inner connection to something much greater than you, to something all knowing and powerful. This knowing is blissful and you will inevitably want to hang on to this blissful state forever. But before you can do this, you have to commit to an extended period of healing your past wounds, all your habitual negative emotions, and all your relationships with others, particularly those with your family and all your romantic/sexual partners.

Seeing your emotions as passing clouds

In this world, one of the hardest lessons we all have to learn is how to manage our emotions. Our education system teaches us nothing about love and compassion. Our long years of schooling may teach us how to write an essay, or solve an equation, but they do not teach us how to handle our fear, our anger or our guilt. Our minds are well trained, but we have no heart, and this leaves us very badly equipped to deal with our feelings and emotions.

Disturbed emotions are a major obstacle on the spiritual path. Moodiness weakens our auric field, and bombards our physical systems with negativity. When we are moody, we cannot love and we cannot be genuinely kind. Would-be Radiant Warriors tend to think a lot about compassion, and often ask, 'What should we do to become more compassionate?' But, until we heal our own moodiness, we are only conceptualising and intellectualising about compassion, rather than actualising it in our daily lives.

Painful emotions are hard to handle, and yet we experience these emotions throughout our lives. You have to learn how to transform all your emotions before you can become a true Radiant Warrior. Once you have been on your spiritual path for some time, you will begin to understand that everything that happens to us is just like a passing cloud. Everything is temporary. All our emotions come and go and no one is angry or sad forever, even though they may fear that this may be the case.

Our emotions are ultimately empty, like a magic display or mirage, and once you fully realise this, you will be able to transcend your emotions with the greatest of ease. When you truly understand that your emotions are projections that create the world that you see around you, you will actually laugh at them. Once you realise that the inside and outside of you are fundamentally the same, you will develop a greater capacity not to engage so seriously with the physical world and all its fantasies and fantastic displays. You will not be so quick to be angry or resentful at what other people do to you. You will blame the world around you less and less for your discomfort.

As you eventually learn to let go of all your anger, blame and resentments, you will simultaneously begin to develop genuine qualities of love, compassion and selflessness. Once you are in touch with the eternal, non-judgemental observer inside yourself, even when your personality-self is in a rage, you will be able to watch yourself and see your rage for what it really is – a projection of your inner mindset. But until you reach this advanced enlightened living, it will take a great deal of discipline and will power on your part to overcome your habitual moodiness.

Allowing all your negativity to rise up to be healed

As a dedicated spiritual seeker, the first step on your healing journey involves allowing your suffering to rise up to the surface to be released. As your negative feelings and thoughts arise, you need to keep reminding yourself that they are coming up to be healed. We all have a lot of 'stuff' buried inside of us. We can even hold negative thoughts and feelings from past lives deep within our systems, and if these are not released, they can cause physical illnesses and emotional difficulties in this lifetime.

When you are having uncomfortable emotions, please do your very best not to push them away. The richness of life comes from embracing everything in the moment, whether joy or sorrow. Before you can transform yourself into a Radiant Warrior, you have to own all your feelings. Your negative 'stuff' is like a large cloud, or thick fog, hiding the light and the truth of God. When you are holding onto hate, you cannot experience God, or joy, or naturalness.

Be very honest with yourself and learn to acknowledge whatever feelings come up for you. Do not try to hide your darkness under a veneer of spirituality, or you will just be like a very smelly dustbin with a thin layer of sweet flowers sprinkled over the top. Do not play being an advanced 'spiritual' person who never gets irritated with other people, or who never experiences hate or fear. There is no such person on earth!

After observing your negativity bubbling up to the surface of your mind, the next step is to commit to transforming it. If you continue to entertain and dwell in negative thought patterns, you will stay perpetually in a hell of your own making. So, first and foremost, Radiant Warriors must decide to change their habitual moodiness on a daily basis.

Bad habits are very easy and quick to acquire, but you will need a long period of disciplined practice to replace them with good habits. Some people can become addicted to smoking after inhaling just one or two cigarettes, but it can take many months or even years of will-power and determination to kick the smoking habit. Being irritated when the world seems to be going against us is actually a bad habit that virtually all of us have accumulated since early childhood.

When we are slaves to our habitual moody patterns and mindsets, when we are slaves to all the irritations of daily life, such as missing the bus or deleting an essential document on our computer, we imprison ourselves in darkness. How do you free yourself from this awful trap? The key spiritual tool for changing your mind is, first and foremost, to learn to observe yourself having all your passing emotions. Then, as soon as you notice that your ego-self has become upset, you can always change your mind.

Healing your negative emotions with love and compassion

Whenever you notice that you are experiencing a negative emotion, such as irritation, guilt, jealousy or anxiety, you can breathe through it, calm your mind, and focus on peace, love or gratitude. If you keep your primary focus on light and love whenever you become aware of moodiness arising within you, that moodiness will usually subside.

When a negative emotion is just starting to brew up inside you, you can learn to avoid getting lost in it, so that it does not have time to escalate. If a feeling like anger has already boiled up in you before you become fully aware of it, find the nearest exit from the situation that is triggering that feeling. After the emotional storm inside you has subsided, contemplate on it. Ask yourself what triggered it off. Sometimes you may need to talk to a spiritual friend to find the answer. But if you are brave enough to go deep into your moodiness, you will inevitably find the hurt or unmet need beneath it and then you can begin to heal that deeper hurt.

Please remember, and tell yourself often, that whenever you are upset, you are being given the perfect opportunity to develop compassion for yourself. As a would-be Radiant Warrior, you cannot just opt for a comfortable existence. When everything in your life is going really smoothly, you will have virtually no incentive to grow spiritually.

When my life starts to become too comfortable, I actually pray for a new challenge to disturb my equilibrium. People often awake when they are having an incredibly hard time, and feel that they just cannot go on in the same old patterns. For example, a number of spiritual teachers, including Eckhart Tolle and Byron Katie, have described how, at a moment of pure desperation, they suddenly awoke into universal consciousness.

Without resistance and pain, you will not learn about healing. Without sorrow and sadness, you will not want to spend all the time and effort it takes to seek ultimate freedom. As you gain more insight about suffering, you will realise that you need to experience the pain of this physical world to enable you to develop your compassion.

Even after you have begun to awake, something will always come along to irritate or upset you. The key is to develop the spiritual will not to indulge in your moodiness and negative emotions. As you become more mindful and more advanced in your practice, you can train yourself to become calm and still when you are upset emotionally. From this place of inner calm or stillness, you can then transform your negative thoughts and feelings.

Whenever you find yourself in a hole, do not dig it deeper. Think instead 'How can I climb back up?' When you step into quicksand, do not struggle. Find a place of stillness and quiet deep within, wherein you can nurture, strengthen and love yourself. When you feel strong and still, you can invite negative emotions into your centre, into that space within you that is dynamic peace. You can fill this inner space with love and acceptance and surround it with a protective pyramid of pure light, violet in colour, or blue like the spacious sky.

When you are centred in this place of pure peace and light, you can invite your painful, judgemental thoughts and emotions to come in, and watch them melt away in front of you. You do not need to do anything. You simply let the light deep inside you heal all those unhealed parts of yourself. You surrender all your wounds and shadows to the healing power of the light.

All our emotional food has to be digested, assimilated and then expelled. If we simply absorb negative emotions into our system without digesting them, they will make us ill, like eating indigestible, or poisonous food. Most people handle positive emotions well and automatically digest them, but very few people have yet learned how to handle their own, or other people's negative emotions effectively. At first, when we are in a negative environment, we need to protect ourselves from being bombarded with negative energy, if we cannot digest it.

However, once you reach a certain level of spiritual maturity, you can use all disturbed emotions to create positive energy to assist you on your spiritual journey. Spiritual masters can digest their anger and use its energy. They can also utilise the energy generated by sexual desire to empower their spiritual practice. True masters welcome their disturbed emotions. They go deep inside them to find the emptiness and true joy within the mind that created them. They see the mind as sacred and whole, and the specific content does not bother them at all. This is their crazy wisdom.

Transforming anger

We all live in a very angry world. Next time you believe that you are really angry about something, think of the amount of anger that inspires suicide bombers! Angry people are always in a lot of pain. They are in so much pain that, whenever they have enough energy, they will naturally want to release it into the world around them, and one way to do this is by becoming angry. Some people, with a lot of pent up pain, express it through being extremely angry at the world most of the time. Other angry people, who have very low energy levels, tend to express their pain through becoming depressed. They turn their anger inwards and bury it under their depressed consciousness.

Anger and depression are twin brother and sister. If you are angry deep down in your system, but have no energy, you may well become depressed. Most of us live our lives somewhere in between these two extremes, which means that we are in a mildly negative, irritable mood most of the time. This is such a habitual state for us to be in, that we do not even realise how much we suffer because of it.

As we go through life, our deep inner anger tends to bubble up the surface. Negative events appear to happen to us, and then we think we have the right to be angry or depressed. You say 'These terrible things have happened to me' 'The weather is so bad, it is making me depressed' 'My partner has left me and now I am on anti-depressants.' 'My son is so lazy, of course I get angry with him.' You habitually make up a story line like this to justify your negative mood, until doing so becomes second nature to you. This is called projection. As long as you continue to do this, you will never transcend your anger or depression and you will never know your true self.

Most spiritual seekers are afraid of their anger, and tend to deny it, but it will inevitably still surface from time to time, because anger is within you. Anger is part of your mind, and try as you will, you cannot just walk away from it. The mind will always seek expression. So, you cannot just hide your anger, or push it down deep inside you, you have to heal it. If you do not do this voluntarily, your spirit will do it for you by force, and certain events will occur in your life that will make you face your anger and fear. When your anger rises up, it can be like a demon, but if you keep cultivating spiritual light, compassion and forgiveness you will eventually be able to face your anger head on and then heal it.

Taking responsibility for all your anger

How do you heal your anger? First, always take responsibility for your anger, rather than blaming it on external circumstances. We choose to have all our emotions, and therefore we are never the victims of external circumstances, or fate, although most people are not aware of this.

Second, when you are angry, do your very best not to shout or moan at anyone. Do not project your bad mood onto someone else, in a vain attempt to make them suffer instead of you. This strategy will just rebound on you sooner or later. Whenever you have an argument with someone, the negative energy will stay in the atmosphere. If you become really angry with someone or something, you will throw reason and logic out of the window, and your fiery emotions can become so strong that you may even burn your house down. Whenever we put energy into our anger, it just grows and grows.

If you ever become so angry that you want to hurt someone, even just with words, please immediately find some space for yourself. Take a nice long walk in nature, or go and sit out in your garden. Do not project your bad mood onto others, or you will create bad karma. When you get really irritated with someone, look for the nearest exit and remove yourself from the apparent cause of your anger. Then find a safe way to express your anger that really works for you. Some people like to scream out loud, others like to bash a cushion for a while or go for a run. Once your rage has died down, contemplate on it and look for the internal, underlying cause of it.

Dissolving your anger in stillness

Very often, we do not really know why we are angry, so we need to sit and contemplate on it. Whenever you notice that anger has risen up in you, spend some quiet, contemplative time by yourself, until you can identify with the part of your mind where deep stillness and peace still reside. When you get in touch with this deep, eternal peace inside you, your anger will just dissolve quite naturally. The more you go into this deep peace, the more you can safely release all your stored hate and anger without drowning in it.

In contemplation, your goal is to focus on a particular issue without intellectualising about it. You think with your whole being, rather than your brain and this type of thinking is not busy. When you feel angry, consult your heart and look deep inside to heal yourself. Usually, if you look deeply into your anger and hate, you will find fear, hurt or unmet needs just underneath the surface.

Whenever you pause to contemplate on your rage, anger or irritation, you should do your very best to bring loving compassion into your awareness. Compassion is a powerful and natural healing agent. So always breathe through your anger with compassion for yourself. Anger seems so natural and normal to most people, but it is not, it is unnatural. Personalities often appear ugly, because they are unnatural and twisted with anger and hate. We all like to project our pain outwards by blaming someone else for our discomfort. We feel good temporarily when we do this, but whatever we project we keep. This is a fact. We have become an angry human race, but this is not our true nature, and the more we can transcend this anger and hate, the quicker we can return to our natural, radiant state of being.

It takes a lot of courage to go beneath our anger to face our deep pain and sense of unworthiness and lack. We all get angry with other people in order to protect ourselves from feeling the deep layers of fear, neediness, guilt and unworthiness within ourselves. Unless we are prepared to cut through our anger to reach these deeper layers of pain, we cannot heal our endless suffering. But it takes great courage to own our own suffering rather than project it outwards, so you should always pray for help from Buddha, Christ, Krishna, or any higher power, to assist you to release and heal your stored anger, condemnation and aggression.

Never try to heal your darkness all by yourself. I guarantee you will not get very far. On the other hand, if you genuinely ask for higher help, all the angels in heaven will assist you to transcend your anger, to heal the hurt that lies underneath it, and to own all your projections, until your mind can remain at peace, even under circumstances that would have previously pushed you to explode with rage.

Transcending your fear

Everything in this world is fearful. So it can seem as though you can never win. If you have someone to love, you are so afraid that you may lose them. If you have no one to love, you are so afraid of your loneliness. In this world, there seems to be no way out of fear. There are so many worldly traps; money, careers, relationships, status, possessions, and they all involve fear. But every effort to transcend the fears of this world counts. Every time you move into the power of eternal joy, peace and love, you make progress on the Radiant Warrior Path. However, the Catch-22 is that you never really want to surrender every scrap of fear in your system, because you are afraid of losing your fearful-self, which is the only identity you know. So, ultimately the final fear you have to transcend is the fear of losing yourself.

If you worry a lot, if you are a very fearful person, congratulations, you have a great imagination. Most people are anxious most of the time. We are always worrying about the future. 'I am so worried about what may happen in the Middle East next year' 'I am so nervous about my son's exams next month.' If someone has no fears or anxieties for a while, they even think there must be something wrong with them. Most people are chronic worriers, but your aim is to become a Radiant Spiritual Warrior, which means that you have to transcend your habitual worrying and anxiety.

Fear is simply a symptom of our deep sense of loss and separation. Without fear, there would be no bloodshed, no wars and no suffering, but because we are all lost, we are all fearful, and when we are fearful, we so easily become aggressive and ready to attack our 'enemies.' Fear is inbuilt into our physical existence. Everyone is fearful and everyone is lost. Children are afraid of the dark. Many babies seem to be born fearful. Adults in our society have also learnt to be very fearful and cautious. Some adults even lock themselves in their houses and hardly ever go out in order to feel safe. But true safety cannot be found in the external, physical world. True safety lies in changing our minds about ourselves, and our identity.

Rising above collective consciousness

So many of us are in the habit of asking 'What if?' 'What if I go out and I get mugged?' 'What if I travel by plane and it crashes?' 'What if I eat this food and get food poisoning?' We can live our whole lives frightening ourselves like this. We impose so many limitations on ourselves because of our irrational fears. How many of us would cross the widest ocean, climb the highest mountain, fulfil our wildest dreams, if only we did not keep saying to ourselves 'What if?'

Radiant Warriors not only have to heal all their own individual fears, they also have to rise above collective consciousness. For example, they have to rise above mass consciousness that is so fearful of war, disease and disasters. Rich Westerners have become very fragile, because they over-value their bodies. Western culture encourages us all to feel weak and sick and fearful.

A few people worldwide die of a new disease such as SARS or bird flu and we all panic. Rich Americans now spend billions of dollars every year on medical check ups and preventative medicine. They spend their whole lives worrying about their physical health, but ironically this does not make them any healthier. It is the responsibility of all spiritual practitioners to release themselves from this fearful mass consciousness.

Every time you focus on your bodily needs and wants, including money matters, health matters and relationships, you will experience at least a twinge of fear, but every time you tune fully into God, or the Tao, you will find a state of mind where no fear exists.

Even advanced spiritual practitioners, who have healed so much of their fearful separated selves, still find that there is always a twinge of fear associated with their physical existence. However, they simply refuse to associate with their bodily fear anymore. They know that some fear will be with them as long as they still have a body, but they do not give into this fear. They keep meditating, contemplating and healing themselves until their fearful dreams in this physical world become happy dreams, and any traces of fear that are still left in their physical systems no longer bother them.

Making friends with your fears

Our fearful minds give such power to whatever it is we fear, but if we do not entertain our fear, the 'fearful' event or person will lose their power over us. We need to realise, first and foremost, that all fear is created in our own mind, even our so-called instinctive fear of death or extinction. We need to respect our fears, but we should not give power to them.

One person can observe a snake and see a beautiful fascinating creature, yet the person next to them will be terrified. So, how can we claim that it is the snake that caused the fear? We may believe that certain external events are universally fearful. For example, if someone knows they are just about to be killed, we imagine that they would naturally feel great fear. But even this is not true. There are many documented accounts of individuals who were convinced that they were just about to die, and suddenly, they felt a perfect peace come over them.

Your mind is so powerful that you can use it to overcome all your irrational fears. Eventually this can become child's play. You can face all of your deepest fears in your mind and, guess what? They will not kill you! So I beg you, please don't be so afraid of fear. If you keep experimenting with facing your fears head on in your mind, you will find out that they won't do you any real, lasting harm. The way to transcend fear is to face it directly, because the more you look straight at your fear, the less you will see it.

Do not be tempted to deny your irrational fears, but rather keep sending love and light to them until they dissolve completely. Whenever you observe yourself going into fear, do something to heal it. We need to make friends with all our fears. However, you should only practise healing your fears when you feel clear and strong, because when you are strong and connected to the light, or the divine within, you can face all of your darkness without running away.

Please be careful not to give your fear extra power by looking at it and then running away. If you attempt to face your fear and then run away from it, you give it tremendous power. So, before you go within to face your fears, pray for protection, pray for divine support and guidance, and then get to know your fear, so that you can transcend it

One very effective practice is to find a symbol for your fear, such as a snake, a spider, a dark tiny cell, or the top of a sheer drop, whatever image is most scary to you. Then, you can go into a meditative or contemplative state, connect up to the light and take this light with you, as you face your symbol of fear head on. If you keep holding this symbol of fear in your mind, whilst bathing it with the light, it will eventually completely dissolve in the light, I guarantee it. A student of mine, who had a phobia about spiders, bravely imagined being eaten alive by a giant spider during several healing meditations and after this, his fear of spiders was greatly reduced.

You are eternally safe

Your fearful, separated personality is ultimately just an illusion. All your pains and problems are experienced by this fearful little personality-self, but what if he/she does not really exist? Who is it that falls out of love and into fear? In reality you can never fall out of love. Only the personality-self, imprisoned in a body, can be rejected, betrayed or abandoned. Through letting go of our ego-based fears by facing them directly, healing happens.

If you are brave enough to go through the dark tunnel of your fear, with love as your guide, you will eventually realise that you are eternally safe. The thick, fearful darkness, or fog, is just a mirage, and you will always emerge into the light at the other end. Your fears are not outside of you, they are inside of you, lying deep within the unconscious layers of your own mind. How can they harm you, if you are infinite and eternal? As an infinite being, you have the power to escape from the self-made prison of your fears whenever you choose to do so.

If you ask for support from the ascended masters, they will accompany you into your dark prison and show you that it is just a figment of your imagination. Once you realise that you have made up all your fears, you will know you can unmake them simply by changing your own mind. The key to this essential healing process is to bring love to all your fears, doubts and anxieties.

Love is a reflection of absolute truth and can therefore heal absolutely anything. If you take your fear into a meditative space and stay with it with a calm mind and an inner connection to universal love and light, you can always transcend it. We are never alone. Christ is always with us. Buddha is always there for us. If you are afraid, and do not feel strong enough to face your fear all by yourself, please remember to tell someone your fear and ask for their support, whether they be a good spiritual friend or an ascended master.

Conquering all your own fears is the most helpful thing you can ever do for your brothers and sisters and the planet earth. Wounded, fearful healers may really want to heal their brothers and sisters, but they cannot until they have completely healed themselves first, because we can never give to others what we do not have. If you do not have one hundred pounds, there is no way you can give one hundred pounds to a friend in need. If you have not healed your own fearful self, you cannot assist others to conquer their fears, however much you sincerely wish to help them. But a true Radiant Warrior, who has faced and conquered all their deepest fears, is a fearless fighter on behalf of all their un-awakened, fear-filled brothers and sisters and a natural healer of all sentient beings.

Setting everyone and everything free

We all have to learn to stop imprisoning others because of our fear. Please do your best never to impose your fear on others, not because you are trying to be a better person, but because whenever you project your fear and guilt outwards, you actually make it more real and powerful, and then you cannot be free. No one and nothing on this planet really belongs to you, and you cannot find true safety by desperately clinging on to anything on the outside of you, whether it is a loved one or a million pounds in your bank account. Whenever you feel fearful, acknowledge your fear, face it with love and compassion and then give it away to God, the Holy Spirit or the light.

You are so afraid of losing all the worldly things that you treasure; your family, your possessions, your physical health. One day, when you lose all of this, your personality self will find it very hard to take, but your spirit will feel free. Of course, you can love your family, your partner, your close friends, but to become a Radiant Warrior you have to set them free. This means learning the great art of non-attachment to all worldly things, including bodies and personalities. Ultimately, you need to learn to live fully in this world, whilst knowing that you are not of this world.

When you die, you will lose everything that you treasure in this world; everything that you love and worry about losing will be gone. So think how important it is to learn non-attachment before you die. One way to practise non-attachment is to imagine losing your loved ones. For example, you can keep imagining going to their funerals, until the fear and grief that you experience in your mind dissipates. Of course, for most of us this is not an easy practice, but it can really assist us to learn dynamic non-attachment.

On the one hand, it is wise to make sure that you look after all that is given to you in this lifetime, and cultivate well all your gifts from God. On the other hand, when the time comes you should gladly give everything back to God. Your children, your house and money, even your body, do not really belong to you. You are just their temporary custodian and once your heart truly understands this, your fear of losing everything will subside.

The world is so haphazard. Wealth, relationships, status, none of them has any real substance. Some people gain millions one day and lose millions the next. One minute someone is planning their wedding, and the next they are run over by a truck. What is the secret of being non-attached to all of this? Learn from the great spiritual masters. They can manifest whatever they need in the material world, but they do not become attached to it.

Lama Yeshe, the head of a Tibetan Buddhist monastery in Scotland, acquired an island off Arran in Scotland, worth well over a million pounds for far, far less than this and then dedicated this island to world peace. Spiritual masters like this live in a miraculous way. There is such grace in it. But they practise day in and day out. So all I can tell you, if you wish to know how to transcend this fear-based world, is that the key is to practise, practise, practise.

Is Lama Yeshe afraid of losing Holy Island? I don't think so! He does not possess Holy Island. He describes himself as merely being the custodian of it, on behalf of the whole of humanity, so how can he be afraid of losing it? But at this moment, you are afraid of losing your loved ones, your house, your income, your body, everything. To develop true spiritual strength, you have to practise day in and day out, there is no other way. After so many decades of enlightened living, His Holiness the Dalai Lama still meditates for several hours every day. Why? Because his inner connection to the light or source is his most important priority.

Connecting to the light

Cultivating this internal connection is even more important than pursuing your life's purpose. 'Seek you the kingdom of God first and everything else will follow.' Even though I would always encourage you to fulfil your true function this lifetime, your own internal connection to the light is far more important. This is why I urge you to connect to the light every day of your life. Learn from The Dalai Lama and other great spiritual masters. The key to a fulfilled, joyful life is to tune into the light first and foremost. If you expose yourself too much to the world and worldly affairs without maintaining this internal connection, you will get lost and fearful again so easily.

I have seen several spiritual teachers who, once they had acquired some power and some followers, got lost in this world again. It is so easy to drown in all of this. It is very sad to see an accomplished practitioner stop growing and become imprisoned again. If you lose yourself in Samsara (the cyclical, illusive realms of existence) it can take such a long time to escape.

So as a potential Radiant Warrior, I ask you to take a personal vow, and really mean it, that no matter how much you love another person, no matter how much the world demands your attention, you will not allow yourself to lose your inner connection to your light or to your soul. Then, continue to ask for divine assistance to keep this vow on a daily basis. When we fall in love romantically, it is so easy to lose ourselves. When we become very successful in the world, it is so tempting to neglect our spiritual practice; to put it on hold just for a while. Please do not do this to yourself, or you will trap yourself in your bodily and personality based fears forever.

Radiant Warriors keep dipping themselves into the truth, until they know that this is all there is, until they really understand that fear is a big lie and only love is real. Beyond everything that you think you are, your body, your personality, your life's purpose, you are simply the extension of the Source. You are an integral part of the wholeness of life that is God, the Tao, the unnameable truth, and your core spiritual practice is to keep releasing and healing all of your fear and all of your pain, until you experience for yourself this eternal, blissful reality.

Exercises

Transforming your anger

Sit quietly and gently ask your higher self, 'What grievance against someone am I now ready to release to the light?'

Go into a meditative or contemplative space and observe your mind holding this grievance without judging yourself in any way for any of your angry thoughts or feelings.

Pray for divine assistance in letting go of this grievance.

Observe the story line that goes with your grievance or anger and ask to see the situation or person differently.

Then tell yourself a different story about whatever triggered anger in your system. For example, if you are angry because someone was rude to you, tell yourself that this person was just someone in great pain crying out for love.

Now sit patiently observing all your angry thoughts and feelings that accompany your grievance and then bravely go beneath the anger to feel the hurt, fear or unmet need that the anger was covering up.

Bathe this pain or neediness in unconditional love and compassion and imagine it dissolving, like a puff of black smoke, into the light.

Transcending your fears

Do not do this exercise unless you are feeling strong and well connected to the light.

Get into a very peaceful meditative or contemplative space.

Connect up to divine light and love or to your higher guide, for example Christ or Buddha.

Pray for help in transcending your fear.

Create a symbol for your irrational fears – something that you find frightening, such as a snake, a spider, an enclosed space or a sheer mountain drop.

Allow yourself to face this symbol of fear head on in your mind.

Observe all the physical sensations, feelings and thoughts that arise in your mind as you face the symbol of your fear.

Then bathe yourself in unconditional love and light and allow the symbol of your fear to dissolve into the light.

Keep repeating this healing meditation until you can hold the symbol of your fear in your mind without reacting fearfully to it.

You may need to repeat this exercise many times in order to release a deep-seated fear from your mind. For example, if you are afraid of spiders, you may first need to imagine that the spider is some distance from you, before moving onto another meditation during which you feel the spider actually crawling onto your hand, until eventually you can imagine that the spider is eating you alive and still feel perfectly calm and safe.

Jane's Story: Part 6

Before I began my healing journey, I would have said that I was certainly not an angry person. After all, I *never* shouted or swore at anyone and if someone really got angry with me, I would just burst into tears or walk away from them as quickly as I could. But since I have begun to observe all my thoughts and my feelings I have had to admit that there is a furious, viscious, attacking 'me' that bubbles up to the surface whenever my buttons are really pushed. It is just that I am too timid a personality to allow that attacking part of me to let rip verbally or physically. This inner rage of mine has surfaced most strongly on several retreats with Jason.

On retreat, Jason can sometimes talk for several hours non-stop and has a habit of talking a little beyond our meal break times. For some reason this has occasionally triggered ridiculous amounts of internal rage in me that has seemed almost impossible to control or dampen down. Every time this rage has surfaced, I have been so shocked and really at a loss about how to handle it. Last time it hit me really badly, I just walked out of our session and screamed into the wind until my system calmed down.

I have tried to understand what lies beneath this surface rage and it feels as though I have a deep fear of being trapped. On one occasion, I saw myself being interrogated for hours on end by two violent men. Maybe this was a past life memory, who knows? On a more physical level I sometimes suffer from low blood sugar levels if I have not eaten for a while, and one of the symptoms of hypoglycemia is irritability. Whatever the true cause of my anger at these times, I have learnt not to blame Jason for triggering my rage. In fact I now smile to myself when it starts to bubble up once again, and genuinely say a silent 'Thank You' to Jason for helping me to release more of my subconscious 'stuff.'

The most challenging aspect of my whole awakening journey to date has been the tremendous fear that I have felt on several occasions. At one point, the fear was so over-powering that I spent the whole night pacing up and down. I was just too frightened even to sit still, let alone go to sleep. How did I finally handle this fear? I didn't. It overwhelmed me and I could do nothing at all except live through it. My only comfort, after it had finally subsided, was that perhaps I had significantly shortened my healing journey by releasing so much deep down fear in such a short space of time.

At other times I have felt very fearful, but not overwhelmingly so, and at these times I have simply faced my fears head on until they subsided. For example, I am quite claustrophobic and on several occasions I have taken this fear into a deep meditative state and asked for the light to assist me to release it.

These challenging episodes and healing meditations have eventually given me so much more strength and trust in the whole healing process. Facing my fears in 'real life' has also taught me so much. The first time I was due to fly out to Thailand for a retreat, my first meditation teacher, for whom I had tremendous respect, warned me that if I went on this retreat I would go completely manic and end up being locked up in a Thai mental institution. I knew that she was not exaggerating. This was a real possibility. I came so close to cancelling my flight, but something deep in my heart told me to go to Thailand.

As I got on the plane that would fly me from Britain to Bangkok, I was literally shaking and crying with fear. I had to force myself to step onto the plane. It took several hours of flying before I finally stopped shaking, but an angel of a fellow passenger, who was a little drunk, chatted away to me and this really helped me to calm down. Throughout the retreat, I was still very scared of going crazy, but I made it sanely through to the end, and this whole experience taught me so much about facing my fears head on, and conquering them with great assistance from my spiritual friends and guides in this world and way beyond it.

Chapter 7

Understanding Relationships

Unfortunately for humanity, special one-to-one relationships, even if we use spiritual language to describe them, can never make us whole·

Looking for love

Virtually every human being on earth is seeking for intimate, romantic relationships because we are all looking for love. We have all been well taught to believe that another 'special' person has something that we need or want. If we are very bodily conscious, we may be looking for a particularly sexy, attractive body. If we are a spiritual seeker, we may tell ourselves that we are looking for our 'soul mate,' but the basic dynamic is exactly the same; we are all looking for another person to fill up the gap that we experience deep inside of us.

When you fall in love, your mind goes crazy and you become so confused. Love on the surface, with candlelit dinners and roses, is so wonderful and no one gets hurt, but once you go deeper, your past wounds will inevitably surface. The more you fall in love, the more your subconscious pain will come up to be healed. If you want to know more about life, plunge into romantic love and get hurt!

Intimate relationships always bring up our stuff. Sexual energy will almost always stimulate jealousy and possessiveness, and so, at some point, after you have fallen in love, your possessiveness and jealousy will arise and kill off the romance. At first you love someone so much, you will kill yourself if you cannot be with them. Then you live with them for 10 years and find that you cannot stand them. What on earth is going on?

Romantic love is just a dream

If you fall in love with someone and believe that their personality and body will give you comfort, later you will hate them for it. When you fall in love with someone, you need more prayers, spiritual practice and protection than at any other time in your life. Why? Because falling in love, and the sexual energy that accompanies this, will bring out all your insecurities.

True love always sets people free, but true love cannot be found in romantic love, because romantic love is always accompanied by emotional games. Most people fantasise about a soul mate or a perfect lover, but fantasies always lead to disappointment. In most intimate relationships, two people are dreaming their own dreams, and so they are not really sharing anything at all. When you think you love someone so much, you are actually dependent on them, and if they leave you for someone else, you will feel tremendous rage. You may even want to kill the person who seems to have stolen them from you.

All this pain is what we call love! I am really sorry to have to tell you this, but every single time you get really close to someone, fear, darkness and pain will rise up sooner or later. If you are not hurt by human love, you are still going through the phase of infatuation. New parents are often infatuated with their baby, but one day that baby will grow up and hurt their feelings. One day that baby will turn into a teenager who hates their parents. Without love you dry up, but all human love hurts. Without love in your life, you will feel no joy, excitement, or enthusiasm, but human love is so painful that it sometimes seems easier to give up and love nature or God rather than another human being.

Sometimes, people who have been hurt so much in the past, decide to play safe. They decide to keep others at arms length, because falling in love again would be too much to bear. But then loneliness sets in and these individuals say, ' Why can I not find my soul mate?' Unfortunately, and you may not like me for telling you this, I have never met a totally problem-free couple. I have never known anyone to fall in love and stay blissfully in love with their partner for the rest of their lives. Does this mean you should give up falling in love? No! If the universe sends you someone to fall in love with, you will have no choice. This is the grace of God, or the divine plan in action. When falling in love with a particular person is part of your karma, you just cannot run away, but you can see it as a heaven sent opportunity to heal yourself.

Romantic love is a powerful illusion

Falling in love with that 'special someone' is one of this world's greatest and most powerful illusions. At first, this illusion is wonderful, but close romantic relationships will eventually hurt you the most. If you choose to have a life-long partner, they are much more likely to be a painful challenge to you, for much of the time, than to be your loving soul mate. The one you share your bed with is usually the person who really pushes all your buttons the most. This person is your specifically appointed saviour, even though most of your romantic attraction to them will eventually die away. Why? Because they will reveal back to you all your unhealed issues.

In our culture, romantic, sexual relationships are held up as the most fulfilling aspect of our lives. Endless books and articles tell us how to meet our perfect partner, how to get them to stay with us and how to keep them satisfied in bed. So many people are longing to fall in love and live happily ever after, but at the same time so many people fall out of love, and wonder why they are so unlucky and why their relationship went so wrong.

Please remember, that many people experience being abandoned, or beaten up, or violated by the one they say that they love, and many others hold so much hatred and grievances against their loved ones that they even become physically sick because of it. There is a lot of heartache in intimate relationships. There is so much domestic violence. At least a quarter of all violent crime in the UK is violence between people who are having an intimate relationship. So, in order to transcend all this pain and heartache, we first have to understand what is really going on in intimate relationships, and then we have to summon up all our warrior spirit and commit to healing our own wounded hearts.

Understanding the nature of romantic relationships

The majority of people, when their fantasies about a relationship are not fulfilled, blame the other person for their pain, but, as a Radiant Warrior, you need to understand why romantic relationships are always such a let down, sooner or later. You also need to know how to heal yourself and your relationship once the pain sets in. We all use our relationships to project our own fear and darkness out into the world. Our close relationships can tell us so much about what is in our own minds and what we need to heal within ourselves, if we are really prepared to examine, with brutal honestly, exactly how we use them.

If we are truly committed to our spiritual path, we can use all our relationships as a tool for healing ourselves. But you need tremendous bravery and understanding to realise that you actually do everything to yourself. In reality, nobody does anything to you without your full consent. If others did things to you, without you having any say in it, you would just be a helpless victim of life, completely at the mercy of others. There would be no way out, and you would be trapped lifetime after lifetime.

The good news is that you are entirely responsible for the pain that arises when you are in a relationship, or when a relationship ends. You actually make up everything that happens to you in this life, out of your own neuroses. You repeatedly attract painful events and relationships into your life, because deep down you think you are a sinner who deserves punishment.

When you are yearning for a man or a woman to make you happy and fulfilled for the rest of your life, please remember that you are just buying into an illusion. There are no exceptions to this. Everyone in romantic relationships will be unfaithful eventually, either physically, or in their mind. If you say to yourself, 'My partner will never betray me' you are living in Cloud-cuckoo-land. Can you cope with this? Romance stimulates all your energy centres, expectations set in, and sooner or later you will be disappointed, because you want your partner to be like your original fantasy of them. You actually fall in love with your own fantasy.

No one outside you will ever really love you just as you are, just as you never really love anyone unconditionally. No one can really love unconditionally from their personality-self. You pretend to yourself that all you want from a sexual partner is true love. I'm sorry to have to say this, but you are deceiving yourself. When you long for a partner, you may be looking for financial security, sex, guidance, protection, excitement or even nursing care, but none of this is true love.

Horizontal love, or love for a special person, is completely different from vertical love, or love of God or the divine. Horizontal love is always closely linked to our deepest fears. As well as making demands, secretly or openly, on the other person, you also keep asking 'What if?' 'What if she fancies my best friend more than me?' 'What if he stops loving me when I get old and grey?' Vertical love is pure, but horizontal love always makes a mess. All you do is bargain with your so-called 'loved ones.' You make sacrifices with them that ultimately do not work, and play out roles that are full of fear and pain just beneath the surface.

Until we awake, we all play out our preferred roles in our romantic relationships. Some people prefer to play victim, and to see themselves as abused or abandoned by those they love. Others prefer to play the role of rescuer, and put a lot of effort into pleasing others. Some people play being indifferent to others, because they are so frightened of being hurt yet again. Indifference in relationships is a protective mechanism. These individuals play it cool and never get too involved or committed. But whatever role we play in our relationships, victim, rescuer or Ms/Mr Cool, we block true communication and true love, and thus we suffer.

Personalities cannot offer each other true love

As personalities, we always try to imprison each other, and our dependency on others always causes suffering. If you rely on just one other person to bring you love and happiness, you will simultaneously hate that person. I have observed and experienced this again and again and again. In the name of love, you imprison someone and want your partner to change so many aspects of their behaviour. In the name of love, you feel so guilty and fearful. You even call it love when you emotionally blackmail each other, and when we are not awake, when we are not enlightened, we all use relationships to blackmail each other.

When you say to your partner, 'I trust you,' don't you really mean, 'Can I blackmail you into staying with me, and behaving the way I want you to behave?' Until we are fully awake, we are all untrustworthy. We change our minds all the time. One minute we love someone so much and the next we think that we hate them. So, if you are wise, you will not put your full trust in the love of another personality or ego-self. Trust others' spirits, because their essence is the same as yours. But, until they know who they truly are, human beings just cannot be trustworthy in love.

From falling in love to falling out of love

All intimate relationships between two personality-selves go through stages that take us from the illusion of falling in love, to the disillusionment of falling out of love. The first stage of these special relationships is infatuation. We find one person who excites us and gives us a tremendous sense of aliveness. When we meet someone who excites us sexually, our boundaries begin to loosen and our heart centre opens, whilst our base centre and solar plexus are churning.

When we meet another body that turns us on, we normally feel giggly and silly. This is all infatuation. Our hormones are activated and we have a strong chemical/physical reaction to this other person's presence. All our reason flies out of the window and our bodies seem to tell us what to do. We long to get physically closer as quickly as possible, even though social conventions may hold us back for a while.

A successful infatuation very often quickly turns into a romance. At this stage, both parties will be on cloud nine. They will both feel so alive, because they have temporarily dropped their barriers. During the early stages of a romantic relationship, both sides worry about whether the other person will find them attractive and so they become the best that they can be.

Neither side reveals their weaknesses. Each lover hides all their physical and emotional inadequacies, and attempts to look their very best. The man may go to the gym more often than usual, while the woman may go on a diet or buy sexy underwear. Each lover performs for the other. Each finds they have so much more energy than usual, and feels as though they could perform miracles. For a short while, it does appear that two minds and hearts have joined together as one blissful whole, but sadly, this is just the illusion of falling in love.

After the romance stage, most couples decide to move in closer and take their relationship to another level. This is a bad move, but we all do it! Romantic couples very often decide to move in together. They cannot resist moving closer, to ward off all the pain of the big wide world. They join together: 'you and me against the world.' After this commitment to closeness, there is usually a honeymoon period in which the couple create mutual dreams or fantasies of a happy future together; marriage, babies, a new home, a dream holiday. During this honeymoon period, disillusionments and disappointments with one another are usually covered up, or pushed to one side.

For a while, most lovers will continue to sacrifice their own needs and desires in the name of love, but sooner or later disillusionment sets in. When we experience this, we feel as though we cannot stand our beloved anymore. We find that there is something wrong with our partner and we no longer desire or trust them.

When such disillusionment sets in, most people in our modern society decide to end the relationship and start looking for another one. Sometimes disillusionment sets in after only a few months together, sometimes it does not really set in for many years. Of course, some couples hang on to each other long after disillusionment has set in. They still live together in the physical sense, but their minds are thousands of miles apart. A lot of people, particularly those with children, stay together physically out of convenience, guilt or fear, but their relationship has become a burden to both of them.

'Special' relationships

In order to understand why romantic love never lasts, we need to understand that all our intimate relationships are, as *A Course in Miracles* explains, 'special relationships.' These special relationships are 'unhealed,' because they are based on bargaining, even though we certainly do not realise that this is what we are doing when we first fall in love. But in all special relationships, our personality-selves are only prepared to give to our beloved as long as we get what we want back from them in return. Traditionally, women have looked after men physically and emotionally in return for economic support and security, but in more modern Western societies, both men and women expect to be sexually and emotionally fulfilled by their partner.

The bottom line of all special relationships is that the ego always wants to get something from them. Before we awake, we always want to imprison our loved ones and we usually attempt to do this by guilt-tripping them. All our close relationships are possessive and prone to jealousy. We say 'You are mine, you belong to me' either out loud or in our heads. We say 'I need you. Promise you will never leave me!'

We all think that human love like this is normal, but in actual fact, it is very painful and unnatural. We think that love is about getting as close as possible to another body, but a body is incapable of love. Your little, separated mind and body do not know what true love is. They just mimic it. Human love can change to hate in a heartbeat, whereas true love is unchangeable. If one day you love someone, and the next day, perhaps because they have left you for a younger body, you hate them, it is not true love. Moreover, when we tell our lover 'I will only ever love you, no-one else,' this is a big lie. Nobody can love only one person for the rest of their lives.

The pain of special relationships

What is really happening in all special relationships is that, unconsciously, we are setting each other up. Somewhere deep inside of us, there is so much fear, guilt and sin, that our egos have to find someone to attack or to blame, in order to project this unbearable pain outwards. We have all had a taste of romantic love, but we have also all experienced the pain that sets in when we begin to project all our 'stuff' onto each other.

When the projection in any intimate relationship becomes full blown, a couple will really start to hate each other. Even the most kind, gentle person can become enraged in an intimate relationship, and sexual partners often become masters at pushing each other's buttons. Most people end up hating their partners, or ex-partners, more than the worst tyrants in the world.

When we fall out of love with someone, we may run off with someone else, and then we will feel so guilty and unkind. Sometimes our partner deserts us, and then we will hate our partner for running away from us. When we fall out of love, the usual pattern is either to blame ourselves, or to blame the other person. In both cases, we will experience fear and inadequacy. Some people then try really hard to get rid of all the pain inside of them. They may well think that if they can just get a replacement partner, they will feel much better, and so they rush from one romantic relationship to the next without ever pausing to ask themselves 'What went wrong?'

Another popular remedy, that many people try, is to punish their 'ex.' Sometimes jilted men violently attack their ex-partners, and a few even kill them. Some jilted wives have cut all their husband's suits up, or smashed their music collection to smithereens. Of course these tactics may bring an immediate feeling of relief, but they never heal the underlying pain and loneliness. Moreover, whenever we hurt someone else in a vain attempt to relieve our own pain, we deepen our karmic debt, and at some point we will experience the harm we did to the other. Our actions will just come back to us eventually. This is not a punishment, it is simply the natural law of cause and effect.

While some jilted lovers seek revenge, others just bury all their hatred and pain deep inside themselves. However, if you do this you will eventually get sick. You may even end up getting cancer, and then you will say 'Why me?' You will have forgotten about imploding your anger towards your ex-partner ten, or even twenty years ago. Good, God-fearing individuals do not want to harm others, so when they are badly hurt by someone they love, they simply bury their anger deep inside themselves, but this pain may well kill them eventually.

We can use all our relationships to heal ourselves

So there we have the merry-go-round of normal human, intimate relationships. We fall in love; feel wonderful for a while, and then we begin to fall out of love and all hell breaks loose. When love apparently turns to hate, we think that we must be particularly unlucky, or bad. What most of us fail to realise, is that falling out of love is inevitable because human love never lasts. Human love is not real. It is an illusion, but the good news is that we can use this love for healing purposes, and when we do this, our destructive special relationships can be turned into a fantastic means for salvation.

Because, as yet, so very few human beings on earth dwell only with God, there are virtually no shining examples of 'holy relationships' (*A Course in Miracles*) for us to follow. Nevertheless, if we truly want to find lasting love and happiness, we have no alternative but to surrender all our close relationships to a higher intelligence or universal will.

Please do not read all this and feel depressed. Although all human relationships are inherently problematic, there is a way to overcome these problems and return to true love.

Climbing out of our self-made imprisonment of needy, grasping human love is extremely challenging, but when you finally reach the top of the mountain you will find that you no longer need another personality or body to protect you from your inner demons. You will be free at last from all the trappings of special relationships: free to love one individual or the whole world with an open compassionate heart and an awakened mind. You will be free to love without neediness, to love without fear, and this is one of the most sublime experiences available to us on this earth.

Exercises

Understanding you own intimate relationships

Sit quietly and think about your past romantic relationships. What was it like to fall in love? What was it like to fall out of love? What did you really want from your relationships? Why did the love die?

Be very honest with yourself as you do this and try to explore the role your own inner fears and self-doubt may have played in sabotaging your past relationships.

Observing your grievances about all your 'special' partners

Think about your past romantic partners one by one and notice any grievances you are still holding against them in your mind. If you are currently in a relationship think about what your partner does that irritates or upsets you.

Your purpose in doing this exercise is not to change anyone or anything. Your goal is simply to become aware of how much pain and dissatisfaction there is in your 'special' relationships, and to notice the extent to which you have failed to find perfect, lasting happiness through your romantic attachments.

Jane's Story: Part 7

I spent over thirty years of my life desperately looking for love in all the wrong places. The first man I fell in love with when I was eighteen was so depressed that he once cut his wrists right in front of me. Then when I was 22, I had my first real sexual relationship with a brilliant politics lecturer who told me his wife had left him. But she came back less than a month after we began our relationship, and he then pushed me to one side. I spent the next 15 years of my life hoping his wife might leave him so that we could be together again, but universal intelligence had other plans for the three of us.

In my mid twenties I managed to live with a sweet man (who had a major drink problem) for nearly a year, but I realised it wasn't the ideal relationship when I had to go into hospital for a few days and felt much happier there than I had at home with him. I could go on, but I think you may be getting the picture, so I will just jump to my last romantic relationship in my early forties with a charming man, who already had two women in his life and just saw me occasionally when he had a very rare free evening.

Even after ten years of almost continuous psychotherapy, I could not find a man to love and cherish me on a long-term basis, and I still could not really understand what was so wrong with me. I knew that my early relationship with my adoptive father had made me wary of commitment and I knew that I lacked confidence in my sexual attractiveness, but these explanations didn't seem to go deep enough.

It wasn't until I read about 'special relationships' in *A Course in Miracles* and listened to Jason's uncompromising talks about relationships that I began to gain some deeper understanding on an intellectual level about what had gone so wrong in all my romantic relationships. I began to see that I had not just been unlucky in love. The fact that all the men I fell in love with were so unavailable, simply reflected my own distrust of men that lay deep within my own mind, and my own subconscious fear of being trapped in a long-term intimate relationship. I began to realise that if any man had actually asked me to marry him, I would have run a mile.

But my gaining this intellectual understanding about what kept going wrong with my relationships, wasn't enough. I still needed to go through my own healing journey to begin to release the inner pain and guilt that the outer world of 'unavailable,' and sometimes abusive, men had mirrored back to me so perfectly. I needed to look deeply into my own wounded heart and unconscious patterns to find the true cause of all my relationship problems.

Chapter 8

Healing Relationships

Your ultimate goal is a holy relationship in which two souls who have found their own wholeness within, share and extend this wholeness with everyone they meet.

Heal yourself first and foremost

You have to love yourself first, before you can love anyone else. The only true relationships you will have as a human being are with your true self and with your God. You have to live with yourself forever, whereas all other relationships are temporary. But how long have you ever spent with yourself? Most people run away from themselves every minute of the day. If they are not with someone else, they will turn on the radio or the TV, or read a novel. How many people can spend an hour with themselves alone, without distractions? How many people are brave enough to face their inner loneliness head on?

You have to accept that until you fully awake, you are alone. You come into this world alone, and you leave it alone. There is no one else to share anything with you, because personalities cannot truly share anything. Until we awake, we will still feel lonely, even when we are sharing our lives with a beloved partner.

If you seek to have a relationship in order to relieve your loneliness and to disguise your lack of self-worth, you will inevitably link up with another lonely, unhealed person and then you will be in hell together. Have you noticed that some people always experience the pain of being abandoned in relationships, whilst others always feel the pain of being betrayed? All human beings have to deal with abandonment and betrayal issues deep inside our own minds.

If you still have abandonment or betrayal issues in your mind, please do not look for an external partner to ease your pain, or you will simply be abandoned or betrayed yet again. We always ensure that our fearful version of love happens to us, even if it is very painful. Someone afraid of being abandoned will always fall for a freedom freak, someone afraid of being betrayed will always fall for a love rat, and someone afraid of being imprisoned will fall for the clingy type.

Only when you can transform all your negative emotions, and find the wholeness deep inside you, can you live a life truly in love. When you can live happily ever after all by yourself, when you can get on well with yourself, calm your emotions and find completion within, then, and only then, you can live happily with someone else, because you won't be the slightest bit dependent on them for your happiness and fulfilment.

The whole of humanity feels a lack inside themselves, but as a Radiant Warrior, your primary goal is to learn how to be fulfilled within yourself, rather than seeking for fulfilment through someone outside of you. You have to commit to healing the gap deep within you, rather than expecting someone else to fill that gap for you.

Healing your inner man and woman

The male / female split is a unique human problem. When you dwell in true love, you will not want a man or a woman to make you whole. Whenever you want something, or someone on the outside of you, it is because you perceive a lack within yourself. Whenever you observe yourself longing for a man or a woman, it is an excellent time to examine the lack within you. The male / female split down here on earth is so fundamental that none of us feels whole. So, we all keep looking for more on the outside of us, to fill up the gap. We keep looking for the perfect man or woman on the outside of us, but we will not be truly happy until we heal our own masculine and feminine side. Only then will the longing subside.

How can you do this? First, if you are still longing for a man or a woman, notice all the wonderful qualities about a particularly attractive man or woman, and feel these qualities inside yourself. Honour and respect the opposite sex, but don't long for them out of a lack of internal balance. If you feel lacking in love, don't look to someone else to give you what you lack. Whenever you feel a strong desire for a man or woman outside of you, go into your heart and observe what is missing on the inside. Whenever you feel lonely and loveless, go in and give love to yourself. Nurture and honour yourself to the very best of your ability. Loneliness actually has nothing to do with our partners, or lack of them, it is an inherent part of our own unhealed psyche.

If you are a woman, cultivate the perfect man inside you, your perfect yang nature. Love the male aspect of yourself, especially if you are feeling lonely. Contemplate on positive masculine aspects, such as masculine energy and drive and then deliberately develop them inside yourself. If you are a man longing for a woman, create the perfect woman inside yourself first. Contemplate on, and cultivate, a positive, feminine side of your nature, for example by deliberately developing your nurturing side.

If you are a woman and you do not like the man within you, you will seek for a man on the outside of you to compensate for your wounded masculinity. Similarly, a wounded man with low self-esteem will endlessly seek the woman of his dreams to make him whole and complete again. Each time you search for an external partner, you will find a man or woman who superficially represents the opposite of what you dislike within yourself. For example, if your inner man seems to you to be weak or pathetic, you may choose a man on the outside who appears to be very macho, very strong. If your inner woman seems distant and cold, you will find a woman who on the surface is very warm and expressive.

The problem with this compensatory pairing is that just underneath the surface, this external male or female partner will mirror the unhealed wounds of your inner man or inner woman. When your 'macho' man reveals his wounded weak inner side to you, you may well feel totally let down and outraged. You will say to yourself 'How could he do this to me? 'How could he hurt me this badly'? When your 'tender,' 'warm' woman behaves coldly to you one day and pushes you away, you may even want to kill her. Yet when you tell your partner how much he or she has hurt you, they genuinely will not have a clue what you are talking about.

Like always attracts like. Unless, and until, we go deep inside ourselves to really observe who we are, and to heal both our wounded male and female sides, we will continue to fantasise about being rescued by an ideal man or woman on the outside of us; our knight in shining armour, our princess with a heart of gold. When our knight in shining armour turns into a pathetic wimp, we are devastated. When our pure princess with a heart of gold turns into a money grabbing bitch, we become enraged.

Over and over again, we seek a man or a woman on the outside of us to heal the emptiness within, and over and over again this external searching ends in pain and suffering. The good news is that there is an alternative path that can free us from this endless round of thwarted dreams. If we are brave enough to heal all our inner wounds, including our hurt and damaged inner man and inner woman, we will eventually become whole enough and free enough to share our wholeness and inner love with the external world around us, including if we so choose, a sexual partner.

Understanding your sexual desires

Sexual desire causes big problems for virtually all human beings. Most of us seek pleasure through sexual fantasy and sexual activity, and most human beings make a terrible mess in acting out their sexual fantasies. If you have not yet experienced difficulties related to sex, I can more or less guarantee that you are in denial. So, would-be Radiant Warriors have to face the complex and fearful issue of sexuality.

So many people use sex to attack others, or they are very defensive sexually. You will always have a difficult time in relation to your sexuality, until you bring all your sexual issues up into the light. Sex has a strong psychological component and a lot of turbulent emotions attached to it. Whenever fear sets into our being, love flies out the window and, whether we are conscious of it or not, all sexuality is tainted with fear.

However, as a Radiant Warrior, you cannot just attempt to suppress your sexual desires. This never works in the long run. Think of the scandals in the Catholic Church that are related to priests being trained to suppress or deny their sexuality. Sex is a problem for all spiritual practitioners, because sexual desire is in all our minds. Someone can be celibate for years, or even decades, and still find that they are tormented by very powerful sexual feelings, images and fantasies.

When we are not dwelling in love, many of us tend to crave sex, because sex is a substitute for true love. You need to understand that when you want sex, you are actually seeking wholeness, or the enlightened state. But even great sex is never great enough to give you lasting satisfaction (as The Rolling Stones reminded us). Even the best sex soon becomes just another memory in your mind.

Healing your sexuality

So how do you heal this major unhealed area in your life? Healing your sexuality has nothing to do with being either celibate or sexually active. The key is to heal your mind, and your body will then naturally follow suit. First, you must become aware of all your fears and desires in relation to sex. You need to look behind the story line of your sex life and deal with the underlying fear and pain. If you can get in touch with the fear in your mind, you may be able to gain some insightful awareness of its cause.

To heal all your fearful thoughts that are related to sex, you really need to be brave and honest and go deep into your fears. For example, you might sit in meditation, connect up to the light for protection, and then imagine that you are being attacked sexually, and feel all the fear that comes up for you. Don't analyse it, but just cut though the darkness of it. If you do not face your fears in this way, you actually give them power.

The mind is so powerful and it creates very deep, strong patterns, so it is far easier for me to ask you to change your mind about sex, than for you to do it. However, until you heal yourself, you will unconsciously seek out sexual partners with whom you can repeat your worst nightmares. For example, if your deepest fear is that you will be abused or used sexually, you will find partners who demonstrate this to you. If your deepest fear is that your sexual partner will betray you by being unfaithful, they will. A very high percentage of married couples will experience the pain of infidelity.

There are no easy solutions to all this pain and suffering. We do not live in an ideal world, and we cannot dictate other people's actions. We even have great difficulty in controlling our own actions in this area of our lives. But ultimately, you have to recognise that mentally, emotionally and spiritually, you do not need a sexual partner for your fulfilment and perfect happiness. Your ultimate goal is to find true love within. This is the only lasting solution or salvation. Dwelling in this true love, you can set everyone free, even though you will still have human feelings, agendas and preferences, including sexual desires.

Every time I feel pain or fear about a sexual issue, I transform my feelings. To begin with I did not fully understand my sexual desires and internal conflicts over sexual issues, but now I have a much deeper understanding of sexual issues and I am no longer fighting myself. I still experience both pain and desire in relation to sex, but I am no longer fighting these passing phenomena.

You have to become fully conscious about your sexual fears and desires before you can genuinely choose whether to be celibate, or faithful, or not. Once you are fully conscious about your sex-related fears, you will not consciously harm others through your sexual behaviour or attitudes. As a Radiant Warrior, you have to take full responsibility for all your actions and reactions in this difficult aspect of life, and become an adult about all sexual matters. If you are sexually active, your goal is always to have sex with love rather than lust in your heart.

If you are going to make love to someone, please do your best not to mix it with guilt. Do whatever it takes to transcend the guilt about sex in your mind. Please do not condemn yourself or others for sexual activities. It is natural for human beings to be sexually active, particularly when they are young and fertile. I never say to my students 'Don't have sex.' They will do it anyway! But I do ask them not to treat their partner as a sexual object, and I advise them that if they see their partner in this way, they will also see themselves as a sexual object, and suffer for it.

Lust is a temporary but very overpowering phenomenon. Young people have more lustful thoughts and desires, but even in very old people, lust can still lurk in the mind. In the long run a Radiant Warrior seeks to transcend lust. First, you can begin just to observe lust in your mind and in your body to see what it is and how it affects you. See how you can stir lust up in your mind. In meditation, or a contemplative state, you can learn to sit still and observe your lust until it subsides, rather than acting on it. Later, as you mature spiritually, you can transform the energy generated by lust into pure energy. To serve God well, we have to use our bodies as a vehicle for transformation. We need to command our bodies rather than vice versa, and we therefore have to transcend and transform all our lower instincts, including our sex drive.

What are 'healing relationships'?

Once you have gone some way to heal your internal splits and emptiness, you may be ready to embark on a romantic, sexual relationship and to commit yourself to healing the pain that will inevitably arise for you within that relationship. When disillusionment sets into an intimate relationship, the two usual options are separating, or staying together in hell and blaming each other for the pain.

If you separate in pain, the karma between you has not been healed, and you may have to get back together in another lifetime to continue inflicting pain and blame on each other. Moreover, if you separate from one special partner without healing your relationship, you are more than likely to just repeat the whole painful process with someone new. On the other hand, if you stay together with your partner once disillusionment has set in, you may well become an enraged victim, with shattered dreams and secret thoughts of hate and revenge.

There is a third option available to all of us, but most of us do not want to take it. This is the option of staying together and transforming our 'special relationship' into a 'healing' or 'holy' relationship in which both partners commit to owning and transcending all the internal pain that is triggered off by their partner. Most people really do not want to do this, because it involves coming face to face with all their own pain and darkness. If you are brave enough to surrender your relationship to a higher power, and ask that its purpose becomes solely one of healing into true love, you can be sure that your relationship will be turned inside out and outside in.

Once you truly commit to the healing path, your relationship will undoubtedly become very fearful for a while, and both of you will struggle, as all your pain comes up to the surface. Then you have to be brave and strong enough to face and heal your own pain day after day, until you clear all your internal barriers to wholeness and true love. If you commit to healing yourself through an intimate relationship, you and your partner will need to cultivate a lot of tolerance of each other for quite a while. At times, you will inevitably feel lonely, depressed and/or angry, as all your inner pain and guilt comes up to the surface of your consciousness, and you will constantly be tempted to blame your partner for your extreme discomfort. At this stage in your healing, you need to keep taking time out from each other, and give each other lots of space.

In order for a close relationship to become a long-term or even life-long healing relationship, both partners have to be prepared to change. If one person in a relationship really commits to a healing path, but the other partner does not want to change at all, you will probably part company eventually, because you will no longer have anything in common. But, if two people commit to healing, the relationship may well survive, and even thrive on a long-term basis, even though you will both continue to project your guilt onto each other throughout the healing process.

How long does it take to heal a special relationship? I do not know, every relationship is different, but probably many years. Most people will just opt out long before the healing process has been completed, because the pain becomes too unbearable.

But if you do separate from your partner, you can, of course, continue the process of healing and forgiveness in your own mind without having to have any further physical contact or communication with your ex. In fact, given the difficulties of staying together through all the pain that rises up in a healing relationship, it is probably far more likely that you will heal most of your relationships in your mind after you have physically separated, rather than whilst you are still together.

To heal your relationships, you have to find the wholeness inside yourself, and after a long, painful healing journey, you will finally discover this. Once you discover the wholeness within, you will relate to your partner, or even your ex-partner, with great compassion and true love. But this love is in no way exclusive or possessive. You no longer need your partner to stay with you physically, and the love you feel for your partner will extend out to everyone in exactly the same way. This is a truly blissful experience.

The irony of healing your relationship to this extent is that you end up no longer needing, or wanting, your partner as you did before. However, if both you and your partner have truly healed, you may still choose to stay together, so that you can both share extending true love out into the world around you.

The ultimate goal

Although healing an intimate relationship through staying together once disillusionment has set in can be very painful, it can eventually lead to a very beautiful state of being, in which you see your partner as an eternal soul, rather than as a personality or physical body. This is your ultimate goal: a holy relationship, in which two souls, who have found their own wholeness within, share and extend this wholeness with everyone they meet. Herein lies the true joy that we are all desperately seeking in our intimate relationships.

But, you have to be a very advanced spiritual practitioner to know that God's love is always with you, and that the loneliness, anger, and even hatred, that inevitably arise in a close relationship are just an illusion. You have to be a very diligent spiritual practitioner to connect constantly to inner joy, peace, love and wholeness, and therefore to have no need or desire for completion through a relationship.

The ego-self is quite happy to latch on to the idea of having a 'holy relationship' with someone. The ego loves to feel special and superior, and will be more than happy to claim that it is transforming your relationship into a 'holy' one. However, it is crucial to understand that the ego no more wants a totally healed relationship than it wants enlightenment, because neither have anything to offer it.

Only your higher self can appreciate the gifts of a healed, selfless relationship, and the joys of pure spiritual comradeship. Your ego will continue to crave a special, exclusive form of love that it can use to project its shame and guilt outwards. Only when this ego-self has begun to dissolve, after a long healing process, can the higher self re-experience and sustain a selfless form of loving that extends out equally to all manifestations of Life.

How to heal your relationships

First of all, know that using your relationships to fulfil your ego's agenda won't work. We are all looking for love, but when we see love as a commodity, something that we can get from someone else, we have got it all wrong, and the outcome is suffering. Please do your best not to use other people's bodies for your own physical satisfaction, and try not to exploit another person emotionally, in a vain attempt to satisfy your own emotional dependency. In particular, do not ask your partners to play the role of your mother or your father. So many of us are consciously or unconsciously looking for a parent figure in a potential partner, to ease the continuing pain of our unmet, childhood needs. Disappointment will inevitably set into relationships like this, because your partner cannot ever be your mother, or your father.

When we become attached to a particular outcome of our relationship, we are asking for trouble. If you want it to be a particular way, if you have specific expectations, you will always be disappointed. By setting up expectations, or fantasies, in this way, you are simply creating the cause of fear and resentment. Whenever you have a secret agenda in a relationship, whenever you are seeking your own self-centred satisfaction, you are not being loving. You are actually attempting to manipulate your loved one.

Out of our own neediness, we always hurt those we love. Out of our own fear, we all attempt to find a special partner to protect us from the world. All special relationships, in which you set you and a partner up against the rest of the world, are poisonous. First, it is you and your partner against the world, then you join up with another family, until it is you and your neighbourhood against another neighbourhood, and then you and your nation against another nation. This is not love. It is hatred, fear and war.

You can begin to heal your relationships, by seeking to understand that you do not really know their true purpose, in fact you have no idea. Only God knows the true, spiritual purpose of all your relationships. Next, you should practise reflecting on your reactions to your partner. Examine all your habitual reactions to them, those irritations, fears and jealous rages, that seem to just happen before you can stop them. If you are good at this, you will still only be conscious of about one percent of your usual, negative responses.

Your reactions to others are primarily based on unconscious patterns, but if you are determined to use relationships to heal, you will have every opportunity to heal. Why? Because, once you learn to examine all your reactions in relationships, you can begin to change them. For example, if you are conscious that whenever your partner is late home, you feel annoyed with them, you can practise being compassionate with yourself for feeling annoyed. In this compassionate state, you can then get in touch with the fear, hurt and unmet needs underneath your anger.

As you allow this unconscious pain to surface to be healed, you can begin to go even deeper, to find true peace, or love, deep inside of you. When you reach this pure, calm, loving space, you can then extend unconditional love towards your partner. The more you practise owning and then transforming all your negative reactions to your partner's behaviour in this way, the more you will transform your habitual responses from fear to love and thus begin to heal yourself, and your relationship,

Don't expect your partner to change for you

What about the other person? Don't they have to work on healing themselves too? Please forget about the other person, and just focus on your own healing. You cannot change anybody on the outside of you. You can only change your view of them. The unhealed person always says, or thinks, 'You did this to me' 'You made me feel this way.' But other people never know how you feel. When they let you down by being 'thoughtless' or 'late' or 'rude' or 'mean,' they are very rarely setting out to hurt you deliberately or maliciously.

Think about how much your partner, or an ex-partner, has tried to change to accommodate you, and you still won't be happy. You moan, 'Why doesn't he talk to me?' 'Why won't she make love to me anymore?' When we are angry at the world, we think that if we can change it, we will change our life for the better. Life does not work this way. You have to change your mind about the world, including your partner, including the purpose of your relationship. If you still use your relationship for what you can get out of it, if you hold it up for blackmail and ransom, your relationship can never be whole, and it can never be healed.

You do not have to ask your partner's permission to heal your relationship. Healing can start from one person. As you concentrate on changing your own mind about your relationship, the relationship itself will change. As you heal, your partner will also heal. This is inevitable, but please understand that your partner in a healing relationship will heal in their time not yours, so try your best not to place any expectations on them.

It may take many years to heal a relationship, and you may have to continue to heal your relationship after you and your partner have physically parted. On the other hand, if both you and your partner become conscious and aware, it will become easier, because both of you can talk to each other about your inner wounds, and your need for healing.

Communicating honestly and compassionately with your partner

Intimate, sexual relationships cause so much pain, that we just have to develop true compassion for ourselves and for others. But please do not be too idealistic about transcending your sexual neediness and setting your partner free. You first have to understand and accept the pain that lies in the human dilemma of sexual relationships, and then develop loving kindness and bravery.

Everyone always has their own unique agenda in human relationships. We never know what the other person is really thinking or feeling. In a healing or holy relationship your long-term goal is to set your partner free, but while you are still not fully healed, you also have to communicate with them. You need to tell them how you feel, without projecting your pain onto them. Without attacking your partner, you have to find a way to honestly express your own feelings and discuss your unmet needs. When their behaviour triggers your deepest fears, you have to be brave enough to share your vulnerability with them, without blaming them for your own inner lack.

Whilst you should do your best to communicate your needs and feelings honestly to your partner, please keep reminding yourself that you cannot rely on your partner for your happiness, or you will inevitably come to hate them. Try never to say to your partner 'I feel so unloved and it is all your fault. You were supposed to love and protect me and give me multiple orgasms. It is so unfair, why did I ever get together with you?' This is all such a game. Rather than seeing your sexual partner as someone who should fulfil your needs and desires, do your best to see your partner as a divine being. Look beyond their physical body and personality to see the divine in them. Experience that divinity being reflected back to you, and then communicate with them soul-to-soul.

No one can make you happy on a long-term basis. In order to be happy, we have to become strong and independent, but without closing our hearts defensively. Ultimately, we need to learn to rely on God for all our happiness, not other people. Meanwhile, you should practise communicating with your sexual partner soul-to-soul, rather than through words. Find your own quiet, peaceful space within, where there is no attack, and then use your mind to communicate with your partner's soul. Share love and light with them in your meditations. Learn to love others without personal agenda, and as you attempt to heal all your sexual issues, always have faith in God and in the healing process that is at the heart of all our relationships.

The more you can experience love, from whatever source, the more others will relate to you with love, because you will no longer be generating so much fear. When you have transcended at least some of your own fear and pain, others will relate to you with less of their own personal agendas, and with more ease.

Initially, the more you experience love and light, the more fear and darkness will rise up to be released. Gradually however, you will experience greater love more and more of the time, and then more subtle layers of darkness will rise up to be healed. As you go through your own healing process, you will see more and more clearly that everyone is trapped. Then you will have so much compassion for human suffering that you will not want to cause a living soul a drop more pain through your un-skilfulness and neediness, particularly not your loved ones.

Forgive and let go over and over again

To heal a relationship needs tremendous amounts of understanding, vigilance and compassion towards yourself, as well as towards your partner. It takes great maturity to stay loving and peaceful at all times, when you are in a close sexual relationship. Most young people just cannot do it. If their partner forgets to ring them, they will explode. You need tremendous bravery, wisdom and maturity to embrace all your experiences and feelings with loving compassion.

There are actually no right or wrongs in this area. I have found that in a healing relationship there is only forgiveness, letting go and compassion, over and over and over again. It takes many years to uproot fear and guilt in relationships. How do you keep going through all of this? You forgive and you let go, one hundred times, a thousand times, or more. You do your best to understand the other. You try your utmost to cultivate the eternal qualities of compassion, loving kindness and generosity to both yourself and your partner on a daily basis.

When we make a mess in a relationship, and we all do, it is because unhealed aspects of ourselves are rising up. Sometimes you need to stay in a relationship to help each other to heal; sometimes you need to move on. Partners always mirror each other, even though they may not be able to see it clearly. See your partner, or your ex-partner as your saviour. When they push your buttons, thank them for helping to heal your neuroses.

Other human beings can only love you in the best way they know how. They cannot love you like Christ, until they become the Christ, and then they will love everyone equally. If your partner turns into a Saint, you will no longer have a partner! All the worldly side of your relationship will disappear, because you cannot imprison the Christ, and Christ cannot mirror your unhealed, hidden fear and pain.

The spiritual purpose of relationships

As you awake more and more to divine truth, you will become more and more fed up with all your projections. You will ask yourself, 'Why am I doing this to myself again?' You will not want to play the roles of victim or persecutor anymore. If you play victim, and say to your partner, 'Don't leave me. I will die if you leave me!' you will ask yourself 'How can this possibly be love?' True love is universal. If two people find God together, their love will not involve emotional blackmail of any kind. They will simply share a very quiet un-possessive love, in which they openly acknowledge each other's divinity.

Ultimately, all healing is based on your inner connection to love, joy and peace. Once you have firmly established this connection, you can withstand the loneliness and the darkness of the ego. The more you get in touch with this inner connection, and inner strength through your wholesome practice, the more you can feel true compassion and say to someone 'I love you' without a hidden, egotistical agenda. Meanwhile, you will inevitably continue to make the error so real by imagining that only someone else can patch up your pain and loneliness and enable you to feel whole.

The spiritual purpose of relationships is to enable you to understand that true love cannot be imprisonment or control. We all have to understand this eventually. So, the lesson for all relationships is that true love is unchanging, and has no opposite. If it is not love, it is an opportunity to heal. Whenever anyone meets another person, there is a spiritual purpose in it, or rather two purposes: first to join in heart and mind to experience the wholeness of love, second, to join together to experience hating each other, so that healing can occur. That's it. All our relationships, with sexual partners, best friends, and worst enemies, have just these two, spiritual purposes.

Learning and healing through relationships

Please do not read all this about healing relationships and think 'It all sounds so difficult, I will give up trying to heal all my relationships, and go and be a hermit on a remote mountaintop.' It won't work. You cannot run away from healing and forgiving yourself and others. Wherever you go, you take yourself with you, and you still have to relate to yourself. You still have to heal all your own neuroses. If you go up to a mountaintop to avoid temptation, when you come back down again your sexual energy will still be there, your jealousy and irritation will still be waiting to catch you unawares.

Our human existence is a learning experience. We cannot ultimately run away from the lessons that our lives are designed to teach us. We cannot avoid the difficulties of close relationships. It is through these relationships that we learn so much about ourselves. Through observing our projections onto others, we can eventually learn all about our own ego-selves. We can then do our very best to heal and to forgive. We can bring ourselves back into connection with the divine love and light that is forever in all of us, shining away all our illusions and mending all our dreams of loneliness and separation.

Only divine love lasts

Only the instant that we join heart and mind with another soul to share unconditional love is real. We have all experienced glimpses of true love and friendship and sharing. Please remember that these moments of true love are eternally real. On the other hand, your expectations and disappointments, your jealousies and frustrations are not real, and you ruin moments of true love through your attempts to manipulate and control your beloved. By trying to hang on to a moment of true love, you actually ruin it.

True love always sets everyone free. The more you love, the more you have to practise letting go of all your attachments, all your desire to imprison someone in your love for them. When you are afraid to lose love, you lose it, because the moment any fear sets in, true love is gone. Moments of true love are a glimpse of your awakened state, but you lose them so easily because you are still afraid of loss. However, always remember that a moment of true love is real and that true love is your salvation.

When you can love someone soul-to-soul, rather than personality-to-personality, you set them free and thus free yourself simultaneously. True love is unconditional and places no expectations whatsoever on anyone. True love is also eternal. The genuine love you give and receive this lifetime will last for eternity. When you connect to this spiritual love, or selfless, soul love, you will be free and you will never attempt to trap or enslave your loved ones. You will always set them free and give them the space to learn their own lessons.

In holy, healed relationships, people who are awake share the love of God with each other and simply extend it out into the world around them. This is what we all long to do deep inside ourselves. This is our true potential. Merging with true love needs tremendous wakefulness and bravery, because you are going into the unknown. However, always remember that God's love is infinitely powerful. When we are fully healed and awake, we can share this divine love with absolutely everyone, and there is no greater joy in life than this

Exercise

Healing your past relationships

You may have to do this exercise many times before you have fully healed all your intimate relationships

Sit quietly and commit to healing all your intimate relationships.

Ask ascended masters such as Christ or Buddha to help you accomplish this task.

Invite each ex-partner into your mind and heart one by one. As you think of each of your partners, feel the trapping in your lower centres and flood these centres with love and light. Do your very best to forgive your partners for any hurt they may have caused you.

Apologise to them, soul-to-soul for any hurt you may have caused them.

Now let them go; cut the cords that still bind you and your ex-partners together and watch them float freely and joyfully up to heaven!

Finish this exercise by doing your very best to extend unconditional love and gratitude to all your ex-partners.

Know that they were the perfect partners for your personal and spiritual growth this lifetime, even if they did not seem like perfect partners at the time!

Jane's Story: Part 8

Reading spiritual texts about relationships over several years had given me some insights into this minefield of human desire and projection, but it wasn't until I took a two year intensive Ling Chi Healing course with Jason that a deeper understanding of my own relationship problems with men finally surfaced. In a deep meditation on this course, I experienced myself in a past life as a soldier of some kind, wearing heavy armour. This soldier (me), along with his comrades in arms, had raped many, many women and then felt totally devastated and full of guilt and shame for what he had done.

Whether I actually was this soldier in a past life or not, this meditation really helped me to see that the problem I had with men started deep in my own mind. Deep down in my unconscious was an inner man who believed he had seriously abused many women and who felt terribly guilty about what he had done. No wonder that in my present life as a woman I had been so keen to see men on the outside of me as the guilty, sexually abusive ones.

Since that meditation my relationships with men have not transformed miraculously. I still have a very deep tendency to see men as the guilty ones, but I do now have a wonderful close friendship with a very caring, kind spiritual man and this friendship is helping me to heal my own inner demons.

I can also now catch myself attacking and blaming various wonderful men in my life and when I observe myself doing this, I gently remind myself that the men I see on the outside of me are just a reflection of my own inner man and my own guilt and confusion about sex and relationships. If I can forgive men for what I perceive as their unacceptable behaviour, I can actually forgive myself for my subconscious guilt and shame in relation to my own sexuality. I still think that I will have to come back for another physical life on earth to heal all my sexual issues fully, but at least I am now 'work in progress' in relation to this key issue for all human beings.

Chapter 9

The Spiritual Art of Forgiveness

True forgiveness has nothing to do with pardoning others. It is a process through which you release all your own fears and darkness.

True forgiveness is not easy

Not one of us will ever be truly happy in the long term until we fully forgive others and ourselves. Whilst you still have even a spot of resentment, or touch of pain, in your system, you still need to forgive. Sooner or later, you have to forgive everyone whom you believe has ever harmed you. Otherwise, you are trapped with them forever. Forgiving others really means setting ourselves free, but this understanding of the true meaning of forgiveness takes time to cultivate.

If you think that you have close relationships with others to share love and light, think again. Until we are fully awake, all our relationships are full of pain and attack, starting with our relationship with our mother and father. In all our relationships we try to gain others' approval by pleasing them, and they try to gain our approval by pleasing us. Then when we are not pleased or approved of, we blame others for our disappointment. This is not true love. It is an immature, emotional game, a vicious circle. In the name of love, we all join the game of manipulation, we all exchange guilt, and play victim and persecutor. Because we are all so good at playing this game, family members, couples, close friends and colleagues so easily turn into bitter enemies.

Based on our own insecurities, we all play childish, unkind games with each other. Even mature spiritual seekers are very good at these games. We all impose guilt and insecurity on others in the name of love. So, we all have to heal ourselves and go within, until our internal connection to true love is so strong that we no longer need to seek any form of external approval or revenge. Once we reach this state, everything we do to ourselves and others will come from true love and we will no longer be capable of hurting even a fly.

Forgiveness is easy to say, but very hard to do, because your pain is so real to you. When you really begin to explore the process of forgiveness, you will discover rage and vengeance rising up within you, and this can be very hard to acknowledge and accept. You may want to forgive a particular person, you may understand intellectually that you are projecting your own stuff onto that person, but you will still protest 'How could that person inflict so much pain on me?' 'How could they be such a bastard/bitch?'

You have to be very skilful, honest and patient when learning forgiveness. You have to become very aware of your own tendency towards self-denial. 'I'm OK now. I am a spiritual person and I have completely forgiven you.' But if you still feel any anger or pain rising up when you next think about that person, you know you have not yet completely forgiven them or yourself.

Whenever you judge, choose again

In this world, you think you learn by distinguishing good from bad. You think you advance by making the right judgements, but nothing is what you think it is. When you judge someone to be either good or bad, you are just making it up. True forgiving actually means learning not to judge. The whole world is the way it is because of a lack of forgiveness. To forgive truly means looking beyond the personality, yours and everyone else's, and seeing only the spirit or light within. When you see everyone as spirit, then, and only then, will you understand why no one can really sin, and why there is no need of forgiveness in heaven.

Whenever you observe yourself becoming angry with someone or something in your life, you should find a time as soon as possible to sit quietly, until you connect to a calm space inside yourself. Then, go back in your mind and re-live the situation that made you angry, irritated or generally upset. For example, if you find yourself thinking about an abusive encounter with someone in your past and still feeling upset by it, go back to that event and, as far as you can, feel all the feelings that came up for you at the time.

Do not run away from your feelings, but at the same time try not let yourself be consumed by the story line of what happened. Just stay with your feelings and know that you will never be asked to experience more pain than you can handle, even if your pain feels unbearable to you at times. Pray for the light, the love of God to go with you into your anger, hurt and fear. Stay with your pain, and hold it in love and light. Ask Christ or Buddha, or your own guardian angel, to be with you as your guiding light. You cannot heal yourself without assistance, but with divine help you can always face your fear and hurt, and discover that they cannot really harm you.

The process of true forgiveness cannot be completed unless there is a correction in your mind. Correction always takes place in the mind, because only the mind can choose again. If you have been sexually, physically or emotionally abused, the hurt will go deep into your mind, and after traumatic abuse, such as rape, the mind will take a long time to heal fully. Spiritual aspirants have to be prepared to feel all their stored up pain and suffering, so that they can let it go. Everybody on this planet needs healing. But the personality-self never really heals or forgives. It constantly judges and condemns. Only the higher self can heal, because once an individual has made a connection to their higher self, this light can transcend all abusive or painful experiences.

Forgiving all your relationships one by one

Once you are a reasonably experienced meditator, you can use your meditation practice to forgive all your relationships one by one, starting with your mother or father and going on to include all your past partners and your current partner. How do you do this? First, connect up to your inner peace and light, then invite each person into your mind and heart one by one, until you feel no more animosity towards anyone in your life, past or present. As you do this, feel the trapping in your lower centres and flood them with love and light.

To begin this process of forgiveness, it is very helpful to step into your enemy's shoes. When someone abandons you, you will say 'I have been betrayed,' but they will say to themselves 'I am right to do this, I had no choice.' If your wife or husband divorces you, or your business partner rips you off, do your best to look at both sides of the situation. Try to see that they did what they did, because they could not help themselves. People rarely set out to hurt each other deliberately. We all hurt one another primarily out of fear and ignorance. Sometimes, two souls conspire to hurt each other in order to assist each other to heal and awake. Sometimes, your higher self may have invited a traumatic event into your life to help you to awake, even though you have no conscious awareness of this spiritual decision.

Rather than blaming others for hurting you, please accept that we all make mistakes. Please try your best not to condemn other people for making mistakes. Get in touch with your soul, and the soul of your enemy, and give thanks to your enemy for teaching you lessons and helping you to grow and become stronger. Know that everything we experience in life had to happen so that we could heal and grow. No one is born into this world with a mission to hurt you deliberately, but those with karmic links to you may have to hurt you as part of karmic law.

The challenges of the path of forgiveness should not be underestimated. It is very hard to forgive your 'enemy.' You cannot just phone up your ex and say 'I forgive you now.' There is too much hurt inside you. You have to wait until you can think about your ex without too much animosity, and the overpowering energy of hate is gone. You need to be very honest with yourself when you are going though the process of forgiveness. Sometimes you may have to admit 'I am not ready to forgive you yet.' Please honour your personality-self and never force forgiveness on yourself, it will not work.

You have so much hurt and pain stored up within, that you cannot just release it in one go. But eventually, you have to forgive and set free absolutely everyone in your life. Apologise to them soul-to-soul and then let them go. Do not leave any negative karma from any past relationship unhealed. Give thanks for all your relationships and transform all your karmic links. Ask great masters and beings to help you accomplish this task and know that through your forgiveness, the whole world becomes a less hate filled place.

Anyone who comes into your mind and disturbs it in any way is a candidate for this healing process. Anyone who comes into your mind as you do a healing meditation is still stirring something up inside you.

Forgiving yourself

Before you can forgive anyone in your life, you have to forgive yourself. 'Why?' you may well ask, 'I haven't done anything wrong.' No, you have just forgotten all the wrong you have done because you are asleep. True forgiveness does not mean forgiving someone else for the wrong they have done to you. Ultimately, forgiveness really has nothing to do with pardoning others. It is actually a process through which you release all your suppressed fears and darkness.

You have been hiding in darkness for a very, very long time, and everyone hiding in darkness has the seed of a murderer deep inside them. Many people, for example, actually feel as though they want to kill someone who sleeps with their partner in order to project and release the murderous anger they feel inside themselves.

So, first and foremost as a Radiant Warrior, you should commit to forgiving yourself for feeling so much pain and for storing so much anger, mistrust and even hatred deep inside your mind. You should forgive yourself for believing that someone else could really harm you and for playing the victim role and forgetting your true nature.

Unless you can forgive yourself, you cannot forgive anyone else, nor can you truly love anyone else. So many people ask 'How can I forgive her/him for what they did to me?' But this is the wrong question. Ultimately, the right question to ask is 'How can I forgive myself, for forgetting my true identity?' However, it may take some time before you reach this level of spiritual understanding of the whole forgiveness process.

Going deep into your own pain and suffering

When your buttons are really pushed, fear and anger will just rise up in you, however spiritual you think you are. But whenever you are blaming someone else, please be brave enough to go beneath your anger, to look deep inside your own heart, and find your own fear, guilt, unworthiness and insecurity. When you think that you are losing everything, for example, when your husband or wife tells you that they want a divorce, you will shake with fear. You may even think of hiring a hit man to kill the person you once loved so much. This is human nature. In order to transcend it, you need to prepare yourself step-by-step for healing and forgiveness.

Every time you justify your anger or attack on the grounds that someone has sinned against you, or wronged you in some way, you will feel guilty, either consciously or unconsciously, and then you will ask for punishment. Deep down in your psyche, way below your conscious patterns of defence and attack, you believe that you have abandoned or betrayed God.

Lurking just underneath the surface of your personality-self is deep pain and suffering. If you have not yet screamed your head off, or cried your eyes out, as part of your spiritual awakening, you are not yet truly on your spiritual path. Every time you experience divine love or light, you will experience fear, pain and darkness later. Fear and darkness are always just below the surface of your consciousness. Until you are awake, you are never in peace. Only true forgiveness can give peace back to you.

True forgiveness, which involves facing and letting go of all your stored pain and anger, means that you will not repeat your negative patterns any more. True forgiveness involves releasing all the violence and vengefulness that you have stored in your system. If you do not do this, you will continue to project your guilt onto others. So, you have to discipline your mind to stop projecting.

Whenever you are poised to attack or blame someone else, you can simply stop and observe what you are really doing. You can press the pause button and practise owning all of your projections. But when you do this, you will feel awful for a while, because you will have no way to release all the guilt and fear that is stuck inside you. Without having someone or something else to blame, the distress you feel will increase, and the power of this distress should not be underestimated.

When you finally learn to stop projecting your darkness, it is undoubtedly very painful for a while, and every genuine spiritual seeker will experience a dark night of the soul. So, you need to develop complete trust in God. You cannot battle alone against your own darkness. You need the help of the light.

The good news is that you can never destroy the love within you, however much you hide from it. But, the only way to rediscover this eternal love, is to open your heart to all your deep down pain, even though, at first, this can feel very uncomfortable and scary. If you are prepared to bring all your darkness up to the light, if you are ready to observe all your darkness with love and compassion, you will eventually see through all your fears and illusions and let them go. On the other hand, without the presence of the light, your fears will simply over-power you.

The process of forgiving yourself is incredibly demanding because the personality-self has so much resistance to true forgiveness. The personality-self really does not want to give up its victim-hood, its superficial face of innocence. Many people do not want to heal or forgive themselves, because they do not want to lose their personal identity that is based on pain and anger. You cannot help someone like this to heal and forgive. They are not ready, but one day they will be.

Moreover, so many people have suffered horrendous forms of abuse. So many people want to be healed, but their injuries, both physical and psychological, are acute. It takes tremendous courage, and many tears, to release all this pain and hurt. Human beings can be so hurtful, but if you observe human kind carefully, you will discover that victims always have a seed of vengeance within their systems, and, if they achieve a position of power, they will abuse the others.

If you have been abused, you will want revenge, and when you are in a position of power you will take it. Individuals take revenge on each other and nations also take revenge on other nations. Anger, hatred and revenge will lie just beneath the surface of each and every one of us, until we forgive ourselves.

If your karma allows you the opportunity to forgive yourself and the world, you are very blessed. If you can forgive yourself for just one lifetime, you are so fortunate. If, momentarily, you can experience the truth, and know that there is no sin, and that you can never be abused or abuse the others, you are truly blessed.

Transcending your ego-self through forgiveness

The more you tread on the path, the more you will really see the dark side of your ego-self. However, you cannot prematurely say 'I do not want to be this ego-self anymore.' You cannot heal yourself by trying to get rid of your ego. This is like cutting off one of your limbs. You cannot be whole like that. You have to use your higher mind to train your ego, and to heal your ego through a process of forgiveness. First you must observe your ego with great honesty and courage, and then you must heal yourself.

This is very challenging, because, sooner or later, you have to accept that every pain you have ever suffered has been self-inflicted. No one ever abused you without your full consent. Your ego-self desperately wants to hang on to being a victim. It does not want to take full responsibility for its choices. But your ego actually chooses to hold on to pain, hurt and anger, and all this has to be undone. This process of undoing can never be rushed. Just be open and willing to surrender, moment by moment, to the lessons life brings you.

Reaching a certain point on your healing path, there will be virtually no more pain to heal, and nothing or no one left to forgive. Once you reach this stage of healing, you can just send love to everyone without conditions attached to it. A person who extends true love like this, at all times, is a totally healed human being, a saint, or a great spiritual master.

I have had some glimpses of understanding how great masters, like Jesus Christ, Ghandi, and Mother Theresa can love human kind so much. They do not really love your body, or your personality. They look beyond all temporary manifestations and only experience divine love. Then they just extend that love out to you and to all humanity. This is your destiny once you have completed the long arduous journey of truly forgiving yourself and others.

Exercise

If you wish to practise true forgiveness, take twenty or thirty minutes, now or later, to go through this healing meditation:

Sit quietly for a while. Close your eyes, bring your attention into your heart and connect up with divine love and light, ask for divine assistance. If you experience any difficulty connecting up to divine love, remember a time when you felt most in love and bring that feeling into your heart.

Once you feel a soft opening in your heart, think of someone whom you do not like, or someone whom you believe has injured or harmed you in some way, or someone whom you just regard as your enemy.

Now find some little spark of light or goodness in the person you are thinking about and gently extend loving thoughts to them. You might say to yourself, for example, 'I offer you God's love and light.'

If this is too difficult for you at the present time, simply ask for divine assistance to heal your relationship with that particular person, and offer the divine or universal intelligence your willingness to change your mind about them.

Now let yourself sink beneath all the chatter in your mind to dwell in peace for a while. Listen in silence to the higher intelligence guiding you to forgive.

Finally, fill your heart with gratitude for the healing that you know has occurred, whether or not you are now consciously aware of it.

Jane's Story: Part 9

This lifetime I have had to work particularly hard to forgive two key people in my life, my adoptive father and myself. At first when I went into long-term psychotherapy, I happily blamed my father for all my problems as an adult. I even played along with one therapist who insisted that my father had sexually abused me in a violent way, even though I had absolutely no memory of any such event actually occurring. It took a very long time for me to realise that my father was not in any way the cause of my current pain and suffering. How could someone who had been dead for many years still be causing me so much pain? Finally I realised that it was actually the stories that I was telling myself about my past relationship with my father, and the impact I imagined that this had had on my life that were the key problem.

During several very powerful 'forgiveness' meditations led by Jason, I was gradually able to face and then release the stored up pain from my difficult early relationship with my father. I remember in one exercise I actually screamed my head off so loudly, as I released some particularly painful memory, that the guy sitting next to me nearly had a heart attack. The most wonderful thing about this forgiveness process was that after releasing a lot of hurt from my childhood, my heart suddenly filled to bursting with love and gratitude for all that my adoptive father had given me. Then, as I continued to meditate on his soul and my soul joining together, I felt the two of us exchanging blissful unconditional love and support for each other.

Interestingly, once I had forgiven my father for what I imagined he had done to me, I uncovered a deep shame and sadness in my heart for all the pain I had inflicted on him. As an adolescent I did everything in my power to push him away from me by being overtly unkind and unpleasant to him. I vividly remembered one incident in particular when he had gone to great trouble to get my favourite and very expensive perfume for my birthday and as I opened it I said scathingly 'I went off this perfume ages ago.'

So as well as forgiving my father for what I thought he had done to me, I also had to forgive myself for the pain I had inflicted on him. I had to see that my unkindness towards him was simply a mistake born out of fear rather than an unforgivable sin. I then had to give myself the same unconditional love and acceptance that I had earlier extended to my father. When I finally did this, I realised, deep in my heart, that in reality my father and I will share unconditional love for each other eternally, long after the silly little hurtful dreams of this lifetime have faded away to the momentary puff of nothingness that they really were.

Part III

The Path of Empowerment

Chapter 10

Spiritual Empowerment and The Body

We have to choose what meaning we give to our bodies. We can see them primarily as a means for experiencing physical pleasure and sensations, or we can see them a wonderful tools for spiritual awakening.

From a spiritual perspective, your body is simply a crucial tool, or learning device, to enable you to learn, to grow and to master life. You need a body in order to establish a path back towards wholeness. You can use your body to experience whatever you want to experience in this physical world. If you sincerely desire to become a Radiant Warrior, your body will be a great asset on your path.

You cannot spread the light in this world if your body is weak or sickly. You need a strong, healthy body to develop spiritually. Indeed, without your physical existence, you cannot grow spiritually, because you can only truly learn from experience. But we have to choose what meaning we give to our bodies. We can choose to see them primarily as tools for physical pleasure and sensations, or we can see them as a means to awaken, and as a means to communicate the truth to our brothers and sisters.

You are not your body

All your dreams of happiness this lifetime are related to your body. Do you long for a more loving partner, a better career, a house in the country? Ask yourself, would these dreams mean anything to you if you did not have a physical body? Your self-importance is all based on your body, and your fear of dying is based on your body. In this world, you see yourself as a body and others see you as one too. We have created a world full of separate bodies, and a world based on bodily consciousness. Normal human conversations are all about bodies: 'Where did you go?' 'What was the food like'? 'Are you enjoying this weather'? 'How's your knee now'?

But when you identify yourself with a body, you are disassociating from your spirit. Your body perceives through its five physical senses, but it does not see the truth. Your physical brain thinks lots of thoughts, but it does not know anything about reality. Only spirit knows. Our Creator did not create a world of bodies that are all born to die. The source of perfection knows nothing of imperfection. The source of love could never create something that can hate. Your body is your idea, not God's. It is your creation. It started in your mind first, and is an effect, or a symbol, of your belief in sin, guilt and fear.

The truth can never be fearful, but bodies are made to be fearful. In my experience, bodily consciousness always has, at the very least, a twinge of fear in it. When you think 'my money' there is always some fear attached to it. When you think 'my wife' or 'my husband' you inevitably fear losing her/him. Your spirit never experiences fear, but your body is in a constant state of fear or anxiety. If you really tune into your body, you can always feel this underlying state of tension or anxiety.

You cannot just disassociate from your body

If you wish to be a Radiant Spiritual Warrior, you cannot just disassociate from your body, it will simply become weak, wobbly and inflexible. A spiritual path that ignores the body is unbalanced. You do not avoid the problems inherent in being in a body by becoming 'spiritual,' but by transcending them. It is not helpful to keep telling yourself, as some spiritual seekers do, ' My body is not real, it is just an illusion.' This may be the ultimate truth, but, at this moment, your body is very real to you, because you are living in a physical world, and while you are in it, your lesson is to manage it successfully.

Some spiritual traditions reject or ignore the body. Some extreme spiritual practitioners have even inflicted severe pain on their bodies in an attempt to transcend the physical. I do not recommend you try this at home! How can you become whole and natural by rejecting or abusing your body? This is just a form of denial. It is like cutting off your toes in response to noticing that you have athlete's foot. As long as perception lasts, your physical sensations such as pain, hunger and thirst, are very real and you need to honour them. You also need to honour them in others. Please do not ignore or belittle others' physical suffering on the grounds that physical existence is just a dream.

We are all light-beings, but most of us have not transformed into light yet, we are still very much flesh and bone. Our physical aches and pains are very real to us, unbearably so at times. Great spiritual masters may be able to live for years on just light and fresh air, but we lesser mortals need to nurture our bodies with good food and pure water. For light to manifest through your flesh, you will need to follow a disciplined, wholesome regime, including exercising your body on a daily basis. Your ultimate goal as a physical being is a complete integration of spirit with your physical existence.

True beauty shines forth from our souls

Whilst you undoubtedly need to strengthen and open your physical body to support your spiritual awakening, you also need to realise that your body is not ultimately who you are. Actually, your physical body does not even belong to you. You do not own it; you just borrow it from the earth for a while. You should nurture your body, but do not spend too much time pampering it, or focusing on bodily attractiveness or bodily achievements. Physical beauty and physical prowess are flash in the pan phenomena; no matter how much time and money you spend on achieving them. True beauty shines forth from our souls.

So, if we really want to be beautiful forever, we need to cultivate the beautiful qualities within our soul, rather than our ephemeral external appearance. If you spend too much time, energy and money trying to make your physical body more attractive, or trying to ward off the ageing process, you will waste a very precious opportunity to grow through your physical experiences. You will die none the wiser. You will also become very fragile and fearful. We rich Westerners have become very fragile, because we over-value our bodies. We now spend billions trying to prevent sickness, old age and death, and yet we feel just as frightened about these phenomena as ever. If you are serious about becoming a Radiant Warrior, it is your responsibility to opt out of this fearful mass consciousness.

Setting your body free

When you associate too much with your body, you suffer. You cannot find lasting happiness through your physical senses. You should love and nurture your body, but you should also set it free, since it does not really belong to you. It is not your possession. You can only seek liberation through your mind, because only the mind has autonomy. If you try to find happiness through the body, sooner or later you will suffer.

The body is born, and then, inevitably, it dies. It is not permanent and therefore it cannot ultimately be real, but we all plunge right into this illusion of the five senses. What we see, taste, smell, feel and hear seems so real to us, and for the majority of people this is the only reality that they experience. The consciousness of most individuals on this planet is all geared into their physical bodies and their physical desires. Some people are even prepared to risk death to satisfy their physical desires and cravings. Heroin addicts who use dirty needles and impure heroin know the risks they are taking, but their desire overwhelms them. There is nothing wrong with seeking physical sensations, but, if you are a spiritual seeker, this cannot be your primary goal in life.

Your body can become a tool for spiritual growth

If you think that you are nothing more than a physical body, then you do not need spiritual training, but we all know that there is more to us than this. If you contemplate on you and your body for a while, you will come to understand that your physical body cannot be the real you. After all, you can loose an arm or a leg, or even all your arms and legs, and you are still 'you.' If you look deeply into a mirror, you will know that your spots or wrinkles are not the real you. Your body keeps changing, but you experience a continuity of consciousness.

Angelic formless beings blissing out in heavenly realms cannot change, or heal, or make any spiritual progress, and so they actually envy human beings who can grow through the challenges of physical life. If you sincerely desire to grow spiritually, your body will be a great asset on your path. So, as you progress down your spiritual path, keep asking yourself 'Why do I have a physical body, what is it for'? You will eventually understand that your physical body is primarily a tool for spiritual growth and, once you have awakened, a tool for communication.

Keeping your body healthy and strong

In order to progress spiritually, you need to look after your physical body to the very best of your ability. You need to keep your body strong and healthy, so that you will have the strength to heal your mind and to feed your soul's growth. You should therefore breathe good air as often as possible and drink pure water to help purify your physical system.

You should always aim to eat foods that give you life and clear energy, and practise eating mindfully whenever possible. This is called eating yoga. Yoga means union, so eating yoga means that as you eat, you transform food into light, until, eventually, you become united with light itself. Bless your food before you eat it and give thanks for it. Every time you eat, enjoy every mouthful and transform it back into nourishing light.

Too much food, especially heavy fatty over processed food, can make your system heavy and lethargic and an attachment to food can trap your mind, but you can make food your friend and you can utilise good, fresh nutrients as food for your spiritual journey.

Please begin to observe the quality of the food you eat and commit to eating only very fresh, vibrant foods, because these will nourish you more. Whenever you eat, you absorb the essence of the food. Food is a manifestation of life itself. Fresh food contains sunlight, and the sun is the father of our physical life. The fresher your food, the more it will put light into your physical system. Organic food will contain more light than food that has been heavily treated with chemicals. Processed food has very little life or light in it.

If you eat meat, choose meat from animals that have been reared in natural surroundings on organic farms. Free-range chickens and eggs will contain far more light than battery reared chickens and their eggs. As you eat, become aware of how your stomach feels as you digest particular foods. Become aware of how different foods affect your physical system and avoid foods that make you feel heavy or out of balance, as this will prevent you from meditating effectively.

Overcoming addictions

If you are very attached to food, if you sometimes crave chocolate or crisps, or any particular food sensation, learn to observe your craving and to see what emotional pain you are covering up by running to the food cupboard. If you are prepared to put some effort into it, you can discipline your mind to resist an addiction to food, or a particular type of food. Ultimately, you are aiming to overcome your addiction to particular foods completely, so that you can face and heal the underlying emotional pain that you try to cover up by guzzling chocolate, ice cream, crisps etc.

Another way to exert mind control over your desire for food is to go on a short fast. Fasting, in moderation, is good for both the mind and the physical body. As we mature, we all accumulate waste and toxins in our physical systems, so it is a good idea to go on a cleansing fast occasionally to purify our systems. The best time to do this is in hot, sunny weather when you can get energy directly from the sunlight. A day or two of eating nothing but raw vegetables or fruit or drinking juices will help to clear your system.

However, as in all practices, be careful to fast in a balanced way and always take extra care if you are suffering from any illness, or chronic health problem. Also, be careful to avoid using fasting just to create a spiritual high. Being ungrounded in this way can seem like a wonderful spiritual experience, but it can be dangerous, and any spiritual experiences, or insights, you gain from severe fasting will not last, unless you can integrate them through a grounded and strong physical body.

Whilst you are transforming your body's vibrations from gross to refined, you should avoid coffee and alcohol as much as possible. You do not have to give either up suddenly, but you should gradually reduce your consumption in a controlled way. If you currently drink a cup of coffee four or five times a day, for example, start with the goal of reducing this to one cup a day. When you have reached that goal, aim to drink one cup of coffee every other day. Eventually, you should be able to drink a really good cup of coffee only very occasionally as a treat. You should adopt the same approach to cutting down your consumption of alcohol. Never have a drink if you are 'dying' for one, because if you give in to these types of cravings, your mind will never be free.

Alcoholism is actually socially accepted within our culture. So many people do not realise they are addicted to alcohol. They see the amount they drink as perfectly normal, but if they were to try and stop drinking for a week they would see the problem. Millions, if not billions, of people in this world are addicted to some form of alcohol. But if you want true health and happiness, if you want to overcome the limitations of your physical existence, you need to develop the discipline to say no to your strong, habitual physical desires, particularly those that have an addictive quality.

It is not ultimately true to say that you are physically addicted to coffee or alcohol or even 'addictive' drugs. An alcoholic can still crave a drink decades after they stopped drinking. How can this craving be physical? All addictions start within the mind. Therefore, the real solution to all addictions also lies in the mind. Bad habits are very easy to acquire, but they take a lot of self-discipline and willpower to transcend. You therefore need to develop the discipline to say no to physical temptations, even if someone offers them to you on a plate.

There is no need for spiritual seekers to force themselves to give up drinking coffee or alcohol altogether, but they must be able to not drink stimulants or depressants whenever they feel a craving for them. Any kind of addiction is imprisonment. You are not being kind to yourself if you indulge your addictions. You are simply perpetuating your pain and suffering. The mind full of desire cannot find liberation. If you are addicted to alcohol, drugs or cigarettes and cannot give either up using your own willpower, then please seek professional help to overcome your cravings. You will not only improve your physical health, you will ultimately free your mind from the trappings of physical existence.

Empowerment through holistic exercise

Ancient spiritual wisdom rarely emphasised the need to cultivate the physical body as well as the spirit. Even today, there are many teachers of meditation who advise their students to stay absolutely still for long periods of time, and to ignore bodily sensations, including even quite severe pain. These teachers do not demonstrate to their students how to meditate more effectively by strengthening and opening their physical and energetic systems through disciplined holistic exercise.

It is revolutionary to teach people that to find enlightenment they need to change their energetic patterns, as well as to still their minds. If your energy is not healthy and vibrant, you will find it extremely difficult to maintain a clear, open mind during your meditations. If your body is not strong, your blood flow will be weak, your heartbeat will be irregular, and your mind will become fuzzy and unclear. It will then be almost impossible for you to integrate the higher energies that are available to you during deep meditation.

This is why I strongly recommend all spiritual seekers to take up yoga, chi kung, tai chi or another bodily-based holistic practice, not as an end in their own right, but as a tool for awakening. Do not strive so much for the perfect posture, as for self-mastery of your crazy mind. Through a combination of meditation, physical practices and energy work, you can learn to calm your emotions, still your mind and strengthen your spirit, until you return home to your natural, enlightened state of being in which your physical existence ceases to be so real to you. This, rather than physical prowess of any kind, should be the ultimate goal of all your holistic exercise.

For me, following a daily exercise regime is an integral and absolutely essential part of mastering the art of conscious living and becoming a full-fledged Radiant Warrior. Wholesome physical exercise is essential both to your physical health and well-being and to your spiritual awakening. Wholesome exercise will enable your body to become more healthy, vibrant and balanced. Because your body is such an important spiritual instrument, you really need to sharpen it and energise it through a daily exercise regime.

If you do not stretch your body regularly it will grow stiff. If you do not use your muscles they will grow weak. Your aim is to keep your body strong and supple throughout your life. People who practise yoga throughout their lives will still be flexible in their 80s. If you touch your toes every day from now on, you should still be able to touch your toes when you are 90. If you do not train your body with endurance exercises, it will grow weak, and you will be physically frail when you are old. When you exercise, your body will open up and when your body is open, you will be happy and at ease. If you do not exercise regularly, your body will close up and your mind may well feel rather sad and trapped.

Wholesome exercise, including tai chi, chi kung, yoga, swimming, dancing and running, will allow your body to absorb the life forces that sustain our physical existence. Different types of exercise are useful for different purposes. Aerobic physical exercise, such as jogging or dancing, will strengthen your lungs and deepen your breath. Your breath is crucial on your spiritual journey, because proper breathing will help you to open your physical system up to divine energy.

You need a very strong and vibrant physical and energetic body if you are to pursue the goal of enlightenment seriously, and this is the key reason why daily physical exercise is a must for anyone serious about their spiritual journey home. It is a myth that you can just meditate and not look after your physical body.

A couch potato, or someone who is always physically exhausted, cannot meditate effectively; they just do not have enough energy for it. If the vitality within your body falls too low, you will not have enough energy to concentrate and without concentration or focus, meditation can turn into a form of lethargic spacing out or escapism. Both chi kung and tai chi can really assist you to raise your energetic vibrations, and to calm your mind. Taoists have always understood this.

Even very simple physical misalignments can be a major obstacle to spiritual awakening. For example, if you cannot sit with a straight spine when you are meditating, your energy cannot rise upward, and basically all you will be doing is a form of relaxation. More experienced meditators also need to protect their nervous systems when they meditate, because they will eventually be able to bring higher energies or light down into their systems. They need to strengthen their energetic and physical systems so that they can handle this very powerful light, or energy. If not, they may blow a fuse and even end up with what appears to be a serious mental imbalance or illness.

The Importance of your energy field or chi

In the West, we are only just beginning to learn about energy fields and how important they are, but in the East, they have studied energy fields for a very long time, and have accumulated a great deal of wisdom in this area that is so relevant to today's spiritual seekers. In the East, they understand that we all have an energetic or chi force that surrounds us.

Everything in this physical world has a unique, energetic emanation. Oak trees, for example, have a very different type of energy than Willow trees. A healthy tree emanates a lot of chi or power. The sun has tremendous chi. Similarly every human being has their own, very personal, energy field. Your unique qualities show up in your energy field. This is just common sense. Your energy body is as real as your physical body, but most Westerners are not aware of it, until they take up an energy practice such as tai chi or yoga.

Chi can be negative or positive. Some people have very negative attitudes about life, but simply do not understand that this is linked to their chi. People do not realise that some individuals will attract so called bad luck into their lives because of their negative chi or energy field. Some individuals spend their whole lives attempting to be loving, rich, or successful, but they just do not have the right energetic field to do this. Their energy field is negative and imploding, and this is why they cannot achieve much in their lives. As an advanced energy practitioner, this is so obvious to me, but most people with negative energy just have no idea why they seem to have endless bad luck.

Everything that happens to you happens inside out, not outside in. This is why it is so important to purify and strengthen your chi. Your unique energy field and vibration will attract other people to you, and you will attract people who reflect you energetically. So drug addicts will attract other drug addicts, whilst those seeking spiritual awakening will attract external spiritual teachers to assist them. This is not just a question of like minds; it is very much about like energy fields attracting each other.

Energy that goes downwards leads to sickness and death. Energy has to rise upwards for healing, health and a strong spiritual connection to occur. Once you learn to bring your energy up from your base centre, through your spine, to your crown, you will begin to balance and open your chakras.

Eventually, as you raise your vibration and open up your whole energetic system through energy work and meditation, you will experience more and more the divine light that is always shining down on you. This light is always there for us, but we have to open ourselves up to it before we can actually experience it. Unfortunately, if you have abused, distorted or neglected your physical and energetic bodies for any length of time, it may take several years fully to rebalance and revitalise your energetic system. You therefore need to be both disciplined and patient to become a master of your own energy field.

In order to live a long and healthy life, you need to cultivate a strong life force. Without an energy field, you do not physically exist. This is a scientific fact. A body with no energy whatsoever flowing through it is a dead body. You can gain great physical strength from pumping iron, but physical strength alone is not enough to sustain your vitality. A number of top athletes have dropped dead at a very young age, because if someone runs out of life forces, they will get sick and die, even if they seem physically strong. Daily life in the modern industrialised world can seriously pollute and weaken your life forces, and so you really need to do some energy work on a very regular basis to become more vibrant, radiant and energetically clear and healthy.

One way to look after your energetic body and raise your vibrations is to spend some time in nature. If you go into the mountains, or walk by a pure stream in the sunshine, you will become lighter and brighter energetically. The sun is an unconditional life-giving force. If you want to become more vibrant and purified, I strongly recommend that you go into nature as often as possible. If you want to experience moodiness, spend some time in a crowded bar or a busy airport.

One of the reasons why so many Westerners are now suffering from illnesses, such as ME, is because they live such unnatural lives in big, crowded, concrete cities. They sit in front of computers all day long, overtaxing their brains, and then spend their evenings in smoky, crowded bars with alcohol-crazed companions. We all use our brains too much and take too little care of our physical bodies, and then we wonder why we get sick. However, it is impractical for most of us to spend all of our time walking alone in the mountains, or swimming off a sun drenched beach, so we need to adopt a wholesome exercise regime that we can combine with our daily lives, in order to strengthen our bodies and raise our vibrations.

Practising chi kung, tai chi, yoga, or a similar type of holistic exercise, on a regular basis will increase your internal chi. This has nothing to do with building the body beautiful. Someone can have a beautiful physical body, but still have a very negative, or very weak, energy field. Without energy, you can have no real peace. On the other hand, when you create positive chi through wholesome exercise such as chi kung, the positive chi will push out and purge your negative chi, and you will become brighter and lighter.

If you can fill up your system with strong chi, you will not get sick nearly as often. But if you allow your auric field to become weak or low, this will eventually manifest in your body as ill health. You should therefore use chi kung and other wholesome exercise to balance and strengthen your auric field on a daily basis. Chi kung is wonderful preventative medicine, it will turn your weaknesses into strengths, and you need so much strength to pursue the goal of becoming a fully awakened Radiant Warrior this lifetime.

Preserving your physical essence or jing

'Jing' is a Taoist term for your physical essence that is closely linked to your sexual energy. The whole 6 billion population of the planet has manifested through this potent sexual energy. If you are a spiritual seeker, you need to learn how to draw this sexual energy up your spine, in order to nourish your charkas. Sexual energy gives you the fuel to open up your heart, so please do not see it as something that you ought to suppress.

Taoists always advise that you have to learn to conserve and transcend your sexual energy, rather than suppressing or wasting it. Sexual energy is the fuel for the rocket to go up. Taoist Masters actually utilise their sexual energy to fuel their spiritual practices. They purify their sexual energy or jing, and then pull it up from their base centre, to create strong chi that they can then transform into spiritual focus, and a connection to the light

Sexual energy is sacred and has great potential. Without it you will lack vitality. In order to cultivate strong vitality you will need to store your jing. Jing is strongest during ovulation and the creation of sperm, and weakest during menstruation and ejaculation. In most people, particularly men, sexual energy leaks outward, primarily through ejaculation. This is why traditional Chinese doctors recommend men to avoid ejaculation when making love, particularly as they get older. If you are a man, I am not telling you that you should never ejaculate, but I am suggesting that if you want to still be a radiant presence in your sixties and seventies you should do your best to avoid excessive ejaculation, so that you can preserve as much jing as possible for as long as possible!

Cultivating an inner smile

As a Radiant Warrior, you should avoid practising chi kung or yoga primarily to amass a lot of energy and strength within your physical body. High-level chi kung, tai chi or yoga masters can accumulate a lot of chi and the powers that go with it, but this energy is not necessarily pure. Building up energy, or power, in your system is not enough on its own. You have to know how to use it for good. So, as a spiritual practitioner, you cannot just accumulate chi, you also have to purify it. This is why I always recommend that each time you start to exercise, you pause and give yourself an inner smile.

If you exercise when you are in a bad mood, you will pollute your system. So, before you begin any holistic exercise, it is a very good idea consciously to tune your mind into a positive attitude. If you have any difficulty doing this, think of someone you love, or a time when you were very happy, and use that memory to create a positive frame of mind. Then, as you exercise, always bring your positive mind into what you are doing, and simultaneously focus on opening your heart with joy. Give thanks to God, or the universe, for your physical existence and your ability to move freely. Cultivate loving kindness, inner joy and an open heart whenever you practise and you will purify your energetic system as you strengthen it.

Opening and balancing your chakras

Chakras cannot be found in your physical body. No autopsy has ever found a chakra, but a good energy practitioner can definitely feel these centres within a person's energy body. Everyone has seven chakras, or energy vortexes, that form part of their energetic or etheric body that runs from the base of the spine up to the crown. Each chakra corresponds to a different level of consciousness, from survival instincts at the base to divine presence at the crown. Each charka links to a different part of the physical body and each one affects us differently on a physical, energetic, emotional, mental and soul level.

Some of your charkas will be open, some not. No one has totally balanced, open charkas, so you are certainly not alone if you are energetically unbalanced. When all your charkas are balanced and open, you will have a glimpse of the divine, natural state of your being, so it is very well worth working on healing all of your seven major energy centres.

Virtually all human beings tend to be imprisoned at the consciousness level of the three lower charkas. Human evolution actually involves gradually transcending the limitations and trappings of lower levels of consciousness. But Radiant Warriors cannot afford to wait for human evolution to release them from fearful physical consciousness. In order to hold light and love within your system, and thus become a radiant presence in the world, you will need to balance and strengthen all three of your lower charkas.

When these lower centres are strong and open, they will naturally fill up with positive chi, and when your energy body is filled with positive chi you will feel radiant and vibrant. You will also have a strong sense of security, self-worth and self-confidence that will assist you to accomplish whatever you set out to do in this world. On the other hand, if your lower charkas remain unbalanced or closed, you may experience feelings of low self-esteem or even a sense of worthlessness. You may continue to believe that you are the victim of life and you will probably feel below par physically and emotionally.

We will now very briefly explore the role of the seven individual charkas, looking at how they affect us positively when they are open and balanced, and negatively when they are closed, unbalanced or weak.

Base Centre

The base chakra is located at the perineum. It is associated with basic survival instincts, life and death issues, fight or flight reflexes and basic physical needs such as hunger and thirst.

Everyone is trapped at the base centre to some degree, and so we all feel unsafe in this world in one way or another. Even people who are very wealthy usually still experience some fear in relation to their security. An unbalanced or trapped base centre can also leave you very weak-willed, and someone with extreme base centre problems may even lose the will to live or become suicidal.

A strong base chakra is essential for maintaining our energetic vitality. Some human beings can be physically strong but energetically weak and people like this may even die young despite their physical prowess. When you are just three to five years of age, you have so much natural energy you can learn virtually anything with ease, but as we get older we all leak energy through our base centre.

One way to maintain your strength and vitality is to keep your base centre sealed. You can do this by pulling in the muscles that control your perineum and anus. You can practise this as you go about your daily life, and no one will notice. You can practise stopping your flow of urine when you go to the toilet. This will help to strengthen the muscles that seal your base centre.

This may sound odd advice in a spiritual book, but really it is so important to create a strong energetic foundation on which to build your life and your spiritual practice. As a life-long Taoist I feel I have to let you know how important it is to preserve and utilise your energy for your long, arduous journey of spiritual empowerment and awakening.

We all need to heal and strengthen our base chakra, at least to some degree. However, I strongly advise you to focus on healing your sacral and solar plexus centres first, because if the base centre is activated too quickly, or before any healing has occurred in the other centres, it can prematurely open up a can of worms, such as extreme fear or anger, that you may find very hard to handle!

Sacral Centre or Dan Tien

The Sacral Centre is located just below the navel point. In the East, this centre is known as the dan tien. This centre is associated with vitality and with the sexual organs and the sex drive. Sexual drive is always there, whether you experience it or not. If you lack sexual energy, you will feel cold and lethargic. On the other hand, if you have too much sexual energy, you may feel constantly sexually frustrated. But sexual arousal per se can be very helpful to an advanced energy practitioner, since sexual arousal generates strong heat and chi.

We all need to balance our sexual energy in order to create a lasting sense of vitality and well being deep within us. But you can only balance this energy centre by yourself. Trying to find a sexual partner to balance you, will not work. You have to heal your own sexual energy first, before you can form a healthy sexual relationship with another person.

Your sacral centre is an energy centre, very much like the centre of the earth. It is a very hot spot, and if you can learn to tap into its energy, you can use its heat to become radiant. One way to do this is to visualise a very bright flame at the dan tien. Each time you breathe in and out your breath fans this flame until it fills your whole torso with bright, warm light. By nurturing an eternal flame at your dan tien point during meditation and chi kung and tai chi practice, you can create heat and a sense of well-being from within.

Energetically, you should nurture and strengthen your dan tien point in order to transform your energy field. If you keep practising nurturing an eternal flame at the dan tien, you will eventually find that you have more and more energy to sustain your meditative state for longer periods of time, without collapsing into a lifeless, trance-like state.

Solar Plexus

The solar plexus centre is located just below the breastbone and is the centre for personal confidence, personal power and self worth. It is also the centre of our human emotions and our personal desires and aversions. A lot of people experience problems with this centre. An unhealed, unopened solar plexus can leave you feeling insecure, weak and empty.

The next time you feel jealous or insecure, check to see how you feel in your solar plexus and you will probably find that it feels sore, tight, tense or uncomfortable in some other way. The solar plexus is always activated when we fall in love. The moodiness we all experience in close relationships does not come from your heart; it is generated in your mind first and then stored energetically in your solar plexus.

The solar plexus is also the centre of absorption and assimilation, so an imbalance in your solar plexus may lead to digestive problems. The stomach will be very sensitive if you are not emotionally balanced. Some people stuff themselves full of comfort food to avoid having to feel their emotional pain, but it is so much better to face this pain and bathe it with light and love. Unfortunately, you have to heal all your emotional junk in order to heal your solar plexus.

The solar plexus is also your lower psychic centre and is therefore very sensitive to external influences. A lot of people instinctively fold their arms over this area of the body to protect themselves when they are in a crowded place. When your solar plexus centre first begins to open, you may feel nausea and you may not be able to drink coffee or alcohol for a while.

Sometimes you may become so sensitive that you can feel other people's fear and darkness, especially when they are physically very close to your own energy field. When your psychic centre begins to open up, you may find that you cannot stand being in crowds or noisy places for a while. You may feel energetically drained and vulnerable if you spend time in a noisy bar, or shopping centre.

If you do go out into the world when you are feeling psychically sensitive, you will end up feeling energetically drained and emotionally vulnerable.

This is why, when you are on a spiritual path, it is so important to keep strengthening your energetic system through daily practice of chi kung or other energy based exercise systems. After a while, if you keep strengthening your energetic and physical systems, you will be able to cope better with noise and large groups of people. But whilst your psychic centre is opening, I strongly suggest that you avoid crowded, noisy places.

As you open up your lower three centres, you will come into your own personal power. When you are strong and balanced in your three base centres, you can open your heart and you will still feel safe and secure. When your three lower centres are finally fully open and balanced, you will feel confident, and have relatively calm emotions. When you are energetically balanced, you will automatically become a kind and loving person. But if you do not develop energetic balance in your lower three centres, you will continue to be moody and even unkind, whether you mean to be or not.

Heart Centre

The heart chakra is located at the very centre of the chest. Compassion, unconditional love, joy and peace are all qualities associated with this centre. But when the heart chakra is not open we can feel trapped, confused, lonely and unhappy. We will also find it very difficult to forgive, even if we want to do so, because true forgiveness can only flow from an open heart.

An open heart centre enables you to connect to true love. When your heart is open, you are happy, when it is closed tight, you will feel miserable. When your heart centre opens, you will also appreciate art, music and beauty. The heart centre is linked with your intuition. Therefore, when making any important decision, you should always consult your heart, because your heart bypasses reason and logic, and logical thinking has just made a mess of the world.

The heart centre is also the chakra of transition where we move from individual consciousness into an experience of the transpersonal and the inter-connectedness of all life.

As a trainee Radiant Warrior, you have to go through the pain of opening your heart. One way to do this is to focus on your heart centre during meditation. You can use the power of your mind to imagine this centre opening up to the light like a beautiful flower. You simply sit and imagine that a lotus, or rose bud, at the centre of your chest is opening up petal by petal, layer by layer, to the light pouring down on it. If you find it helpful, you can visualise this flower at the centre of your chest as having soft, luminescent pink petals, as pink is the colour usually associated with the heart centre.

When you first open your heart centre, you will inevitably feel vulnerable, because of all the times your heart has been hurt in the past. When your heart centre first opens up, you may even find yourself crying buckets of tears for no apparent reason. You have closed your heart through the fear of being hurt again, but without an open heart you will never find true love. Deep inside your heart is your primordial innocence. This innocence has great power. It can move mountains. But if your heart is still closed and fearful, your mind will stay fearful, because your mind always fulfils your heart's desires.

There are several different stages to the opening of the heart centre. When their heart centre first begins to open up, some people feel as though they have been reborn as a small child. You may feel fragile and vulnerable and need a lot of support and understanding as you go through the early stages of opening and balancing your heart centre. You may also need to avoid aggressive people and violent films during this stage of your opening.

You will probably go through a stage where you cry very easily, so you need to really nurture yourself, until you begin to feel strong again. Once your heart centre is more open, love and compassion will come in to naturally heal your past wounds. Eventually, all your fears will disappear for a while and you will experience a great sense of well-being, and even a welling up of bliss that extends outwards from your heart to envelop your whole being, and the world around you.

Throat Centre

The throat centre is located in the centre of the base of the neck, and is the chakra for expression, creativity and communication. This chakra is also a bridge between our lower, thinking mind and universal mind or higher intelligence. When we tap into this universal mind we will find that we are infinitely creative. Everyone can learn to tap into this unlimited source of creativity, but opening your throat centre usually takes some time and disciplined practice.

You cannot just say to someone, 'Be creative!' If their throat centre is blocked, their creativity will also be blocked. An open throat centre helps us to express the qualities of our soul and enables us to connect to transcendent wisdom. When your throat centre is open, you will want to express yourself creatively, perhaps though music or writing or art. On the other hand, if your throat centre is unbalanced or blocked, you may be susceptible to glandular fever or hormonal imbalances.

Singing will help your throat centre to open, as well as certain chi kung exercises such as The Six Healing Sounds. You can also focus on opening your throat centre during meditation by imagining a bright star at the centre of your throat and by breathing clear, healing bright light in and out of this star until it shines incredibly brightly.

Third Eye

The third eye is like a vertical eye that is located in the middle of the forehead, between and just above the eyebrows. The third eye is very hard to describe because it is so abstract, and you have to experience an opening in your third eye for yourself before you can really understand its important function in the awakening process. An open third eye helps you to expand your consciousness. When your third eye is open, you may see worlds within worlds, worlds beyond this one. You may experience a lot of inner light and ultimately, when your third eye merges with universal consciousness, you can even perform miracles.

The third eye seems so mysterious because it has nothing to do with this world, but when it finally opens fully, you will experience tremendous benefits and all your worldly anxieties will no longer make any sense to you. When we can experience divine grace pouring through our open third eye, negative karma is naturally cleared and deep healing can also take place without any conscious effort on our part.

To help open your third eye during meditation, you can focus on seeing a vertical eye in the centre of your forehead that reaches up into infinite space above it. You can then practise gently breathing bright light in and out of this vertical eye.

Your third eye can be very tight and contracted, and when you first focus on it, you may experience a headache. If your third eye opens up too quickly you may also experience throbbing in your temples. This is just a sign that subtle energies are trying to open up this centre. If you experience discomfort as this centre opens, you can simply massage your forehead gently to ease the tightness.

If you have no energy in your third eye, you will not be able to focus during your meditation. On the other hand, if your third eye opens up too suddenly, you may experience a lot of spiritual light without being able to ground it. Some people can even go crazy if their third eye opens up suddenly, particularly if they have yet to open and strengthen their three lower centres. This is why it is so important to practise opening and balancing all your charkas, for example by breathing bright light in and out of them, rather than just seeking spiritual highs.

Everyone is so different. Some spiritual seekers who are very open energetically need to concentrate on grounding so that they can integrate the light safely. Others need to open and relax more and allow the light to heal them. Once you can focus gently and harmoniously within your third eye, your consciousness will begin to open up and become polished like a mirror so that life itself can reflect back into your consciousness.

Crown Centre

The crown chakra is located at the centre of the top of the head. Finer energies will come into our systems as we open up this centre and eventually, as this centre opens more and more to the light, we will experience oneness with life itself. This experience cannot be described, but once you have tasted it, you will know the bliss of enlightenment, and in this state of bliss, you will be in complete harmony with all that is. You will experience a state of being that is sometimes called simply 'I Am' or even 'I Am God.'

When your crown centre first starts to open you will probably feel a tingling on your scalp. As your crown centre opens, it will stimulate your brain cells and your consciousness will expand. You can be a genius when you are connected to universal intelligence, but you have deliberately closed yourself off from this universal consciousness for a very long time and now you may have to make some effort to open yourself up again. If you have ever abused alcohol or drugs, you may take longer to open and heal your crown centre. You can assist your crown centre to open by breathing light in and out of it during a meditation. Whilst you do this you can also imagine this centre opening up to the light like a thousand petal lotus.

But please do not over-stimulate this centre prematurely, as you may not be able to handle the higher energies that will start to pour into your system. If your crown centre opens up too quickly before you have strengthened your lower centres, you may feel very ungrounded and unable to think clearly or to function normally in the world. If you ever begin to feel like this, I strongly suggest that you stop meditating and stop any other practices that may be stimulating the opening of your higher centres, until your system calms down.

As your crown centre opens and your brain becomes more receptive to universal wisdom, you may become clairvoyant or much more intuitive. This is just a side effect of spiritual unfolding. Please do not make the mistake of confusing psychic abilities with spiritual maturity. The two do not always go hand in hand! Someone can be very psychic without being very advanced on the spiritual path and it can be dangerous to dabble with psychic phenomena before our energetic systems are strong and our heart is purified.

When your crown centre is open, you will not have to struggle in life. You will naturally be able to draw down universal life forces to replenish yourself, including your physical body. You will never miss an opportunity to fulfil your true purpose in life and you will be very clear and bright on the inside. Spiritual will and light will come down into your whole being and your mind will become still. This spiritual light will purify you and speed up your spiritual evolution and you will gradually transform your personality-self over a period of years. It does take time for your system to get used to higher vibrations, but eventually you will be able to hold higher, purer energies of chi life forces for longer and longer stretches of time.

Once your higher centres are fully open and clear, you will inevitably experience divine light pouring through you. You will begin to shine like a diamond. This is your divinity manifesting itself and filtering down into your physical existence.

When you reach this stage of spiritual awakening, others will be attracted to your radiance and you will be naturally connected to universal wisdom and love. You will dwell in the eternal now and you will be able to look on any dis-ease or suffering and naturally transform it into health and wholeness. You will have begun to transcend physical, personal consciousness and you will more and more dwell in the higher transpersonal realms of pure consciousness. Ultimately your consciousness will merge back into God or the Tao. You will simply be 'I AM' or 'Divine Presence,' and your amazing journey back to the light will be over

Exercises

Overcoming your addictions

Take a minute or two now to think about which foods or other substances you habitually crave.

Make a commitment to cut down your consumption of either caffeine, alcohol, sugar, chocolate or any substance you habitually crave for the next five days.

For example if you drink two cups of coffee a day, drink only one cup a day. If you drink alcohol every day, go at least one day without a drink.

As you do so, keep a record of your thoughts and feelings and do your best to send a lot of love and compassion to that part of your mind that seeks to escape from pain through physical addictions or pleasures.

Opening and balancing your chakras

A simple way to begin to heal and open your chakras is to sit in a meditative position and concentrate on breathing bright light in and out of each centre in turn, starting with the base. As you focus on each centre in turn, point your palms and fingers towards that centre. This will assist you to bring your mind to that centre.

Breathe in and out at each centre for nine or eighteen slow and deep breaths. As you breathe in, imagine that the centre is being filled up with very bright, pure healing light and then as you breath out imagine this light gently opening or turning the centre.

At first, you may feel very little during this practice, but if you continue it on a regular basis you should eventually become more aware of energy turning at each chakra and/or you may experience heat or other sensations during your practice.

Some practitioners like to use different colours to strengthen and heal their energy centres. You can imagine bathing your base centre in pure red light, your sacral centre or dan tien with orange, your solar plexus with yellow, your heart centre with soft pink or green, your throat centre with sky blue, your third eye with indigo and your crown with violet.

Jane's Story: Part 10

In my childhood and early adulthood, I really did not like being in a body. I therefore tried to ignore my body by living almost exclusively in my head. While other children were out playing tag or hopscotch, I would curl up in bed with a book. I clearly remember being very cross when I was about eight years old because as a child I was only allowed to borrow three books every week from our local library, whilst my Mum and Dad could take out five books each.

In my early adulthood I hated my body so much that I developed anorexia and although I never became dangerously under-weight, I lived for several years on nothing much more than crispbread, slimming biscuits, apples, and small chunks of cheese and carrots. Thankfully, I slowly grew out of this crazily punitive behaviour and I now eat a relatively healthy diet apart from one or two 'vices' such as Starbuck's coffee and Pringles crisps.

My main problem with my body is that it is both physically and energetically rather weak and this has meant that at times I have not been able to integrate or hold the spiritual light that I have experienced pouring down on me. Indeed, at the end of my first ever retreat with Jason, I went dangerously 'high' as my third eye and crown suddenly opened up, whilst my lower centres remained very closed and weak. This meant that the spiritual energy that I was experiencing so powerfully could not ground through my system. Eventually I had to take some prescribed medication to bring me back down to earth.

Since then, I have worked very hard to strengthen my physical and energetic bodies through a combination of Infinite Tai Chi, Infinite Chi Kung and Chi Yoga exercises. Progress has been quite slow and even painful at times, but I can now go into a very deep, or high, meditative state and come out of it feeling fully grounded and very safe and present in my physical body and this physical world. My lower three charkas are still not as open as my higher chakras, and I may never be able to channel the light as powerfully as some of my fellow Infinite Tai Chi practitioners, but I nevertheless feel that my progress in strengthening my energetic and physical systems is a minor miracle. I know that if I keep up my yoga practice, even though I still don't particularly enjoy doing it, I can make even more progress towards developing a strong radiant body as a tool for further spiritual growth and awakening.

I have also noticed that when my body is tired, my mind tends to be grumpy and my meditations are very flat. So in the last few years of my spiritual journey, I have made it a priority to get enough sleep. Sometimes, after a particularly intense retreat, I may sleep for eleven hours a night for several weeks on end. So be it. I no longer buy into the world's rules about such things. If my body needs more sleep for a while, I got to bed early and get up late. Then, when my energy naturally returns, I can become a little busier in the world once more.

Chapter 11

Cultivating Radiant Qualities

You are sheer potential. Whatever you practise you become.

If you truly want to transform yourself from a constant worrier into a Radiant Spiritual Warrior, you will not only have to heal all your past wounds and fearful emotions, you will also need to cultivate a range of positive qualities, especially loving kindness, compassion, generosity, inner joy, trust and bravery. If you think of your personality-self as a computer, you can imagine that you are re-programming yourself with positive thoughts and qualities.

Every effort counts, even though your personality traits are only temporary. In this world of duality, we all develop some characteristics based on fear and some based on love. This duality is very, very real. When you are jealous, you cannot be generous, when you are miserable, you cannot extend joy into the world around you. Some people are born with certain qualities, or characteristics, that makes their cultivation this lifetime much easier, but to cultivate radiant inner qualities usually takes a long time and a lot of disciplined effort.

Most people act selfishly most of the time, but when we constantly think about ourselves and our own problems and desires, it is all too easy to become fearful and contracted. If you are mindful about your life, you will soon see that when you are self-centred, you are not joyful and expansive. So, overcoming our tendency to be self-centred is not a moral issue. It is about learning the difference between true joy and egocentric grasping after pleasure that never lasts. If you cultivate selfless love, understanding and compassion for yourself and others on a daily basis, you can begin to interpret your experiences differently and to break out of the endless patterns of attack and defence, of being the victim and then being the persecutor.

At first, you may gain some intellectual understanding of concepts such as compassion, but this is just a starting point. Gradually, as you keep practising, these words will take on a meaning deep inside your heart, and deep inside your soul. Eventually your heart and soul will be transformed, and this transformation will permeate your intentions and your behaviour.

When you finally return to your natural state of being, which is sometimes called the enlightened state or self-realisation, you will no longer have to strive to embody positive inner qualities, you will just be them. But until you reach this stage of your spiritual journey, these positive qualities within you are just high ideals, or potential, and you have to practise cultivating them on a daily basis.

As a Radiant Warrior, you never strive to change anyone else. You only strive to change yourself. Cultivating these positive, spiritual characteristics, or inner qualities, is a wonderful way to heal yourself, to grow spiritually, and to move into the light.

This world we live in is fifty per cent light and fifty per cent dark. Half of your whole existence is light and bright, the other half is darkness. When you are in a bad mood, you hate everyone in sight. When you are fearful and insecure, you worry about every aspect of your life. Fifty per cent light and fifty per cent dark, it is that simple. So we have to cultivate those qualities that will enable us to live in the light.

Please do your best to understand and accept that you make up your own world. Whatever you experience on the inside of you, that is what you see around you. This is called projection. If you are moody or fearful at any given moment, this is what you will experience around you. When your mind is full of fear, you look out and see a very frightening world. When you feel kind, loving and secure, not only do you feel good inside, but you will see the world around you as a kind and loving world. You will experience everyone you meet as loveable.

If this all sounds unlikely to you, think about the last time you fell madly in love. Did not the world seem like a really wonderful place to you for a while? Then you fell out of love, and for a while the whole world seemed so awful. This process of projection is so fundamental to the way in which we experience the world, that by cultivating radiant inner qualities, you not only transform yourself, you completely alter your perception of the world around you. Instead of seeing a fearful, dangerous world, you will ultimately perceive a peaceful, harmonious radiant world of infinite possibility

Loving kindness

You already know that you should be loving and kind to others. In fact, deep down, you always want to be loving and kind. You know how much better you feel when you are being loving, than when you are being fearful, or hateful. The problem is that most of the time, you find this so hard to do.

You have probably known since you were a small child that you should 'love your neighbour as yourself.' However, whenever you are in a bad mood and your neighbours annoy you, at that moment, you hate them. When you are fearful, and someone offers you love, at that moment, you push them away. The heart of your problem is that you cannot be loving and kind to others at all times, because you are so often moody, and because you are not always kind and loving to yourself.

To cultivate loving kindness therefore, you must start with yourself. You are so close to yourself, you cannot ever run away. You can run away from the world, or from following a spiritual path, but you cannot run away from yourself. So it is logical to start this practice by being kind to yourself. You think you can be kind to your best friend, your neighbour, or your cat and not be kind to yourself? That is self-deception. Apparent kindness to others can be a smoke screen to cover up our own pain and neediness.

If you are not loving and kind sometimes, it is because you are fearful and not connected to your loving heart. When you feel loving and kind, you are always coming from your open, fearless heart. To cultivate loving kindness, you should therefore practise centring in your heart rather than your head. Our brains and our hearts are only fifteen inches apart, but most of us think, speak and act from our heads, not our hearts and thus we do not always think loving thoughts, speak loving words or do kind deeds.

To become a Radiant Warrior, all you need to do is to make the 15-inch journey down from your head to your heart. These fifteen inches are the difference between heaven and hell, because unless you make a conscious effort to connect them, your heart and head will want different things, and you will be in perpetual conflict and inner turmoil. But when your heart is open, and your mind stays connected to your open heart, loving-kindness will become second nature to you.

As you begin to learn to centre in your heart during meditation and other mindful moments during your day, you should always practise being kind to yourself first, and then gradually extend this loving kindness to those around you. Is this a moral precept that you ought to follow? No, it is actually a natural, internal transformation. You have to change yourself and your world from the inside out, because the world you see is simply a projection, or an extension, of yourself.

Please understand that in our natural, true state of being we are all kind. However, in this crazy world of fear and separation that we think we inhabit, we all learn so well from our society, our culture, and our traditions, to be cruel as well as kind, and to hate as well as to love. Above all, we learn to make constant judgements about others and ourselves, and these judgements are very often negative. We therefore need a constant reminder to ourselves to be kind.

In our crazy world, kindness is associated with being soft and gentle, but this is not at all how it is in reality. In reality, kindness is a power from the universe, from God, or the Tao itself, and this kindness is very strong. True kindness is a natural extension of your true self. Once you really connect to life, you will be automatically kind, and you will continuously share your kindness with everyone you meet.

How to cultivate loving kindness

For those spiritual seekers who have not yet reached this level of spiritual awakening, guidelines such as 'Cultivate loving kindness' are most helpful. How can you cultivate loving kindness to yourself and others on a daily basis?

First, you can observe your thoughts. Whenever you notice yourself judging or condemning yourself or others, you can change your mind. For example, if you notice yourself thinking 'My boss is so unkind' or 'My ex-partner is so mean' you can pause and attempt to replace these negative judgements with a kind thought. You might say to yourself ' I know my boss is overworked, I hope he has a wonderful time on his week off next week' or 'My ex-partner seems to me to be mean with money, but perhaps he is really fearful about his financial future. I wish him a wonderfully abundant future.'

It is relatively easy, if we are mindful throughout the day, to notice when we are being judgemental about others, but beating ourselves up is such an ingrained habit, that you may have to work harder to catch yourself being unkind to yourself. So please make a real effort to notice every time you are unkind to yourself.

If you constantly say to yourself, for example, 'How could you be so stupid?' or 'I am so lazy,' change the record. Do whatever it takes to replace these habitual, unkind thoughts with kind ones such as 'Everybody makes mistakes sometimes, don't worry so much' or 'Its perfectly OK to rest when you feel tired.' If, as you do this, you observe another voice in your head saying something like 'What rubbish!' just send love and kindness to that part of yourself too and know that it is just another fearful thought that is crying out for love.

Whenever you hear a voice in your head being unloving and critical about something you have said or done, send love to the part of you that is so unkind, critical, fearful and out of love. Then send love to the part of you that you have just criticised. Whenever you make a mistake in your life, however big it may seem to be, do not condemn yourself. Do not say 'You bad, horrible person, you will go to hell for what you have just done.' Change your mind! We all need to learn to love our shadow side and to see ourselves as simply unskilful at times, rather than innately or habitually sinful.

To cultivate loving kindness, just keep being aware of when you judge yourself as a bad, sinful person, and then think instead in terms of where you are still unskilful. If you notice yourself habitually snapping at your mother, for example, do not tell yourself you are an unloving, wicked son or daughter. Start to see yourself as an unskilful son or daughter instead. Then cultivate ways to develop your skilfulness in this area of your life. You might decide to read some self-help books on parent/child relationships, to go on a course about family relationships, or to find a good therapist, and thus develop the skill of being able to relate to your parents in a kind and loving way.

Whilst you are developing the skill of loving-kindness, you will have to forgive your unskilful behaviour over and over and over. How long will it take to love and forgive yourself and others unconditionally – a lifetime, several lifetimes? Don't worry about it. Just keep practising on a daily basis. Keep practising self-directed loving-kindness, until it becomes an automatic response to all your mistakes, all your areas of un-skilfulness.

The second way to cultivate loving-kindness is to notice your behaviour towards yourself and others and to change it whenever you become aware that you are not behaving in a kind, loving way. If you very rarely treat yourself, make a list of all the things you love most, all the activities that bring you most joy, and commit yourself to giving yourself at least one treat everyday. This need not be an expensive new habit. You might treat yourself to a walk in the park or a long hot bath. You might ask a friend for a small favour, instead of assuming that you would be seen as a nuisance.

Similarly, practising loving-kindness towards others does not have to be costly or time consuming. At the end of your meditations, you could simply spend one minute sending loving thoughts to all your friends and relatives. As you advance in your practice, you could also spend a short time each day sending loving thoughts to those whom you do not like very much, and even to those whom you regard as your enemies.

We are all so well-versed in criticising others and ourselves, that it can take quite a long time to develop the inner quality of pure loving-kindness, but every little effort counts. If you gently practise being kind to yourself and others on a daily basis, I guarantee that you will quite quickly find that loving thoughts and actions begin to come much more naturally to you, and that this habit of loving-kindness soon begins to transform your life and the lives of all those around you, in ways you cannot even begin to imagine.

Compassion

Disciplined practitioners can train their minds to become very powerful, but unless they also cultivate great compassion, they can misuse this power and cause great harm in the world. So cultivating compassion as you awake is a must.

Compassion is an eternal quality that dwells deep inside every one of us. Inside every person, including you, there is an observer, a soul or an intelligence who observes you and your suffering. This observer is always amazed to see how you continue to suffer and to feel trapped and imprisoned. When you perceive yourself to be trapped, you will inevitably try to imprison others and make them suffer too. You need to realise this.

Maybe you think 'I suffer by myself. If I suffer that's my business. What has it got to do with the world?' In fact, that cannot be true, because you actually have no independent existence. As you cultivate desirable spiritual qualities, such as compassion for yourself and others, you change the whole of humanity. You change your mother, your father, your partner, your children, your society, your nation and the whole planet earth. Every time you pray with compassion in your heart, somebody will benefit, without doubt someone, somewhere will benefit.

When you persistently go deep inside yourself through meditation, prayer or deep contemplation, you will eventually get in touch with your true heart and true soul nature. From this centre of your being it is so natural, so automatic, to gain deep insight into the nature of human suffering, pain and injustice. When you look back out at the world from this deep centre, you know that all people who are not awake suffer, even those who appear to be so rich and powerful. You know this too from examining your own life. You too have suffered. You have felt some kind of emotional, physical or mental pain, some kind of disappointment. So it is natural for you to feel compassion toward life. It is automatic.

Compassion that comes from our personality or ego-self is often tinted with our belief in our own victimisation. It is tinted with our anger and our fear, or self-pity. Universal compassion, on the other hand, is pure love. True compassion has nothing to do with self-pity, or sympathising with others from a superior standpoint. This is the personality-self thinking it is being compassionate.

True compassion is not a fake, sugary feeling; it simply wells up from your deep understanding of human existence. Your own suffering, and your conscious observation of it, will enable you to develop the quality of compassion. As you come to know yourself, you come to know the others. You will simply know that we are all in the same boat. We are all going through the journey of life, of birth to death. Inevitably, at times on this journey, we will all experience some moments of satisfaction, joy or pleasure, but we also experience lots of moments of pain, suffering, disappointment and loss. When you realise this through your own spiritual practice, compassion just oozes out from deep within you.

Being truly compassionate is a must for your own freedom and liberation, because when you experience true compassion, there is a wholeness and naturalness to it, whereas pity or sympathy are made up, artificial feelings. When you experience the reality of loving kindness and compassion, you will know how different these qualities are from any emotions that you make up. There is a beauty and softness, combined with great power, in true compassion. Connecting up to this universal compassion will empower and energise you to transcend all problems and difficulties. Pity and sympathy do not have this impact. But you cannot just understand this in an intellectual way. You need to experience it first in your heart, and then through a knowingness in your mind.

When you experience true love and compassion deep within you, the experience is so deep and rich that when you come out of it, even your own strong feelings and emotions seem to fade. All those personal feelings and emotions that go up and down, from day-to-day, and moment-to-moment will all fade in colour. This does not mean that after you have experienced true compassion, you will never again experience anger, irritation, lust, fear or jealousy, but it does mean that these temporary feelings will fade in colour and lose some of their power over you. They will not touch you so deeply or disturb you so much.

Three stages of cultivating compassion

First, make every effort to develop the quality of compassion inside you. Every time you meet someone who is suffering, you can cultivate your compassion. You can say to yourself 'You and I are both suffering. We are in the same boat. We are both trapped and in prison together.' Develop compassion for your own pain and suffering first, then extend your compassion to those less fortunate than yourself.

Can you begin to open your heart to all those billions of human beings who suffer so much in this world? Have a go, and see how much suffering you can embrace. As well as sending love and light to all suffering beings on the planet, you should also do what you can on a practical level to alleviate the suffering of the poor, the starving, the sick and the homeless. You do not have to give everything you have to those less fortunate than you, but if you see someone in need, act compassionately toward them. If you see a beggar on the street, do not turn away from them in disgust. You do not always have to give a beggar money to show your compassion; a smile or a kind word may sometimes be equally compassionate.

As you begin to develop the inner quality of compassion, be careful not to be tricked by your ego mind. You cannot reason yourself into being compassionate. True compassion springs naturally from an open, loving heart. It emerges automatically as you heal and unfold. Don't demand compassion from anyone, including you. Be patient, practise diligently and your natural state of love and compassion will return to you. But don't waste your time faking compassion. If love and compassion are not flowing naturally form your open heart, you should focus on healing your own pain and blockages rather than on helping others. Always focus on healing yourself first, before you attempt to heal the world.

As you advance on your spiritual path, you will reach the second stage of cultivating compassion. Here you will begin to understand the power of illusion, and your compassion will include all human beings, even the most rich and powerful. At first, you may think that it is much easier to love the poor and helpless, than to love someone as rich and powerful as the President of the United State of America or Bill Gates. However, eventually you will understand that everyone suffers sooner or later, unless they know who they really are.

Worldly goods and pleasures are nothing. They never last, and those people who appear to 'have everything' are simply going through very temporary experiences. Even the mega-rich can be so fearful about losing their wealth, their health or their loved ones. The rich and famous may smile sweetly for the cameras, but on the inside most of them are nervous wrecks. The only truly blessed people are those who have embarked on a path of self-discovery. So, spiritual masters always include the rich and powerful in their compassionate prayers.

The suffering of humanity can be overwhelming, and normal human beings can easily become numb and withdrawn in response to it. Doctors, for example, very often become distant and withdrawn from their patients, because they are overwhelmed by so much suffering. Then, they may appear to be cold and uncaring. If you watch too much news, you too can become desensitised to suffering. But, as you become more advanced as a spiritual practitioner, you have to open up to the suffering of the world without letting it overwhelm you. This is an advanced spiritual practice, but eventually you will be able to take in all the suffering of the world, bring it to the light through meditation, and then bless all those involved, the victims and the victimisers; the innocent victims of war and the perpetrators of massacres.

The ultimate level of compassion is that of enlightened Masters or Bodhisattvas. Their compassion comes from dynamic emptiness. This compassion is spontaneous and transcends duality. It is constant and flows indiscriminately and directly from divine love, God or the Tao.

Inner joy

Your ego-self constantly seeks happiness and excitement from the outside world. You say to yourself 'What's happening out there to make me feel good?' 'Whom can I meet to make me happy?' Your soul, on the other hand, wants only to experience the joy within, that is unchanging, eternal, and God given. The human emotion of happiness is only temporary, and is different for every individual, so it cannot really be shared. Inner joy, on the other hand, can be shared with the whole world. So promise yourself to be joyful every day of your life, and commit to sharing this joy with the world around you.

You will need to practise cultivating inner joy on a daily basis. To find your true joy, you have to still your mind and go inwards. When you are in deep meditation or prayer, the inner joy you experience is sometimes so great that tears of gratitude will pour from your eyes. Joy is in life itself, but again until we experience and know this directly, we have to make every effort to cultivate and develop it.

To start with, you can cultivate inner joy not only through meditation, but also by raising your subtle energy or vitality. As you open up your energy centres or charkas, inner joy will sometimes just rise up your spine. The more you practise chi kung exercises or tai chi, for example, the more you will open up your energy centres and develop a flow of chi within. As you develop this chi flow, you need to bring an inner smile into it. This inner smile will bring light, perfume, refinement and brightness into your different energy channels and charkas, and transform your habitual mindset from negative to positive.

When you combine an inner smile with meditation or with exercises such as chi kung or tai chi, you can create a very sunshine-like quality within your energetic system, which you may experience as a feeling of joy. Ultimately, as you go ever deeper into this inner smile quality, you will literally transform your internal chi or energy into light.

So, it is very important to cultivate an inner smile whenever you are doing energy work or energy practices. As you do this, all your anxieties and worries will disappear. If you do not apply this inner smile to your practice, you will not brighten yourself up internally. You will not rise upward and expand your consciousness until you experience pure bliss. You may sit and look as though you are meditating, you may think that you are doing a lot of spiritual practice, but if you do not do this joyfully, if you are miserable whilst you practise, you will actually poison yourself.

If you just follow a spiritual formula, without brightening yourself up from the inside out, you can actually make things worse. Your inner smile and internal joy enable you to remember who you really are. They help you to remember your eternal, natural state of being. As you experience inner joy, you will see more clearly the duality or contrast in our physical existence, the light and the darkness. But as you go even deeper into inner joy, you will find that eternity is there. Even if your body is in pain, eventually, you will still experience deep, inner joy. Then you will remember that you are not a body, but an eternal soul or spirit.

Most people think of joy as a type of physical pleasure, emotional comfort or an energetic high. They do not realise that there is a much deeper and everlasting type of joy. For a Radiant Warrior it is different. Just by focusing on inner joy alone, you will begin to reflect your eternal, or real state of being. As you do this, you will naturally want to share joy and love with the world around you. This natural sharing of joy has nothing whatsoever to do with your personality, or your passing emotions. Inner joy will just naturally shine through you, and out into the world around you.

Generosity

A lot of people do not understand what generosity means. Not so many people can achieve 'Give all to all.' While you live down on earth, you do have to find a balance in relation to giving and receiving. Even spiritual masters still have to practise this. However, when you reach a certain point of knowing, you will truly understand that you cannot lose anything, and that God always gives you everything. Then, and only then, you can be truly generous. True generosity has a sense of ease and freedom in it. Serving others without calculation is actually as natural as the wind. It may be quite normal in our world for individuals to act selfishly, but it is not natural. When you are centred in divine love, you are so generous you appear to be crazy.

But you will not be generous if you believe that you have to earn a living through hard work, and that the only way to be safe and secure in this world is through accumulating your own wealth. You will not be truly generous if you think that you are too old, or too young, or that you may not be in the right place at the right time. If you are well educated into the beliefs and thought patterns of our society, you cannot be genuinely generous, because you still entertain the idea that you can lose out. Someone else wins the lottery and you say to yourself 'I've lost again.' You still fear that you may have to struggle to get what you want, or wait a long time until your boat comes in.

How to cultivate generosity

How can you cultivate generosity wisely? There are two useful principles to follow. The first is based on the natural law: 'You cannot give what you do not have.' If you do not have faith in life itself, it is so easy to get lost, and at that particular moment you cannot be generous. Generosity is not about giving something away and then believing that you haven't got it any more.

In order to be truly generous, you need to understand the principles of giving and receiving. You need to understand the dynamics of the flow of energy that is involved in giving and receiving. You need to develop an awareness that in reality giver and receiver are actually one, and that what ever you do for others, you do for yourself. Whenever you smile at someone, you are smiling to yourself. Whenever you give money away, you are actually giving it to yourself, not your personality-self, but your true self.

However, to begin with, you should not give out blindly. When you are in doubt do not give. So the second principle to follow is: only give when you are in love, when you feel abundant, when you feel highly motivated and inspired. Only give when you have not got that negative feeling of loss, or the idea that someone might take advantage of you. You can only be truly generous when you feel clear, comfortable, natural and whole. If you have any doubts, do not give at that moment. Instead of giving when you do not feel comfortable about it, it is far better to pray, to do some spiritual practice, and ask God to assist you to remove those negative feelings and fearful scarcity consciousness from your mind.

Before we are awake, many of us habitually give to others in an attempt to gain something back from them. Therefore, before giving anything to anyone, you should examine your intentions behind your giving. Your intention is far more important than how much you give to others. Many people use gifts to blackmail their friends and loved ones. They give large gifts with the intention of buying love or friendship. They give to charity, because they feel guilty about having so much when others are starving. Please, never give because you want to be seen as a good person, or simply to assuage your guilt. Do your best to avoid giving large gifts because you think it is expected of you, for example at Christmas, or on a friend's birthday.

Always consult your heart before you buy someone a gift and ask 'What is my motive for giving this present?' If you give someone a present out of guilt or fear, you will actually poison that person! So please try not to buy into the world system of compulsory gift giving, however uncomfortable this practice may make you feel for a while. Only give to others from your heart. One flower given with true love, and with no ego agenda attached to it, is a far better gift than a very expensive bouquet bought because you felt it was expected of you. As a Radiant Warrior you need to be brave and refuse to conform to the pressure from our consumer-driven society to buy expensive, but loveless gifts, every time the shops proclaim another gift-giving occasion is nigh.

On the other hand, do not walk away from people who are in need. Do what you can to help feed the hungry and house the homeless. If people are unhappy, be their good friend, as long as they do not sap too much of your energy, listen to them. Showing genuine kindness to others is a form of generosity. Comforting those in pain is a wonderful type of generosity. Another way to be generous is to share your knowledge and wisdom with those who are ready to receive it. The hunger of the soul is different from the hunger of the body, and great spiritual masters are very generous with their time and their teachings. They will give these out endlessly to those students or disciples who are yearning to receive them.

We all like to give, we all enjoy sharing with others, but when we feel threatened, when we feel insecure, we have a tendency to become stingy. When your mind is trapped in illusions, at that moment we you cannot give. This is one of the great benefits of spiritual practice. When your mind re-opens in deep meditation, you will feel tremendous love and compassion inside yourself and you will realise that you just want to give love and kindness to the whole of humankind.

Always give out of abundance and love

But before you reach this level of awakening, you need to understand that whenever you give, you are not just giving out gifts, you are giving out the intention behind your gifts. You are giving out whatever you believe deep inside your mind. So, if you believe that when you give something away you lose it, you are affirming and projecting scarcity consciousness. If, on the other hand, you believe that by giving something away, this actually enables you to have more of it, you are affirming the natural law of abundance. If you believe that whatever you give out will increase what you have, you will naturally be generous. If you believe that what you give to someone else you lose, you will not be naturally generous. It is as simple as that.

Whenever you give with unconditional generosity, you do not just give to one person, you give to the whole of humanity. When you are truly giving, all the powers from heaven and earth assist you. Being generous does not mean that you have to give away everything that you own. Being generous is not just about giving material gifts. It means that if you experience peace, you share it. If you experience inner joy, you always find a way to pass it on to others. This will actually enable you to experience even more peace and joy, not less.

You cannot share or give anything to others until you have got it yourself. This is why those who wish to become light workers and save the world, need to develop their own internal qualities first. You cannot share love, unless you know love, unless you open your heart totally to love, and bathe your whole being in love. Only then can you share this love with the world. If you have doubts about sharing love with others, that is actually what you share, your doubt. If you are suspicious, this is what you share. You cannot give peace to the world unless you are peaceful in your heart. Those who demonstrate angrily against unjust wars actually fan the flames of hate and fear. Fighting for peace never works. Only those who can contemplate their 'enemies' with an open, peaceful forgiving heart can truly extend peace to others.

Most of us long to share love and joy with others. However, a lot of people say, 'I would like to give love to that person but she is just not lovable.' Or, 'I want to love him, but I just don't trust him anymore.' Because of past hurts, you close up your heart to others. So, in order to cultivate the quality of generosity, you have to heal and forgive all your past hurts. You have to heal all your relationships past, present and future. This is not easy, not easy at all, but it is an essential part of becoming a loving, compassionate and generous person.

Understanding the cycles of life

In order to learn the art of generosity well, you also need to understand the cycles of life. The divine plan works through life and enables you to progress towards total abundance, but sometimes the divine or higher plan makes you poor. You may also find situations in life when you are not in a position to give. These times are trials because, seemingly, by the world's standards, you are poor. However a true Radiant Warrior knows that they cannot really be poor.

As a Radiant Warrior, you know you are here to share the light, to share the richness, abundance and depth of life itself. You are here to extend the creative power of the one mind that we all share, and to demonstrate that you are the manifestation of infinity. When you fully know and accept this, then, even when you are apparently living in poverty, you are still very rich. Not many people can live out this truth. But you must understand that everything is being given to you by life for your greatest good.

If there are times in your life when you experience material poverty, when you do not feel abundant, you simply need to understand and appreciate the many cycles in life and the dynamic cycle of change. You need to remember that without autumn and winter, there would be no spring and no summer. This deep understanding and knowing will enable you to share more freely and wisely. It does not matter what you are sharing – money, love, or peace – you always need to be aware of the cycles of this movement of energy. When you understand these cycles, you will know that sometimes you have not got anything to give out, because you are going through autumn or winter, and you just need to wait for spring to return once more.

Because life always goes in cycles, you need to accept that there is a time to save and accumulate, and a time to give and to share. If you never save any of what you harvest, you will never have enough wheat in your granary. But once your granary is full, you have to start wisely to empty it. There is no point having a full granary if you do not ever take out any wheat. This is another natural law that you should follow as you cultivate generosity.

You must learn the art of knowing when to share your gifts and when to build up your talents and assets. But at the same time, practising wise generosity on a daily basis will assist you to transcend your selfishness and help you to create abundance in your own life and the world around you. 'To give is to receive,' and the more we practise and cultivate true generosity; the more our own life will overflow with great riches and natural abundance.

Bravery

In order to follow the spiritual path right through to self-realisation, you need to be bold and brave. Do not play small and say 'I am just a housewife' or 'I am just a computer programmer.' Who on earth benefits from you playing small and insignificant? Who benefits if you always insist on taking a back seat? You need to overcome your littleness and be brave.

If you are going to follow a spiritual path to its conclusion, there are a thousand and one courageous questions that you have to ask yourself. You actually have to do battle with yourself, because your personality or ego-self really does not want to get enlightened. Once you are truly awake, there is no such thing as the ego-self or deluded-self, so, of course, your deluded-self does not want you to be in an enlightened state, because it does not want to die. Therefore, as you continue to go through the process of healing yourself, as you continue to establish yourself on the path, your ego-self will continue to challenge you and give you a really hard time.

You need so much courage to keep going on the spiritual path, because you have to face all your fears. You have to face all your own shadows. Spiritual courage is not about conquering the world; it is about facing up to your own unkindness and even cruelty. We have all damaged others and ourselves so much out of our own ignorance. That is why you need to cultivate bravery. You think you need to be brave to fight an enemy on the outside? You believe that as a trained light worker, you are going to fight terrifying, external, dark forces? No, the worst enemy is within you.

When you are healing yourself, you have to face the fact that you are your own worst enemy. At times, you will experience tremendous doubt and suspicion. You have so many fears that sometimes in your meditation or deep prayer, you will experience such fear rising up, for no particular reason, and then you will just sit there and shake and shake with fear. Why? Because everything inside you that needs healing has to come up to the surface. Every part of you that needs to be healed has to come up into your conscious awareness to be released, and that is sometimes very hard to face.

Bravely facing all your internal fears and doubts

You need to prepare yourself, mind, body and spirit, to feel the fear and keep going, to feel all the fear, all the doubt, and still love the spiritual path you are on. There is no one on the outside who makes you so fearful, it is always what is inside your own mind that makes you afraid. It is not easy at all to face every fearful, angry, vicious aspect of yourself. You have to cultivate such bravery to go through all your own insecurities and to face up to whatever you have to do.

For example, you may be dying from within, because you are in an unhealthy intimate relationship. You may have been with your partner for many years, but now you know that if you do not get out of this relationship, you will die spiritually. If you decide to be brave and leave your partner, you will feel so insecure, so scared, so guilty. Or your personality-self may just want to run away from a painful relationship, but deep in your heart you know that you have to stay for healing to happen. Again, you have to be so brave to face the pain that always rises up in intimate relationships, without either blaming your partner for all your anguish, or simply running away into the arms of a new love.

Even though, in reality, all our fears are just illusions, in this world, fear can feel so real to you. It is as though it takes away all your power and all your strength. When you have not got any real challenges in life, you can be brave. But when you come face to face with a real challenge like divorce, cancer, death or bankruptcy, you will really wish you had already cultivated spiritual strength. We all have a lot of different levels of fear and shadows.

True courage and bravery come to us only after we have cultivated a deep, compassionate understanding of all of our fears.

All serious spiritual practitioners have transcended hardships. Courage cannot be found in a spiritual textbook. If you listen to the life stories of advanced spiritual practitioners, they have all experienced times of great hardship, whether physical, emotional, mental or spiritual, and these times have assisted them to build great strength of character and bravery. Advanced practitioners such as His Holiness the Dalai Lama, Thich Nhat Hanh and Mother Theresa were all brave enough to walk on stormy seas. See them as role models. First, you can pray for the courage to heal yourself, and later you can pray for the courage to heal the world.

When you are facing life's difficulties, chaos and confusion, you need to pray and meditate more. When the mind re-opens, when the heart re-opens, then you can see that you are just trapped in illusions. There are no problems in reality, but in this illusory world, they can seem so real to you that you will shake with fear and anxiety.

In a deep meditative space, you can see everything so clearly, and you will come out of this space with a solution to all your illusory problems. Of course, it can take some time to clear your mind, to shed your scales like a dragon, and to see the light inside. But each time you bravely persist on your healing journey, each time you are courageous enough to face your inner demons head on, your strength and courage will increase, until one day you will become a master of all your own fear and doubts and a truly courageous master of life itself.

Exercises

Committing random acts of kindness

One very practical way to develop your loving-kindness is to commit 'random acts of kindness' without seeking any recognition for them.

For example, you could put some extra money in the parking meter when you leave, as a gift to the next person to park in that spot. Or you could secretly plant some bulbs on a communal piece of land, or tidy up a public place that is usually strewn with litter.

The key to this practice is to think up innovative ways of being kind to others without them knowing, so that your personality-self cannot use this practice primarily to gain approval or friendship.

So now, think of a random act of kindness that you could perform with relative ease within the next few days and then set a time and a place when you will actually do it.

Cultivating compassion

At the end of your daily meditation, take a few minutes to think of a person, or a group of people, whom you know to be suffering.

Do your best to open your heart to their pain and then, from the centre of your compassionate heart, send them unconditional love and blessings.

As you advance into this practice, include a blessing for someone whom you may see as 'having it all,' or whom you perceive to be behaving badly. Do your very best to see this person's underlying fear and pain and bless them unconditionally without wishing to change their behaviour in any way.

Cultivating true generosity

Commit to noticing how you feel when you buy someone a gift during the next thirty days. Be very honest with yourself and ask yourself 'What is my motivation for buying this gift?' 'Am I buying it out of guilt or a sense of social obligation?' 'Am I trying to buy someone's love or approval with this gift?'

If you do notice that your motivation behind gift giving is not always heart-centred unconditional generosity, please do not judge yourself harshly. Simply begin to notice the difference between 'giving to get' and giving with absolutely no strings attached to your gift. Know that simply becoming more aware of your different modes of giving will greatly assist you to become a more truly generous person.

Jane's Story: Part 11

Before I began to awake, I would have described myself as a reasonably compassionate, kind and generous person. But I can now see that a lot of my apparent generosity and thoughtfulness towards others was based on an inner neediness and a fear that if I did not please others they would abandon me. As an adopted child, I was always desperate to make my adoptive mother happy, and I can now see that underneath this behaviour was a fear of being rejected and abandoned by her. Hard though this has been to admit, I now have to accept that my personality-self wants to please others primarily in order to protect myself, and is therefore only giving to others in order to get something back from them.

On the other hand, when in deep meditation I go beyond my personality-self and link directly to higher consciousness, I sometimes experience a completely different type of loving-kindness and generosity that is based on an inner knowing that I already have everything and that I am eternally safe. When I am in this amazing space my heart just seems to overflow with love, compassion and generosity and I would quite happily give everything I own away at that moment (so please never ask me for a big favour when I am deep in meditation like this!)

Whenever I experience unconditional or divine love and light pouring through me, at that moment I am naturally so loving, generous, joyful and brave. However in my daily life I still have to focus on developing all the qualities of a Radiant Warrior, particularly the quality of bravery. There have been times on this spiritual journey when I have prayed, 'I cannot go on another step, just leave me here and let me die,' but something so much greater than me has kept me going despite my own weaknesses.

I really believe that I am being guided along the path by an infinitely patient higher intelligence that knows far better than I ever could where I am going and what is my next best move. If I do seem to have been brave at certain times on the journey, it is only because I have surrendered to this higher power and prayed, 'Thy will be done, not mine.' This surrendering has given me the strength to go on when my personality-self has more or less collapsed into a quivering wreck of anxiety and self-pity. This higher authority has lifted me up on His shoulders and carried me across obstacles on the path that I definitely could not have surmounted by myself.

For example, on my last retreat with Jason, I began to be irrationally terrified that the spiritual light that was pouring down on us was going to harm me in some way, or even annihilate me. At six in the morning I went for a walk to try and calm myself down and found myself crying and praying 'Oh God please help me to overcome this terrible fear.' When I got back to my room, I opened *A Course in Miracles* completely at random and there, staring me in the face, was lesson 48 *There is nothing to fear*. My heart just filled up with love and gratitude for this amazingly appropriate divine message and after that my fear began to subside.

Experiences such as this have taught me that I do not really need to be an especially brave or compassionate or generous person to tread on the spiritual path. I simply have to be humble enough to ask for help when I am afraid, or feeling unloving or mean. I simply have to have absolute faith that whatever help I need to progress along the eternal path back to the truth will always be given to me beyond my wildest expectations.

Chapter 12

Manifesting Abundance

Please live a happy, abundant life. You do not serve yourself or any other living thing if you are poor and miserable.

Abundance is natural

Everyone on this planet is looking for happiness. All 6 billion of us want the same two things, health and happiness. This search is inbuilt in human nature and is an instinctive expression of self-love. It is not selfish to want to be happy and abundant. If you are unhappy, you will upset everyone around you, whereas your true nature is a pure joy that is in no way self-centred.

Why do so few people achieve what they want in life? Why do so many people fail to achieve their goals? America is the richest country in the world, and yet within five years, eighty percent of new American companies will have failed. The first reason why so many people fail to fulfil their dreams is that that they lack belief in themselves and the world. For example, they want to be rich, but they have a poverty consciousness. They believe that they are the helpless victims of the world around them. They do not believe that they are the masters of their own destiny.

In normal life, your habitual mindset is predominantly negative, and you interpret events negatively. You need a lot of spiritual training to change this. Radiant Warrior training will assist you to be constantly mindful of the many ways in which you sabotage yourself. You want love, but you are afraid of getting hurt. You want to make money, but you are so used to thinking that you are poor, that you defeat your own plans. So many people wear themselves out vainly attempting to make enough money in order to feel secure. But if you are free, in love and creative, at that moment, whatever you do will bring you abundance. We all have tremendous creativity. Everything is possible because creativity is in the collective psyche. But if we are fearful, and invest in scarcity thinking, we will never know our true creativity

If you are not perfectly happy and fulfilled in your life, you need to examine all of your negative belief systems that keep you trapped in unhappiness and struggle. For example, if you habitually tell yourself that it is so hard to make a good living, please start telling yourself that making an excellent living doing something you love is simplicity itself. Your underlying beliefs always determine the outcome of your efforts. Change your underlying beliefs and you will change the outcome, sooner or later. Please discard all those beliefs that do not serve your highest good and your greatest happiness. You always have a choice. 'Life is hard' or 'Life is a joy.' The more you learn to manifest your heart's desires with ease, the more you will build up your faith in a benevolent universe.

Do not deny your deepest desires

You cannot say that you only want spiritual experiences, and think that this is the path to wholeness or self-liberation. Attempting to deny or suppress your deepest desires, because you think they are not spiritual, can be a very slow, unhappy path to awakening. So please be honest with yourself and really understand and accept your deepest desires. We are not all Mother Theresa. We are not all ready to live a completely selfless life. Radiant Warriors do not give up the world prematurely. They learn to live very successfully in the world, whilst seeking always to transcend it.

The material world traps us so easily, that it may seem easier just to renounce the world, but this does not work in the long run, because you cannot just renounce your unfulfilled desires. They will keep coming up to haunt you, even on a remote mountaintop.

You do not have to be poor and celibate to become enlightened; this is a major misunderstanding of the spiritual path. To stabilise an enlightened state of being, you need dedication, discipline, mindfulness and love, not sacrifice. Wanting *per se* is not harmful. The greatest art and music has been manifested out of the artist's desire to create. There is nothing un-spiritual about becoming successful and fulfilling all your desires. Being a high-flying entrepreneur is great training in life. If you think that rich, successful people cannot find God, think again!

Wanting to make a lot of money does not necessarily mean you are a greedy person. Many spiritual seekers are very confused about money issues, and seem to believe that being poor is a spiritual virtue, whilst being very rich is a sin. This is a complete misunderstanding of spiritual mastery. Do you think Mother Theresa was poor? No, she raised millions and millions of pounds for her work in India. Is The Dalai Lama poor? No, he supports many thousands of Tibetan refugees and employs a very large staff.

Nobody benefits from a negative, miserable, poor person. They are simply a burden on everyone else. If you are broke and depressed, no one will want to know you, and no one will benefit from your life. So please always see yourself as an abundant, generous, rich person, and do your very best to manifest abundance in all areas of your life.

You cannot just sit back and say, 'I trust in God. God will make sure that I succeed in life.' If you do this, you will become lazy. God's grace is given in equal measure to every soul on this planet. But poverty consciousness comes so much more easily to most of us than abundance consciousness. It is far easier to play victim, than to change your mind, and take full responsibility for your life. I know that this is a very politically incorrect message. It is currently fashionable to see the world's poor as helpless victims of the rich and powerful. But, we have been seeing the problem of poverty in this way for quite some time now, and nothing much has changed. The problem of poverty has certainly not diminished.

From a spiritual perspective, poverty is not primarily an economic problem. It is a problem that starts in the mind. As a spiritual practitioner, please do not feel sorry for the poor, this is not true compassion. If you want to help the world's poor, learn to change your own mind first. Teach yourself that you live in a world of abundance, with more than enough for everyone. Then, when you manifest abundance in your own life, find a way to share it so that you empower individuals to create abundance for themselves. Bill Gates has done far more to help the poor than many of his critics, who condemn the rich and glorify the poor as virtuous victims of globalisation and the capitalist system.

One friend of mine took early retirement and still saw himself as abundant with so much to offer the world, so he set up a charity in Cork called SEA Change that is now giving interest-free loans to poor entrepreneurs, mainly women, in several developing countries. None of this would have happened if he had simply felt sorry for the world's poor. It all happened because he truly believed that he could make a difference and that what the so-called poor in the world needed was a hand up rather than a hand out.

You cannot run away from money issues

Money makes our world go round. You cannot run away from money issues in our society. Our attitudes toward money closely reflect our beliefs about ourselves and others. Virtually all of us have some healing to do around money issues. Money represents security to most people in our society, and most of us need to heal ourselves before we can feel totally secure, whether or not we have a large sum of money hidden away for a rainy day.

You cannot say, 'I am a spiritual person, I could not care less about money issues.' Whether you are consciously concerned about money or not, you still have to deal with it, and money is a major issue in our lives, usually even more of an issue than sex. You do not make love every day (I am making an assumption about you here), but you do spend money every day, or virtually, every day. Every time you save money or spend money, your actions, thoughts and feelings are telling you something about yourself and your life.

Money is a big issue for all of us, whether we like it or not, whether we want to look at it or not. We can learn a lot about ourselves by closely examining our views about money, and our behaviour in relation to money. Whether you are out having fun with friends, or staying at home on your own, whether you are working or unemployed, whether you are rich, poor, or in between, dealing with money will undoubtedly trigger your fears and insecurities.

Making a lot of money does not have to be selfish. It can be about sharing abundance with love and generosity. How can you ever become abundant if you condemn the rich? Why not ask 'God, if it is for my highest good, grant me abundance that, I may share it with my beloved brothers and sisters.' But do not pray from a position of lack. Know that in reality, you have already been given everything. Infinite abundance is your birthright, as a son or daughter of God. However, in order to fully realise and manifest this total abundance, you will have to forgive yourself completely, and release all thoughts about your unworthiness. If deep down you believe that you are unworthy of God's love, His abundance cannot come to you.

Do you believe it is your birthright to be abundant? Are you really worth it? Your birthright is to have complete happiness and fulfilment in your life. *God's Will for me is perfect happiness* (*A Course in Miracles*), but who truly believes this about themselves? Very few human beings believe this. When you reach this point, you have almost cracked it, and everything will be accomplished on your behalf. This complete faith in the benevolence of God, or the Source of all that is, is at the core of all spiritual accomplishment. It comes from a place of absolute stillness and oneness in which everything is already accomplished. You have to train your mind to know that you are worthy of God's love, or your underlying thoughts and beliefs will block your natural abundance and sabotage your potential success time after time after time.

Why are some people's lives so easy whilst others' are so difficult? It is primarily down to their belief systems. Because you feel so guilty on some level of your being, you have a secret wish to suffer. Guilt is always asking for punishment and therefore, until you heal all your hidden guilt and shame, you will continue to create pain and suffering in your future, including strong feelings of lack.

You have to watch all your thoughts and behaviour very carefully if you do not want to suffer in the future. If you believe 'Everybody loves me' you will experience a lot of love in your life. If on the other hand you believe 'People only pretend to love me because they are after something,' or 'I am unlovable,' this is what you will actually experience, time after time, until you change your mind.

There is no such thing as bad luck

Most people, when life seems to deal them a bad hand, say 'Why me? What have I done to deserve this?' 'Why am I so hard up when people around me are so well off?' 'Why can everyone else find a partner, but not me?' The secret is that you always create your own life, you just haven't realised it yet.

In this life you do not get what you want, you get what you are. If you are loving, you will attract love. If you are generous, you will attract generosity from others. Every moment of your existence, you are creating your future experiences. You are determining whom you are going to meet, how rich or poor, healthy or sick you will be.

For every action there is a reaction. The fruition of all your past actions is known in the East as karma. Karma has nothing to do with retribution, or revenge for your past sins. Karma is simply the power of your own creative mind; it is the extension of your mindset. Your intention now will create your future experiences. There is no such thing as good or bad luck in life. Most people constantly complain about their lives, but they do not plant good seeds. They do not work diligently to overcome their weaknesses and unskilful areas. They do not look within to heal their unhelpful beliefs about themselves and the world around them.

If you have no real purpose in life, if you are not continuously planting new seeds, life can become very boring and your energy will dissipate. Don't envy the super rich who have no real purpose in life, apart from spending their money on the latest 'toys.' Think about an apple tree. Every year it will produce big, sweet, juicy apples with no effort, but if you never put any fertiliser in the soil, after many years, its fruit will turn sour and small. If you enjoy a luxurious lifestyle without putting anything back into the world, you will use up all your good karma and waste your precious energy.

If you are fortunate in life, don't forget to plant more good seeds. Do some good deeds for others, or, after several years, your good fortune will dissipate. Don't just think about yourself all the time. This will not work. If you want more money, give some money away. If you want to be successful, help others to be successful. When you become rich and secure, keep giving back to society. This will create good karma. If a very rich person gives just 10 per cent of their wealth back to society, they can make a real difference.

Most people believe in good and bad luck, but as a genuine spiritual seeker, you will learn that there is no such thing as luck in life. There is no such thing as something for nothing. If you want to become rich, you have to plant the right karmic seeds. How many people have you fed in your past? How many people have you helped to become abundant?

Most people want so much to be happy, but they continue to plant seeds of harm and suffering. They want to be rich, but they borrow money from their friends and never pay it back. They want to be loved, but they constantly criticise and distrust the opposite sex. Then, when they continue to dwell in lack, they say, 'Oh God why is this happening to me?' and God will reply (although they probably won't hear Him) 'You have created this, it has nothing to do with me.' If your life is not giving you happiness and fulfilment, please realise that you made it exactly the way it is, and only you can learn the art of un-making it.

If your life is not how you want it to be, there is only one effective response: change your mind. If you want more happiness in your life, for example, see yourself as a happy person right now. Do something right now that you really enjoy doing, and focus on feeling the joy of it. If you want more love, find the love on the inside of you first. Open your heart and pray for an experience of true love. Once you have fully experienced something inside your mind, you will always find a way to experience it on the outside. When you realise just how powerful your mind is, it will really scare you. You will realise that you have so much power and that your fulfilment or lack of fulfilment in life is all down to you.

Learning to manifest abundance

Virtually everyone on this planet says 'I want to be rich,' but this is very different from saying 'I really, really want to be rich' and fully committing all of your energy to manifesting wealth in your life. Whatever you really desire in your life will eventually manifest, as long as you follow up your desire with developing the requisite skilful means to manifest it. If you want to earn more money, study other people's success and learn from them. What sort of people become rich and stay rich? Observe them carefully and then start to imitate their thinking and behaviour patterns. If necessary, go for training to acquire the skills that they have acquired.

Everything that is accomplished in this world needs action. If you think that doors are not opening for you, put some action into your dreams. Put more energy into making them come true. Most rich people work very hard indeed. Americans are amazing, because they put so much energy into manifesting their dreams. The downside of all this activity is that many of them burn out, but their 'can do' attitude is very inspiring. In England, I have observed that most people have to have a cup of tea and a biscuit before they will do anything.

If you want to manifest your dreams, be prepared for hard work. Visualise the life you want to live, and then work out all the steps you will have to take to get from A to B. Invest time, energy and money to train yourself in your chosen field. Everything is a manifestation of energy. You can wish for anything you like, life will not oppose you, but if you do not have energy, drive and focus it will not happen. If you are half-hearted about your dreams, forget about them! Lazy people do not get good opportunities. It is your life, and no one else can manifest your dreams for you. Your mother may want the very best for you, but she cannot live your life for you, she cannot pass the exams you need to pass, or learn the new skill you need to succeed in your chosen field.

Be resourceful in relation to making money. When you are resourceful, you feel safe and when you feel safe, resources are always available to you. A lot of people lack money, because they lack resourcefulness. There are six billion people in the world and they all have needs and desires. If you can find a way to service them, to fulfil their desires you will be rich. Ask God 'Train me to become resourceful. Help me to strengthen myself and to improve my skills.'

Do not play small

As a trainee Radiant Warrior, you must learn not to play small and helpless. Never tell yourself you cannot afford something. What a crazy affirmation! If you really desire something from the depths of your heart, work hard until you get it. Learn from very successful people. What makes Bill Gates so different? What makes the chairman of Tesco tick? What is in their minds?

You do not have to become a corporate executive, if that is not your life's purpose, but you should practise thinking big, rather than small. Thinking small kills just as many brain cells as thinking big, and benefits no one. Why fantasise about earning £30,000 a year, when you could fantasise about earning £300,000 and use up exactly the same amount of brain space? But, if you are going to think big and make it big, you have to really believe it first.

This physical world is actually all a game of make-believe, so why put any limits on your mind?

Most people muddle through by playing small in life. If you are ready to own your own power, make sure that you clear all the junk out of your mind first, or you will sabotage your success. When you fail to get what you think you want in life, you have to realise that what you want consciously is just the tip of the iceberg. This is why reciting positive affirmations rarely solves all your problems. What you create in life is based on many, many layers of your mind, most of which are not normally in your conscious awareness.

Becoming aware of your sub-conscious programming

Your mind, like everyone else's mind, is conflicted. In many situations, part of your mind really wants something and another part really does not want it. For example, you may think you want a man or a woman, but another layer of your mind may be determined to sabotage this agenda, because you are so scared of intimacy. You want to be less lonely and think that getting married would ease your loneliness, but at the same time you dread being trapped in a long-term relationship. On the surface you may really long to be rich, but deeper down you believe that you deserve to be poor. If, when you think about being rich, a voice inside your head tells you 'You are just daydreaming,' your mind is against you.

Until you become aware of these layers of your mind, you may well not get what you think you want in life. If, deep down, you believe that it is a struggle for you to make money, lo and behold, it will be a struggle. So you have to examine your belief system very carefully and then re-programme your mind. You have to train your mind to be on your side so that it always supports the wishes of your heart. Do not let your mind put a full stop to all your dreams. 'I'm too old' 'I'm too unfit' 'I'm too stupid.' Please do not entertain your negativity by allowing your mind to rabbit on like this. Kindly tell it to shut up.

Never let your deep down belief in your own unworthiness and your unconscious guilt sabotage your success in life. If you continue to entertain your own unworthiness, you will inevitably sabotage your desires. You will say 'Who am I to think I could drive a BMW?' For goodness sake, millions of ordinary people are driving around in fancy cars. But of course, we all have this underlying sense of unworthiness in varying degrees.

A lot of people really want money, but they can't get it. A lot of people really want good health, but they stay sick. So many people long to be loved, but when someone comes along and offers them love they cannot handle it. Some people are so afraid of love, that they drive all potential partners away by behaving outrageously. So, we all have to heal our underlying unworthiness before we can really lead a successful and abundant life.

To make your dreams come true, you have to remove all the obstacles from your subconscious mind. For example, if you habitually think that making money is difficult, you have to tell your mind 'Money comes easily to me.' Once you truly believe this, the money will flow towards you with the greatest of ease, but your mind will struggle against all your attempts at re-programming. It will try to hold on to its habitual thought patterns. So, you need to make a very strong commitment to take responsibility for your thoughts and to keep changing those that do not serve your highest good. Sometimes you will have to dig very deep into your subconscious until you find a well-hidden belief that is stopping your success.

Most people will have beautiful creative ideas at some point in their lives, but they lack the focus and drive to bring these ideas to fruition. Some people never act on their dreams, because they are so afraid of failure or rejection. Many people have big chips on their shoulders and are afraid of real, lasting success. They will sabotage the most beautiful relationship. They will screw up the most amazing career opportunity.

We all constantly trample on our own dreams, but most people then blame others for their lack of success. They blame the government, the rich, the poor, or even the weather for their misfortune. They never think to look within for the true barriers to their success. There are so many obstacles inside our minds to fulfilling our dreams, but with conscious awareness and disciplined self-enquiry, we can observe and then transcend all these obstacles, until we are leading a miraculously fulfilling life.

As you clear all your subconscious blocks to success, you also need to remember that what you think you want in your life may not be for your highest good, and therefore may not happen. If you are serious about being on your spiritual path, it may feel at times as though you are being asked to sacrifice your most cherished goals in life. For example, you may have to go through a bankruptcy before you can tread on the path, or you may have to give up your dream of a 'normal' family life with a devoted partner and two lovely children.

When I was a young man I longed to be a really successful entrepreneur, but if these dreams of mine had come true I would not now be a spiritual teacher. The world will always disappoint you if you are due to awake this lifetime. Your relationships won't work; your business plans won't work, because these are not your true life's purpose. You may say to yourself 'I am a good person, why am I suffering so much?' 'Why has my business or relationship failed despite all my efforts?' Your business or relationship will fail because it is not your true path this lifetime. If you are ready to awake, all the worldly paths may just not work out for you.

Surrendering your dreams to a higher power

The more you are spiritually connected, the more you will be able to manifest what you want or need into your life. Of course, there are degrees of strength and conviction. When your system is full of light, doors will open for you, but if you are feeling down, you simply will not have the energy to manifest a bright future for yourself. Moreover, however talented you are, you cannot do everything. We all have personal limitations, but if you have faith in the universe, rather than just relying on your own limited abilities, you can undoubtedly achieve great things. Understand your personal limitations, but have faith in God or divine will.

Whenever you are anxious about the future, give your worries up to God. You have to give priority to establishing your faith in your connection to the divine, because this faith can move mountains. But always be realistic in what you pray for. Sometimes we just cannot handle what comes to us. For example, if you know that you cannot handle a lot of energy, do not pray to win millions on the lottery. Some people can be ruined by having too much money, or too much power.

We very often do not know what is in our best interests, but God always knows. We may not get what we want at one point in our life, and then, ten years down the road, we are so grateful that we did not get it, because finally we can see why it would not have served our highest purpose or good.

So, always hand your desires and goals back to the universe or the divine. Always pray 'Thy will be done, not mine.' Your prayers will always be answered, but the outcome may not be what you expect, because the divine cannot support your illusions. The divine cannot support lies and self-deception; it can only support the truth. If your loved one goes off with someone else and you think you have been abandoned, you may pray to God for your loved one to return to you. But God knows that, in truth, no one has abandoned you. In truth you and your lover are still one. Your lost love is just an illusion or nightmare that God knows nothing of and cannot share.

New Age spirituality is often all about getting what your personality-self wants, for example through 'cosmic ordering.' But when someone truly awakes spiritually, they will want absolutely nothing because they will be complete and fulfilled beyond comprehension. Great spiritual masters want nothing from this world. They just connect to the light all of the time, and are thus inherently rich beyond normal human beings' wildest fantasies.

Defining your own success

A Radiant Warrior does not buy into our culture's dominant view of success. Some people with very little money are truly successful, because they are so happy following their soul's calling. But everyone is different. You have to work out what success means to you. You have to find work that you love to do.

There is no one definition of success, but it is certainly not about having the money to buy a load of toys, such as fast cars and grand houses. Material possessions such as these can imprison you. You have to keep working to maintain them, and they can become a real burden and a trap. If you are a stressed and miserable rich person, you are not successful. If you are materially poor, but you have transcended your own weaknesses and connect daily to your inner joy and peace, you are a highly successful person, even if the world is not yet ready to see that.

You may believe that in order to become highly successful, you have to be hyperactive and competitive, but this is not so. If you think you have to become sharper and have a competitive edge to succeed in life, one day you will collapse in exhaustion. Our culture and education system strongly encourage individual competitiveness from a very early age, but this just wears people out. No one else has your unique gifts. No human being is exactly like you, just as trillions of snowflakes all have different patterns.

You actually have no competition in life. Rather than focussing on external competition, the key to success in all walks of life is to take time to be still and go within. When you find dynamic inner peace, the whole world will work with you rather than against you. The vast majority of people find it so hard to be still, even for a minute, but when you can be still and let your turbulent emotions subside, you will find clarity and you will be able to make clear, intuitive decisions. In this still centre, you can receive answers to all your questions and transcend all your worldly problems.

Dynamic stillness will guide you through everything, even a life threatening illness. Most people do not understand the treasure to be found in stillness. In stillness you can cultivate all the inner qualities needed to manifest your goals in life. As you connect to your soul nature and to the power of universal or divine consciousness, you will begin to fulfil your unique purpose this lifetime. You will accomplish what only you can do.

The power of gratitude

Our appreciation and gratitude can reverse our tendency to sabotage opportunities through our negative mindset. For example, so many people say 'I would love to do xyz, but I just cannot afford it.' So many people constantly tell themselves 'I've got no money' and yet the world is full of money. The world is full of opportunities to make money. By complaining that they have no money, individuals block abundance within their minds, and then wonder why it does not manifest in their lives.

If you are not experiencing abundance in your life at this moment, it is time to explore thoroughly all your negative thought patterns around abundance. Perhaps you habitually tell yourself, for example, 'I am not qualified enough to earn good money' or 'I do not deserve to be rich.' Instead of giving yourself sabotaging messages such as this, I strongly suggest that you give thanks for your abundance *before* you experience something.

Focus on becoming aware of how abundant you already are. You do not have to spend lots of money to experience abundance. Go for a walk on a lovely sunny day, and give thanks for the flowers you see and the birdsong you hear. Open up your cupboards and see how much food you have, how many pairs of socks you own, and then laugh at your belief that you are poor. Give thanks on a daily basis for your abundance and watch it grow. If, at some point in your life, you are feeling poor, spend some money on an inexpensive gift for someone or buy something from a small business to support its success.

Letting abundance flow naturally

Money is just a form of energy, and if you free up the flow of it outwards, it will flow back to you. In my daily life, if I ever start to feel poor, I give out some money and watch it flow back to me. Being generous confirms that you are abundant. Accumulating a lot of money in the bank is a waste of time. If you do not use money wisely, the energy of it will simply stagnate. If you think that piling up loads of money in the bank will increase your security, think again. Remember what happened in Argentina in 2001 when the economy collapsed and almost overnight everyone's savings become virtually valueless.

Being greedy or mean with money simply confirms your lack. Giving generously to others confirms that you are abundant. A very helpful maxim to follow is 'Always give what you want to receive in life.' If you want to become wealthy, do your best to empower others to become rich. This principle applies not only to money, but also to all other aspects of your life. If you are feeling a lack of love in your life, focus on giving your love to someone who needs it. If you want good health, help those who are sick to recover.

The secret to success and abundance in this lifetime is always to fill your heart with gratitude for what you already have. Love whatever you are doing in your life now, and if you are not yet fulfilling your life's purpose, see your current work as a stepping stone. Sometimes in daily life, you will have to do things that are not your personal preference. For example, if you are a mother or father and your children are driving you mad, you cannot just throw them out; you have to get on with it. But please do your best to develop a positive 'can do' outlook on life.

Becoming a full-time happiness seeker

Everybody says that they want to be happy, but most happiness seekers are part-timers. So many people have so many excuses for being miserable. They say to themselves, 'If the sun is shining then I will be happy.' 'If my dinner is cooked just the way I like it, then I will be content.' One student of mine, on a retreat in Thailand, found herself getting really worked up just because her breakfast eggs were overcooked one morning.

If you still let little things like this make you miserable, you are not yet a serious happiness seeker. Those who are really serious about being happy insist on happiness regardless of external circumstances. They insist 'I will be happy whatever the weather.' 'I will spend this day in love, whether you are nice to me or not.'

Cultivate the sunshine within, even if it is raining on the outside. When your daily life is challenging, do your best to get on with it without indulging in a lot of moaning and groaning. Try very hard not to screw up your face when your children or your customers annoy you. Keep smiling. Don't indulge your spoilt child within.

Following your heart and your true purpose in life does not mean that you will feel good all of the time. Even when you are doing the work you were born to do, it will not always be easy sailing. Do your best not to moan and complain about your current work or relationship. Daily challenges at work, or in your relationships, will teach you patience and courage, so always give thanks for them. Realise that you can never be in the wrong place at the wrong time, you can never miss the boat, so have trust that your life is unfolding perfectly.

Know that God has already given you everything

Most people pray to God from a sense of lack and despair. Most people pray 'Please God send me some money so that I can pay my debts.' 'Please God let me get that job so that I will have a decent income.' This type of prayer is actually a form of begging. If you pray like this, you are affirming that you lack something and that you are not really worthy of it. Rather than praying out of a sense of lack, it is far more effective to pray with appreciation and gratitude in your heart. Know that God gives you everything, and that all you need do to become perfectly abundant is to remove all the obstacles to abundance from your own mind.

Ask God to help you to remove all your obstacles to abundance and love and to assist you in overcoming all your anxieties and fears about the future. Love and fear cannot coexist. If you ask God to give you some money, you are actually affirming that you are in need and living in lack. When you pray about money, the most effective prayer is one in which you ask God to remove your obstacles to making more money, or ask to be given clarity about how you are blocking your own success.

If you have true faith and trust, the whole universe will open up and conspire to make your dreams come true. Great spiritual masters can manifest events or matter instantly. They know, for example, that money is not real, that making and losing money is just a game, a virtual reality. If you practise the art of appreciation and trust on a daily basis, your life can become very rich and fulfilled. Every time you entertain the view that the world is against you and that life is unfair, you sabotage yourself, but the more you observe your mind working in this way, the more you can change it.

Committing to happiness every day

Please commit to happiness every day of your life. Each morning decide how you want your day ahead to be and give thanks for it. Thank God for already receiving a day filled with happiness, love and abundance. Try your best to fall in love every day with a piece of music, a flower, a baby. If the outcome of your day is different from the one you planned, you can always use this experience to examine yourself with great honesty and compassion, so that you can heal your internal blocks to love, peace and joy, and start again. Keep remembering what you want. For example, 'I want to live in a peaceful and abundant world' and then transform every situation in your mind that does not fit into your ideal world.

If you go out in the morning and immediately become irritated by the heavy traffic, or the litter, remind yourself that you want a peaceful world and that you have the power and responsibility to change your own mind until all you see and feel around you is peace. Every evening, examine your thoughts and actions from the day just ending. Clear your karma each day by undoing any unskilful actions within your mind and by sending love, forgiveness and light to yourself and anyone else involved in your unskilful behaviours.

Each evening ask 'How could I have handled that situation better?' or 'How would a great spiritual master have handled that differently?' Or even 'What would Jesus Christ have done in that situation?' Then change the story line of what happened in your mind, so that it will not keep coming back to you. Finally, before you go to sleep be sure to forgive yourself for the mistakes you made during the day and give genuine thanks to God for all the wonderful things that have occurred, including the challenges that have helped you to grow and to heal.

Ultimately you will go beyond the need for daily disciplined practice. The wind does not have to practise blowing, nor does the sun practise shining. They are their own true nature, but until you go back to your true natural state of being, you need practice. Wanting to be abundant in every area of your life is not enough. You have to surrender so much of your personal agenda.

Please do not be too attached to getting what you think you want from the external world. Your primary goal should always be to feel abundance in your heart and mind, regardless of your external circumstances. Whenever you are fearful about your security, and your perceived lack, feel the fear and doubt and keep practising anyway. Every great spiritual master and saint had to face their own shadows. Eventually peace, joy and abundance will be with you in every step you take, and you will have found heaven within, whilst still living physically on earth.

Exercise
Making your dreams come true

Sit in a meditative position and calm your mind. Go deep within. You can use your breath, you can use your heart's feeling, just tune in as deeply as you can to touch your soul.

Once you are in a deep meditative space, open up as best you can to receive true abundance from life itself. Visualise this abundance as a very bright incandescent light, and then hold this light and let it naturally extend through your mind and through your entire being.

Now see yourself radiating light just like a golden sun and then extend this light into your worldly dreams and projects.

As this brightness touches your deepest dreams, desires and projects it will transform everything for you.

As you intuitively feel that in this moment everything has already been accomplished on your behalf, open your arms and fill your whole heart with gratitude for the infinite grace that you have received.

Do not allow your lower mind to entertain any doubt.

If doubt does arise cancel it out. Simply delete it from your mind.

Now surrender your lower mind's expectations of any specific outcome from this abundance mediation.
....

Please take note if the outcome of this process is not what you expected. The universal purpose always has a greater plan for you than anything your lower mind could envisage.

If you regularly repeat this meditation, you will develop great trust in divine wisdom. You will know that all is being done on your behalf.

It may take you some time before you truly understand that all events, encounters and unfolding situations in your life are always for your highest good and for the highest good of others. But this process will eventually enable you to develop what we can call 'discerning wisdom'.

Your personal, worldly desires are always tinted with some guilt or fear. Even if you go through a deep visualisation and positive affirmation process that promises you that you can have whatever you wish in this world, somewhere deep inside, you will still find a sense of lack. This sense of lack may be obvious or very subtle, but from this place of lack you will continue to search fruitlessly outside yourself to fill up the gap within.

In contrast your soul is yearning only for genuine love, peace and spiritual joy. It does not go out to seek or to search. When you deeply touch this infinite love, peace and joy deep within, you will truly know that God has already given you everything.

Jane's Story: Part 12

I have never experienced material lack or poverty this lifetime. I have always been more of a saver rather than a spender and therefore I have never been in debt. I remember when I was an undergraduate, most of my university friends would run out of funds by the end of the academic year, but I always had a small amount of my grant left. So money has not really been a major issue for me this lifetime. I always balance my income and expenditure carefully, and seem to have plenty of funds for doing the really important things in my life, which currently means going on retreat with Jason five or six times a year.

I still have a preference for luxury living. I love cashmere jumpers and I travel business class to Jason's retreat in Thailand each year, but I do not yearn to be rich. I know, from experience, that buying more and more material 'toys' does not make me happy. In fact, I have noticed that the more I indulge my material desires the more I want. I therefore try to be as mindful as possible when I go shopping and frequently say to myself 'Yes, that's very nice, but I am not going to buy it today, maybe next week.' If, after several conversations in my head like this, I still find myself desiring something, I may well buy it, as I don't believe that totally suppressing my desires will make me more spiritual. However, I do see the process of observing my endless material desires and then attempting to exert some control over them as a very useful spiritual practice.

Although I definitely see myself as materially abundant, in other areas of my life I have not always felt abundant. For example, I have struggled for most of my life to feel loved and although I have always had plenty of friends, it has taken me decades to begin to accept that these friends really do love and care for me.

I have always had a tendency to see the glass as half empty, rather than half full and it has taken quite a bit of effort on my part to train my mind to see that half empty glass differently. One practice that I have found very helpful has been to keep a 'thank you' diary. For several months I wrote 10 'thank yous' a night for all the wonderful things that had happened to me that day.

If nothing immediate came to mind I would write 'thank you' for the basics, like the abundance of food in my fridge.

I am not a great fan of positive thinking books that tell you that you can become a millionaire almost instantly just by repeating some positive phrases, but I do know that cultivating gratitude changes things. After I had kept my 'thank you' diary for a while, my life just seemed more joyful and abundant in all sorts of ways. Maybe my life had actually changed for the better, or maybe I had just become much more aware of how blessed I was.

After the success of my first 'thank you' diary, I decided to keep another one just about men. I knew that I had a strong tendency to see the worst in men, so I decided to focus my attention on all the wonderful things men did for me and to keep a daily diary of positive thoughts about men. Again the results were quite dramatic. Suddenly, I was surrounded by caring, thoughtful men, who kept surprising me with their generosity and kindness. I wonder who had really changed, the men I knew or what I was noticing about them?

What both these practices really taught me was that I can choose how I experience life. I can decide whether to see life as infinitely abundant and infinitely available to me, or I can slip back into my old way of thinking in which I was the victim of a cruel and dangerous external world. Sometimes I do still fall back into this negative way of thinking, but more and more I tell myself that the choice is all mine and that I choose to live in a joyful, peaceful world full of abundance and beauty. Miraculously, my half-empty glass now just seems to keep on filling itself up and my life just keeps getting more and more free and fulfilling.

Part IV

The Path of Surrender

Chapter 13

Developing Trust

Life is not a formula that can be learned from a book. You have to be brave enough to throw yourself off the cliff over and over again until you trust that life will not let you crash to pieces.

Everyone on earth has doubts

Without trust you cannot perform miracles. Radiant Warriors must learn to place all their trust in something that is out of this world. They have to trust an infinite power that is in them, but not of them, and to start with this entails blind faith.

But once you have experienced for yourself the awesome power of God, you will not trust your own petty strength ever again. You cannot use your own petty power to plan your spiritual journey. It will never work. None of us have a clue where we are going or why. Our own little intelligence cannot possibly guide us through the maze of spiritual healing and awakening. So we need to learn to trust a higher intelligence. When you become aware of this incredible power beyond yourself, you will finally find something real in which you can trust.

Trust is one of the most powerful qualities that you have to acquire before you can do God's work down here on earth, but it usually takes a very long time to cultivate. Even people who have done a lot of spiritual practice, and have experienced some pretty amazing spiritual moments, still experience doubt. Then they wonder 'How come I have had all these spiritual experiences and still feel such doubt?'

Developing trust on your spiritual path will really test you. You do not know the way to your journey's end. You are like a blindfolded man or woman walking down a path, facing great uncertainty. When you are blindfolded and cannot see where you are going, you have to surrender totally. All your skills and knowledge disappear and you are no longer in control of your life. Your inner teacher is like someone leading a blind person, but this inner guide has infinite patience and wisdom. You have to learn to trust this guide, to trust this process. Higher intelligence will always take you down the path that will be of highest benefit to you, even though the journey may not always seem to be an easy ride!

Learning to trust the dance of life

Even after you have been following the Radiant Warrior Path for a very long time, you will still have doubt simply because you are living down here on earth. Unfortunately you have to know the darkness inside out and outside in before you can really know the light inside yourself. Why? Because when you really know them both, you realise that both darkness and light are part of the dance of life, and you understand that you can trust life. You can trust the movement of the Tao, the impulse of your soul.

Once you realise this, then you can step bravely into the unknown because you have seen it all, not because you know the future, not because you know what is going to happen next, but because you have already seen and experienced all there is to see. You have seen everything in duality. You have seen your darkness and fear, and you have seen your glory and your light. Then you trust. It will take a long, long time to develop this trust of life, particularly when you are facing danger. You need to trust life every time you jump into a car, because there may be an accident. Every time you fly off for a holiday, there may be a plane crash. Ultimately you will trust life even in the midst of your plane actually crashing.

When you have seen all the ups and downs of life, you learn to trust the process. As you gradually go back to your natural state of being, you become like a drop of water flowing through a river to the sea. As you return to the sea, you will face all kinds of obstacles. You will cascade down a waterfall and tumble through a ravine, experiencing all the ups and downs and excitement of the torrential flow. But you know that even in the midst of the excitement of life, nothing can change your true qualities, your eternal essence. You just continue to flow gracefully through all the ups and downs of life.

When you really understand the true nature of your mind, you will find that one aspect of your mind is just like water. There is a continuity to it. You are continuously experiencing life, whether you like it or not, but sometimes you still feel so unsure. You cannot see clearly. Sometimes you are just like a drop of water in a very still pond, when suddenly the rain lashes down and the wind whistles round. Then the water begins to rise, and this still pond bubbles up and up, until it becomes part of a raging torrent of water that rushes you through to the next stage of life. However, if you understand your true nature, you still know that essentially nothing has changed, that reality is changeless.

Eventually, you will flow back into the sea and be absorbed high into the atmosphere, and from that high vantage point, you can look down on the ocean and the rivers and the streams, and you can see the quiet times and the turbulent times and so forth, and through it all you continue to transform, whilst deep down, your true nature stays exactly the same.

Seeing the whole picture

If you know all this about life, you can always trust. Why? Because when you look down on the whole of your life, you can see the complete picture. When you can see the bigger picture of life, then, and only then, you can develop trust. When you are down in the midst of it, you keep praying, but you still stumble and fall and feel fear and doubt. But when you have experienced all this long enough, you know that you will also experience times of peacefulness and clarity. You will remember, when the water gets stirred up and is so muddy that you cannot see clearly, that this is just part of the dance of life, the ebb and flow of the currents of life, and you will just trust the process.

We have all heard so many times that we are really the light, that we are all the perfect, unchanging sons and daughters of God. But you have to go deep within to experience the truth of this for yourself. Then, when you are swept along in a fast current of life and you feel fear, you know that is okay. You experience doubt again and know that is okay too, because you have been there before. You experience confusion and darkness and you know that this is just a passing state of mind.

When you can see the whole picture, it is perfectly all right to experience fear, doubt, confusion, anxiety and anguish. It is self-denial to say that the mind is never doubtful whilst you still have a physical existence, but you can learn to master your mind and all aspects of existence. This is why the spiritual path is a course in mastership. You have to learn that you have been in the darkness many times, and will be there many times more, and yet you are still, at heart, absolutely fine.

Placing your trust in God

The trust you need to become a fearless Radiant Warrior is not about trusting your personality-self. This aspect of yourself is just temporary and eventually it will disappear. Do not place all your trust in your own endeavours. When you have been on the spiritual path for long enough, you will begin to realise how unreliable and moody you are. You will learn to place your trust not in human endeavour, but in God, the Source or the Tao.

To give your trust absolutely to something so intangible and abstract as God is quite often a very scary process. Money is easier to trust, because you can actually see and touch it. But your safety lies in the truth, not in your pension fund. You just have to keep trusting in God, until you are convinced. This trust is moment to moment and involves not knowing. Because we usually only trust in something we know well, to trust something that is not explainable in normal, every day terms takes courage and faith.

This trust is very hard to teach, or even to convey in words, because it has to come from personal experience of the divine. Words are so limiting, and it is so hard to describe that moment of enlightenment, that blissful state of being, that state of oneness, in which the whole of life is fully revealed to you.

All that any spiritual teacher or master can do is to help create the right conditions for you to experience this for yourself. When you have a taste of the divine, you know it. Sometimes the clouds are there, and life is very hard. Sometimes the doubtful suspicious part of your mind can be very loud and strong. Occasionally your doubt may hit you hard, just like a custard pie being thrown right in your face. But you still trust life itself.

Your practice becomes your lifeline, and, as your inner connection grows stronger, your faith will increase. This has absolutely nothing to do with a belief in Christ, Buddha or God. It is the direct experience of Christ, Buddha, God. True spiritual masters have tasted the divine, and that is what they trust. To become a Radiant Warrior, you need to trust; not the world, but the power that holds the whole universe together. Once you experience this, once you have a taste of this, then you know. Then you trust.

Meanwhile, the trust or faith you need to cultivate on your spiritual path can be developed in three different stages.

The three stages of developing spiritual trust

In the very first stage of your spiritual journey you aspire. You have read some spiritual books and they have opened up your imagination, or you have met someone who stimulates a desire in you, and you want to seek. You are not yet on a spiritual path, but you are inspired to seek out a spiritual teacher or master. You want to know more. At this early stage you need blind faith. You have no real idea what you are doing, or where you are going, but you are inspired to seek. At this stage you can cultivate trust in the divine by giving thanks regularly to God for all that you have. You can even give thanks when you ask for something that you think you have not got yet, and practise knowing that you have already received it.

In the second stage of your spiritual journey, you have started to do some spiritual practice, and you are beginning to feel some benefit from it. You may say something like 'Wow, I've seen the light' or 'My heart is so open, I love every one who comes into my mind.' At this stage, your faith is getting stronger. At times, you may feel so certain, but this certainty still comes and goes, you have not stabilised it yet. During this stage, when you have doubts, you should practise more. You should keep praying to God or the divine to remove all your doubt and fear rather than increasing your doubt by indulging it. Cultivating trust day by day, come what may, is a core aspect of spiritual training that will develop your strength and bravery.

In the final stages of your spiritual journey, you have seen the face of Christ or Buddha, you may even have had a glimpse of God Himself. You know that your spiritual practice is carrying you forward and changing you. No matter what, nothing can shake your trust or faith. Your faith is very, very strong, not fanatical, but strong enough for you to really trust the process. This is so important. This trust or faith will enable you to become a true healer, a miracle worker, a teacher of God. In order to become a Radiant Warrior or light worker and raise the vibrations of this planet, you have to develop this level of trust. There is no other way.

Keep taking leaps of faith

Radiant Warriorship means facing all your fear head on. It means developing great strength and trust so that you can keep taking leaps of faith and transcending your fearful mindset. The 'you' who is so cynical and doubting is not the real you at all. So please have the courage to plunge in and make leaps of faith, so that one day you can perform miracles.

Advanced Radiant Warriors have so much trust in life that they know that they will be carried every step of the way on the long journey home. They do not have to calculate before taking the plunge. Their life is always so full because they always say 'yes' to life. When they feel the inspiration to move on they just pack up and go. Whatever happens to them in life they say 'fantastic!' They do not entertain doubts or anxieties. They know that everything that ever happens to them is for their highest good and they follow divine inspiration.

When Eckhart Tolle first awoke, he gave up a very well paid, prestigious career, followed his intuition, moved to America and began to write *The Power of Now*. Eventually he completely ran out of money, but then he won just enough with one lottery ticket to enable him to finish the book. Now he is a very rich man.

Advanced masters always wait for divine inspiration before they act fearlessly. For example Mahatma Ghandi always waited for inspiration before taking any political action against India's British rulers. Great masters do not respond to external pressure. They go within and wait patiently for the divine impulse that tells them to act.

You too can develop this level of trust in life, and when you do so it will appear as though your life simply unfolds miraculously. Even when your life becomes challenging, you will perceive the miracle within the challenge, and at this stage of your spiritual development, your unshakable strength and trust in a power much greater than yourself will become a great inspiration for all those fearful souls who have not yet reached your level of spiritual maturity.

Exercise

Sit quietly and look back at least five or ten years and gently remember a time during which you were very unhappy or when life seemed particularly challenging. Maybe your girlfriend or boyfriend at that time had just dumped you, or maybe you had just failed to get your dream job or discovered that you had a serious illness.

Ask your intuitive heart, 'How did that experience help me to grow personally or spiritually?'

See if you can now understand why that challenging time was actually perfect for your personal and spiritual growth and awakening.

Now give thanks for the situation that you once thought was a disaster.

Tell yourself that you cannot possibly see the bigger picture in life, but that life itself is now guiding you perfectly down the path to awakening. The outcome is certain. Your doubts along the way have absolutely no impact on the perfect working of the perfect plan for your personal and spiritual journey.

Jane's Story: Part 13

I would not say that I was naturally a very trusting person. My personality tends to be quite cynical and I am certainly not one of those New Age seekers who believes that angels are always helping them to find parking spaces. If anyone had told me twenty years ago that I would become a serious student of a channelled book (*A Course in Miracles*) I would have bet them thousands of pounds that they were wrong.

Blind faith has never worked for me. I have to develop faith based on my own experiences. Spiritual fairy stories are just not my cup of tea. I prefer cool hard logic and empirical evidence. Over the last ten years, it has been my own unforgettable experiences of the divine that have most persuaded me to place my trust more and more in a higher intelligence that seems to be guiding me every step of my spiritual journey.

At times on this journey, I have had some amazing experiences. Occasionally I have felt as though Jesus Christ himself was directly talking to me and specifically guiding my every thought and deed. At other times, when my energy centres have been less open and my vibrations much lower, I have experienced no such personal connection to the divine, but the way my life has continued to unfold has convinced me that, whether I am consciously aware of it or not, I am being led down the spiritual path by a guide who is infinitely wiser and more caring than anyone or anything I could conceivably imagine.

More often than not, it is the little things that convince me that I am not in control of my life or my spiritual awakening, and that everything that I need to heal and awake will be provided for me by a much higher power than my own little brain. Who would have thought, for example, that a shortage of ice cream in Phuket, Thailand would lead to a major healing for myself and a dear friend? (Sorry but it is too complicated to explain here.) After this healing occurred, my friend and I both had a good laugh about the way in which miracles can occur.

No human mind could possibly have engineered the perfect conditions for this particular healing to happen. No human mind could have known that a shortage of ice cream in a particular ice cream parlour in Thailand was essential to facilitate two souls' spiritual awakening! But we are now both convinced that there are no accidents on the spiritual path. As far as we are concerned, that shortage of ice cream in one shopping centre in Thailand was divinely planned!

Chapter 14

Undoing Your Personality Self

Your personality is not ultimately real. One day, readiness to let go of your personality-self will just rise up from the depths of your soul.

All your problems are about 'me'

All the problems you have in your life, including your fears about the state of the world, are based on 'me': 'my' problem, 'my' body, 'my' house, 'my' marriage, 'my' divorce. When there is no me involved, then and only then, you have no problems. When I associate myself with Jason Chan, I have problems. When I shift my consciousness and no longer misidentify myself as Jason Chan, suddenly all my problems disappear, not because I am denying my problems, no, at that moment I really do not have any.

All the people I meet through my work, all their problems are related to their belief that they are a little separate self that they call 'me.' Once you transcend that me, you will experience the divine self, or spiritual self, that cannot suffer. It can take time to have this realisation, but all our human problems, all the world's problems, are associated with 'me' – *my* country, *my* religion, *my* race, *our* holy war.

In this realm of existence, our ego is automatic. If we did not have an ego, we would not be here on earth. But, once you are conscious that you have an eternal-self as well as an ego-self, you can observe your ego and all its games. You can heal yourself by undoing yourself layer by layer, until you return back to your wholeness. When you identify yourself solely as an ego, or isolated little personality-self, you are so limited and judgemental and trapped. You are like a drop of water that has no idea it is an integral part of the whole ocean.

When you identify yourself as a separated, lonely, weak little body you become so fearful. You think that you can be destroyed in the second it takes someone to pull the trigger of a gun, and this generates so much fear deep in your system. You think you have separated from your Source, and this creates so much guilt within you. However, just as it was your desire to separate from God in the first place, so now, you must truly desire, above all else, to return to God or Oneness. You must want this beyond all worldly things including wealth, power, career success and wonderful loving relationships.

The spiritual path is a path of undoing

When you are on your spiritual path, learning is the opposite of gathering worldly knowledge and wisdom. Spiritual learning is about relinquishing all that you think you know about yourself and the world you see around you. The genuine spiritual path is actually a process of undoing yourself. What you think you are is simply a set of beliefs, or a mindset, that can be undone.

The idea of undoing ourselves may be a new concept for the majority of us, because we have all developed very fixed ideas about ourselves and others. However, eventually, if you keep pursuing your spiritual path, you will discover that you no longer know who you are. You will loosen all your ideas about yourself such as 'I am rich' or 'I am poor,' 'I am an angry person' or 'I am a spiritual person.' Your fixed ideas about yourself will become softer, and you will begin to realise that the little self that needs protection and attacks in order to defend itself is not the real you.

You have to experience this process of undoing for yourself. It is not a philosophy that you can pick up second hand from books or spiritual masters. You have to undo yourself layer by layer, including all your perceptions about yourself and others. This undoing includes letting go of the stories you tell yourself about your past.

Your fixed ideas about yourself and others always come from the past. Some of these ideas will not even be in your conscious awareness, but they will filter through to affect your habitual thinking and behaviour patterns. For example, maybe your mother never cuddled you when you were a baby, and this unconscious memory now stops you from being a physically affectionate person. In order to free yourself from this trap, you need to bring this memory up to the surface of your consciousness, so that you can heal it and let it go. This undoing process, or releasing of your past, eventually enables you to be authentic.

Engaging in life without becoming trapped

When you know who you really are, you can still play being a normal human being and engage in ordinary human activities, such as running a business or having a sexual relationship. You can still play the roles of a dutiful son or daughter, a loving mother or father, or a passionate sexual partner, but you will not get trapped nearly so often in your temporary roles or identities. When you are authentic, you no longer have to prove yourself, and you will not need so much external validation or approval. It is only your insecure small, false self that needs approval.

A free mind can expand into a vastness in which it needs absolutely nothing. A free mind can engage in human life without attachment and therefore without fear. When you are awake, you are no longer trapped in your past, or your body, or the image of yourself. This is the potential inherent in all of us, the potential to expand our minds beyond our bodies and our brains. The natural mind is never separated or isolated; the natural mind just extends infinitely. It is simply love in action.

Letting go can feel uncomfortable

Returning to your true self may be very natural, but it usually involves some pain as you shed all the false layers of yourself that have protected you for so long. As you progress on your spiritual journey, you will sometimes have to go through a process of letting go that you may well experience as uncomfortable, or even disorientating. This letting go process always entails a temporary sense of loss.

Sometimes letting go may happen by force, for example when someone you love dumps you, or you are made redundant. These enforced changes will really test your trust and commitment to your path. All you can do, when facing such losses, is to nurture yourself through these challenging times with love and compassion. You may find it helpful to remind yourself that you will eventually transcend these trials and re-find the light on the other side.

Once you have surrendered to the divine, the outcome is never in any doubt. Only the time you take to transcend all your limitations is down to you. As you grow spiritually, you will come to know yourself less and less. The old fixed image you had of yourself will begin to dissolve, and, at times, you may feel pretty confused, and even fearful. At times like these, it is so useful to remember that whatever is worthwhile involves challenges, and that each time you transcend your fears, you will strengthen your inner faith and trust.

Veterans on the path even welcome tough challenges, because they have learnt from experience how much they grow at these times in their lives. But if, at any time, fearful challenges get too much for you to handle, you can always pray for assistance and ask for your spiritual healing to be slowed down to a pace that you can handle. Several of my students tell me that this prayer has really worked for them.

The spiritual path is never a straight line up to heaven. You will inevitably take two steps forward and then one step back. As we progress on our spiritual path, we all have to face major challenges, or trials. Please do not blame God when you seem to be going through endless challenges in life. Your true self actually gives you these challenges not God. Why? Because you have no idea how much power and love is there within your true self, until you triumphantly go through challenges that help you recognise your own strength and power.

Living without your ego

Eventually, after a long and challenging process of undoing your ego-self, you will arrive at a state of existence in which you function without your ego. What is it like to experience life without a 'me'? I will give you some clues, a preview of what it is like. When you transcend this little 'me,' you can love as much as you want to. You smile and laugh virtually all of the time. Occasionally you can play at being a little me, a personality, an image.

However you know it is not the real you. When you are consistently connected to reality or Oneness, you can still dance in illusion for a while. You can play at being a very successful worker during the day, and at night you can play at being a romantic sexual partner. You can play at being a famous artist or a brilliant scientist. You can play whatever role you would like to play, but you are always aware that the real you lies behind all the different roles you adopt.

Most people get so stuck with just one old image. They make their story so real that they don't realise that they can change it whenever they want. You too are stubborn like this. For example, you may be absolutely convinced that you cannot forgive someone who hurt you many years ago. However, when you transcend this little me or ego-self, you can forgive the whole world. Is it easy to transcend the ego? No, it is not easy at all. But once you do, your true self will reveal itself to you more and more, and selfless action will become as natural to you as breathing.

The dangers of acquiring spiritual power

Before you reach this point of true selflessness however, the power you gain on the spiritual path can be very tempting to misuse. When you become strong and confident in your spiritual practice, spiritual pride can set in. At this point you may well start to disrespect and criticise your spiritual teachers. You also begin to judge most other people are less spiritual than you. You think you can do everything by yourself. If you begin to think like this, please hear alarm bells. When some apparently humble seekers finally reach the point of power, they can go crazy. They can believe they are specially chosen to do God's work, and they delude themselves into believing that everything they do is saving the world. These individuals can be very psychic and charismatic. They may have real healing powers and many followers, but they can do great harm.

Spiritual powers can so easily inflate the ego, and when well-trained spiritual practitioners turn into 'dark lords' and misuse their powers for their personal gain, lots of people suffer at their hands. You need great humility to go all the way on the spiritual path. The Dalai Lama has such humility. He says 'I am just a simple monk,' whilst millions of people worship him as a god. Humility is not being over humble, but it is about never abusing your personal and spiritual power, and never taking the credit for divine grace and God's gifts to you.

Without disciplined spiritual training and constant mindfulness, you will continue to make the wrong choices. So, in order to avoid the danger of misusing spiritual power, you need to keep purifying yourself and your intentions. It is imperative at this stage in your spiritual journey to keep checking your motivation with great self-honesty. You also have to keep giving back any powers you may acquire to life itself. Keep giving all the credit for your spiritual powers back to God, and keep opening your heart with great gratitude for His grace and guidance.

Saving the world

You may think that achieving world peace and harmony simply through changing your mind is an impossible task, but what is strong enough to make an unjust, warring world, is equally strong enough to let it go. Eventually the whole of humanity must change its mind and choose peace, without waiting for others to change their minds first. As a Radiant Warrior you have chosen to lead the way. You have agreed to set an example by setting aside your egotistical goals, projections and your constant refrain of 'What about me?' You have volunteered to surrender selflessly to the will of a much higher spiritual authority.

Throughout the history of humankind, leaders have been driven by their egotistic goals and throughout history, wars and conquests have inflicted terrible pain and harm on billions of people. Human hatred runs very deep. Hatred is in the collective psyche. For millennia, we have had religious conflicts, racial disharmony, genocide, terrorism, brutal repression of opposition groups, nations hating each other, and so on, all born out of ignorance. The ego is very dark because it always acts out of fear, ignorance, excessive desire or greed, insecurity and a drive to harm others and, subconsciously, itself.

When you have not actively participated in overt forms of violence for a while, you say to world leaders and terrorists alike, 'Why are you doing this?' We all either deny responsibility for the world's suffering, or justify our part in it. Every attack, whether on an individual, or a whole race or nation, is always justified by the attacker. No one ever claims to be waging an unjust war. In every war both sides know that God is on their side.

Until you awake, if you have power in the world, you will inevitably play the role of perpetrator or persecutor. If you are powerless, you will play victim. We all keep swapping these roles. In one round we are the aggressor, in the next we are the defender. These patterns in human behaviour just keep repeating themselves. Only the means of inflicting damage on others have evolved. From throwing spears at one another, to destroying whole cities with nuclear bombs, the ego always rules the world cruelly.

Saving the world by changing your own mind

What can you do about all this? First and foremost, if you want to save the world, start by changing your own mind, over and over again. Moment by moment you can choose truth over illusion. You can choose to forgive, rather than to attack, and to love, rather than to hate. Each choice we make is a decision for or against peace, for or against ourselves, and for or against the whole human race.

Every moment you have to choose: life or death, love or hate, peace or war, reality or perpetual nightmares. You cannot hedge your bets or compromise on this; you cannot have a bit of both. Love and hate are opposites that can never be resolved. You cannot love God, but hate terrorists or the President of the United States. You cannot pray for world peace, but fight your neighbour over the ugly fence he has erected without your permission.

Humankind creates wars through its own shadows. You may claim that you want only world peace, but you still harbour hate and conflict within your own mind, and pretend that your thoughts are private and therefore no one else's business. Do not ask for peace on the outside, until you are completely peaceful on the inside. If you ask God 'Why do you not create peace on earth?' He will tell you that perfect peace is eternally within you.

You will need a lot of help at first to make the peaceful, loving, forgiving choice time after time. The decision for God has to be constant, and this will not always be easy, because when you think you are being attacked, you will want to retaliate. But when you can open your heart and stay connected to your true self, or transcendent natural state, forgiveness will come automatically to you, and peace will prevail.

If you are truly committed to becoming a Radiant Peacemaker, keep focussing on your desire for perfect love, and keep asking for harmony and peace to be the outcome of every situation, or relationship, in which you find yourself. As you consciously connect to God or life at all times, death will gradually disappear. As you choose love in all circumstances, hate will fade away. Consciously choose to be joyful regardless of what is going on in the world around you, and sadness and sorrow will diminish to nothing. Consciously choose to forgive rather than to condemn, and the sinful world you now perceive will dissolve into the light.

Always choosing forgiveness does not mean that you can no longer discriminate between right and wrong actions. Nor does it mean that you cannot act appropriately to defend yourself and others from attack. But it does mean that you do not judge and condemn those whom you perceive as committing wrong deeds. You do not have to be smart to make these choices, but you do need sincerity, commitment and bravery to choose truth over illusion.

Choose for everyone's highest benefit and change will happen. Commit yourself to unconditional love, and you will be shown the way. Reclaim your power by making a commitment to God, and you will be guided to fulfil your highest purpose this lifetime as you gently undo your ego-self and re-connect to your true self that knows nothing of conflict, but dwells eternally in peace and love.

Exercises

Dis-identifying from your personal problems

Sit quietly and think about your personal problems or concerns.

Now connect to the light and pray for help in letting go of all your personal problems –just for a while

You may like to use the power of your mind to see each problem floating up into the sky like a helium balloon disappearing into the sunlight. Or you may find it helpful to imagine that you are watching your life as though it were being acted out on the stage, while you sit in the audience.

Sit in the auditorium and observe your personality-self playing a role on the stage. See your personality-self acting out a particularly worrying situation or event. Notice how unreal and actually quite amusing this worrying event seems to be when you watch it as though you were watching a play or a film.

Now do your best to completely let go of thinking about your personal problems. Simply let them fade into empty space or dissolve into the light.

Relax your thinking mind and rest in dynamic peace.

Finally, fill your heart with gratitude, peace and joy and tell yourself, 'I am not my personality-self, I am an eternal being experiencing myself as a personality in a body, but this experience will not last.'

Who am I?

Sit quietly and contemplate the question 'Who am I?'

As your thoughts surface, gently remind yourself that you are not just a personality.

For example if you think 'I am a middle aged woman' or 'I am a young man' smile to yourself and remember that you are not your age. When you were four, you were still the same 'you' as you are today, so how can you be your age?

If the thought surfaces 'I am a healer' or 'I am an accountant,' again smile to that thought, and remember that you are more than just your career or your chosen roles this lifetime. After you retire from your work or career, you will still be 'you.'

Once you have watched your thoughts about who you are for a few minutes, still your mind as much as you can and simply feel your 'being-ness' that is beyond your ego-self.

Just be in the moment, breathing in and out, resting in awareness and gently let go of all your fixed ideas about yourself. Rest quietly for a few minutes in this peaceful state of being.

If more thoughts come into your mind, just let them float past you, and return to experiencing a state of inner peace and expansion.

Jane's Story: Part 14

The longer I tread on this spiritual path, the less fixed my personality seems to be. For many years, I had a very strong identity as a university lecturer, but five years ago I rather reluctantly gave up that role to follow my heart's desire to follow a full-time spiritual path, and since then I have not found another defining role to play.

Now I sometimes teach tai chi, but I do not identify myself as a tai chi teacher. Sometimes I play the role of spiritual student, but I do not totally identify myself with that role either. Sometimes I play the role of *A Course in Miracles* teacher, and doing so gives me incredible joy and fulfilment, but this role still does not define me.

My life just seems to flow quite naturally from one activity to another, sometimes with fairly long periods of rest in between. I used to rush from one activity to another, but now I am so blessed to be able to stop and just look at the flowers for a while, or sit quietly and soak up the sunshine.

I still have strong likes and dislikes, but more and more frequently, I catch myself smiling at my personality-self as she huffs and puffs about something trivial that has really annoyed her. Sometimes I become very aware that my personality-self is like a dream figure wandering about in a rather crazy dream world and I just watch myself going through all the usual human thoughts and emotions, without any longer drowning in them.

Unfortunately, at other times I am still far less mindful, and at these times, I quite easily slip back into totally identifying with myself as the innocent victim of a cruel and heartless world. I simply lose myself in my negative thoughts and feelings and when this occurs I cannot be truly loving or compassionate, however much I want to be. But on the whole, my life is now so free and joyful that I am filled with gratitude for everyone and every event in my life that has helped me to awake just enough to know, at least some of the time, that I am not really 'Jane Rogers' and that my true self is limitless and immortal.

I have also experienced just enough spiritual power to understand its dangers. It is so easy for the personality-self to hijack spiritual awakening and I really have to watch myself to guard against any tendency to feel superior to 'less spiritual' individuals, or to compete with my spiritual friends in a crazy game of 'who is the most spiritually advanced amongst us.'

Thankfully, whenever my ego does become rather puffed up on my spiritual journey, I seem to receive almost instant correction. For example, after the last spiritual retreat I attended, I was feeling rather proud of one particular spiritual experience that I had 'achieved,' when I realised just how unkind and uncaring I had been at one point to a fellow member of that retreat.

Immediately my spiritual pride was well and truly punctured, and I deflated rather like a pricked balloon, as I heard a voice in my head saying 'You think you are so spiritual, but you cannot even be as kind to a friend as any normal person would be.' Whilst this insight was rather uncomfortable for a while, I was soon very grateful for this correction that kept me from straying too far from the very narrow path of awakening without inflating my ego.

Chapter 15

Selflessly Serving Others

Serving others without calculation is as natural as the wind.
You are here to heal the world and bring peace to the world.
If you are not serving others, you are not happy.

Everyone has a true purpose to fulfil

As Radiant Warriors, we all have work to do down here on earth. Once you have reached certain levels of opening and healing, you will understand that there is a divine plan for you, a true purpose to your physical existence. Everyone has a true purpose this lifetime. If you do not fulfil this purpose, you will know that there is something missing in your life. This purpose is connected to a selflessness that arises naturally from deep within you, once you begin to transcend your egotistical existence.

Someone can be strongly spiritually connected and yet be no use to the world whatsoever. You can convince yourself that you are blessing the world by, for example, meditating all day long and repeating 'My light is permeating the whole universe,' but children will still be dying of hunger in their millions. You are here in this world for a reason. A lot of people become spiritual seekers primarily to comfort their personalities. Like the 1970s hippies, they adopt a very easy-going lifestyle and say that they are spiritual, rather than materialistic, but very often they are still neurotic, rather lazy and fundamentally self-centred.

As you grow spiritually, you have to watch out for the danger of becoming addicted to spiritual pleasures. Spiritual bliss can become addictive. You may think that you have given up all your attachments, because you no longer crave sex, alcohol or social recognition, but can you give up your attachment to spiritual light and bliss? You can actually become imprisoned in a spiritual palace, surrounded by love and light, imagining that you are saving the world, by shining your inner light onto it.

Get real! What planet are you on? Millions of people on this plant are dying now from hunger, disease and war. Collectively on planet earth, we are a long way from heaven. When you awake, you cannot just abandon your suffering brothers and sisters. You have to understand the hell human beings make on earth, and do your very best to get people out of it. This is the spiritual agenda for the 21st Century. Today, spiritual masters are coming down from the mountaintops, to work among the masses. This is no easy task, and those who have awakened have to guard constantly against being pulled back into fearful mass consciousness.

Do not say to yourself 'If I am spiritual enough I need do nothing, God will take care of everything on my behalf.' This is just self-deception. If we do not wholeheartedly pursue our true purpose this lifetime, we will waste our life, remain unfulfilled, and fail all those who are meant to benefit from our awakening. It is no longer enough to find your own heaven and retreat into it. The world, and the whole of humanity, needs many more light workers. We urgently need many, many souls to awake and to stay in the 'normal' world in order to transform the consciousness of the planetary system.

If everyone had tranquil, peaceful minds, we would live in a completely peaceful world. So we have to transform our own consciousness one by one. But without power, strength, discipline and a lot of self-healing, you cannot transform anything, not even a mouse. If you really want to help others, you have to empower yourself first, and then extend this empowerment out into the world. You cannot help the weak by rescuing them, or simply giving them the things they lack. Just giving food aid to starving nations is not a lasting solution to world poverty. In the long run, you just make the poor more dependent and therefore weaker. As a Radiant Warrior your goal is to empower others as you have been empowered

You cannot advance spiritually, solely by serving other people, and trying to solve their problems. If you observe the armies of people who sincerely want to help the world, you will see that they always see the world's problems as outside of them. They say 'The world is an awful place, but it is not my fault.' 'The world is at war, but I want peace, so I cannot be responsible for what is happening.' Of course, the world we live in is replete with very awful problems such as famine and AIDS and genocide. Children are dying every second from 'solvable' problems, but it is self-denial to see the world's problems as only on the outside of you.

Those who fight against evil in the world can be extremely angry individuals. Anti-war protestors very often actually fan the flames of violence. They project their own pain and suffering outwards, and end up contributing to a violent and fearful collective consciousness. Those working tirelessly for good causes may be genuinely motivated to save the world, but they may then go home and shout at their partner, or, at the very least, express angry thoughts about those whom they hold responsible for the problems they are trying tirelessly to alleviate.

Radiant Warriors do not attempt to fight against so called 'evils' in the world. But, reaching a certain point in their spiritual development, all spiritual seekers will naturally desire to serve the world around them. Why do you need to serve the world? because as you deepen into your spiritual path, you will find that there is nothing else to do.

When you fully understand that your interests and those of others are exactly the same, you will just naturally want to help your beloved brothers and sisters. Divine inspiration will guide you, and the whole world will benefit. Playing at being a little, separate personality eventually becomes boring. As you awake, you more and more see physical life and physical pleasures as quite pointless. Why invest so much time and energy in something that is not permanent, in something that is inevitably going to disappoint or even disappear sooner or later?

Surrendering to the divine plan

Genuinely serving the world is never the ego's plan, but it is divine will. Your ego may want to save the world in order to aggrandise itself, but this is just yet another attack in disguise. Your good intentions are not enough. To want to do God's will on earth is completely different from having all the skills to do it. Doing God's will takes tremendous effort and energy. Until you are completely at one with the divine itself, you have to practise continuously purifying yourself and then plugging into universal consciousness and letting it guide you. The more you surrender to the divine, the more you will establish trust and faith.

As you more and more merge yourself back into this divine state of oneness, you will increasingly realise that you do not need to make any plans of your own to serve the world. Unlike worldly leaders, those who serve God do not have to worry about making five or ten year plans. There is just divine planning at work, on a level and scale that the individual human mind cannot begin to comprehend. If you think that you are not good enough to serve or to save the world, don't worry about it. The divine plan will work through you and turn your greatest weaknesses into strengths.

Great saints can sit knitting and save the world. An ordinary housewife who sits and knits is just wasting time. What is the difference? One is constantly tuning in to God's will and cultivating this divine connection, the other is just killing time in between their birth and their death. Great saints and masters do not have to do anything to fulfil themselves. They choose to serve humanity because they choose to serve God. They see God in every human being, and they serve God in every human being.

Because they are awake, the great spiritual masters no longer see billions of separate human beings; they see just one fragmented Son of God who is suffering. They understand that the divine plan is to reunite this fragmented Son of God into divine wholeness and unity, and they commit their whole being to assisting God in this process.

Serving humanity will not bring you rewards in the usual sense. Your ego-self will not gain from healing the world, but when you are awake you just have to become part of the divine plan. No other path or pastime will give you any lasting joy or satisfaction. There are no personal rewards whatsoever for saving the world. In fact, humanity won't thank you at all for wanting to heal them. They will probably hate you for it, and try to destroy you.

In past centuries, great masters and saints who preached nothing but love were tortured and killed. Christ was crucified because his complete lack of ego and hatred was seen as a terrible threat to a world based on self-interest, hatred and attack. Today a great spiritual master is more likely to be destroyed by an exposé in the popular press, but the basic process is exactly the same.

If you want to help the world, you cannot play small, but equally you must guard against becoming arrogant. No one can fail to do what God appoints him to do. At times, illusions of despair may seem to come to those who commit to do God's will, because the spiritual path is undoubtedly long, steep and extremely challenging, but you must learn not to be deceived by illusions. You must always remember Who walks with you and guides your every step.

The ultimate outcome of all your sincere endeavours to follow God's will is guaranteed by Him. Do not be afraid. Look up to heaven and see His word writ large among the stars. Look up and find your certain destiny that the world would hide from you, but God would have you see. God is not complete without you, and as you awake and heal yourself, God gives thanks to you for all your effort and dedication.

Healing others

An unhealed healer cannot help anyone. In fact they can be downright dangerous, because they have too many shadows that they have not cleared, and therefore continue to project their guilt out into the world around them. Self-understanding is a must if you want to save mankind. Without purification, and years of self-healing, you may want to heal others, but it just won't work. Giving other people your advice or your opinions is not true healing or helping. Helping others from a position of superiority and specialness won't work.

Healing skills or tools by themselves are not enough. You may be a highly trained and skilled acupuncturist, herbalist or homeopath, but if you have not yet healed your own inner darkness, the therapies you offer will not work on a long-term basis. Anyone who is not dwelling in pure love, joy and peace virtually all of the time, still needs to work on healing themselves before they offer any sort of healing to others.

Good intentions are not enough to spread the light. You also have to take some action. You cannot just sit around and say 'God will do everything for me.' You have to get up and make something happen. But your spiritual healing and unfolding are more important than what you do in the world, and it takes time to mature spiritually, so please do not rush into action prematurely. The light does not need your help. It will always find a way to reach those who are ready to receive it. Your sole responsibility is to accept divine correction or atonement for yourself. God will then use you to spread the light, but you do not need to worry about how or when this will happen. The means will be given to you.

Divine timing is not your timing, so do not prematurely insist that you have to spread the light. Heal yourself as much as you can first. Don't rush, and opportunities will just open up for you when you are ready to use them safely and effectively. Yoga, tai chi, meditation, spiritual healings and spiritual teachers are now becoming quite mainstream in Western societies, whereas 20 years ago they were considered very weird. So don't be shy about what you are doing, but just expand your light-work gradually. Be patient, but combine this patience with very active practice and alertness. Fill your time productively, and when the time is right, you will be totally ready to get up and go. Never slacken off in your practice, or try to go back to your old way of life, because you will find that there is nowhere to hide.

The true healer, or spiritual guide, is one who no longer believes in nightmares of any kind. A true healer has left their allegiance to fear far behind. One instant of joining in unconditional love without any tinge of fear or attack is all that is necessary for healing to occur. A healed healer naturally gives others strength, courage and love so that they can face their fears and heal themselves. As a Radiant Spiritual Warrior, you have to be very strong and loving to be able to face and vanquish others' fears. A sick, suffering person always sees themselves as separated from God. Your role is to show them that this is not true.

Once you truly heal yourself, life will be beautiful, and you will become a natural healing presence in the world. Your soul will eventually shine through and set the others free too. Once you can hold divine love and light for prolonged periods of time, you will become a miracle worker who can transform lives from darkness back into light. Once you have healed yourself, you will naturally heal others and spread light right around the world. Once you have connected with your eternal inner peace, you can offer true peace to others. I pray that you will not stay part of the collective fear that is ruining planet earth. I urge you to rise above it, and from that place of infinite grace, reach out to give your brothers and sisters a helping hand.

Performing miracles

Provided that they have purified themselves sufficiently, everyone has the capacity to give and receive miracles. You have to be ready at all times to allow miracles to happen through you, but you should never attempt to initiate them. You have to let the light lead the way. It is your task to make yourself ready to perform miracles, but God always leads the way. Your role is to become *'miracle minded'* (*A Course in Miracles*) which means that your ego or 'me' consciousness is kept right out of the way. You cannot say 'I want a miracle to happen.' When you try to make a miracle happen in this way, you block it.

To perform miracles, you have to learn the art of opening and surrendering. You have to become a God-inspired healer, without wanting things to happen in your own way, or in your own time. Everything that comes from true love is a miracle, but it is so hard to surrender totally to the power of love like this, because we all want to be in control. You cannot become a miracle worker unless you truly believe that everything is possible, and if you observe your mind closely, you will probably find that you do not fully believe that you can create your own wonderful reality.

The world is not yet ready to understand miracles. The human mind is very fixed in its own way of thinking. The world calls it a miracle if a sick person who is about to die recovers, or if a parent prays for a missing child to be saved from harm and they turn up safe and well. But true miracles are not always like this.

We all tend to think that the removal of physical pain, or the postponement of a death is a miracle, but once you reach a certain level of spiritual advancement, you will begin to understand that pain can be a miracle and someone dying can be a miracle, if they die in peace, or if their death triggers a deep healing in someone mourning their loss. Going through a really hard time, such as a bankruptcy, or divorce, can be a miracle for some individuals.

Miracles always happen for your highest good and not according to the world's agenda.

Only when you surrender to God, and relinquish all your expectations, will you get a glimpse of what miracles are really about. To perform miracles, first and foremost you have to have complete faith in divine love. When love is in action, miracles happen. When love is received, miracles happen. You cannot consciously perform a miracle. If you try to do this you are performing magic and it will not work because it is based on illusions. You can never know what is the best outcome for anyone, or indeed for the world as a whole. You cannot know whether the best outcome is for someone to recover from a physical illness, or whether the best outcome for the world is an immediate end to all wars.

A lot of psychics and clairvoyants are fixers, not healers. People buy their wares because they want to be fixed. This fixing mentality is a fundamental human weakness. Do not pray to God to take someone's pain away, or for a specific outcome to a world problem. Do not pray for any particular outcome at all. Pray only to sustain everyone concerned with love, light and inner peace. A true miracle is an expression of love based on complete trust or faith, but before you can understand this, you have to go though a long healing process of purification, forgiveness and letting go. The more you heal yourself, the more you can become a pure channel that the Holy Spirit can use to perform genuine miracles.

Miracle workers need to undergo years of external and internal training. They have to allow self-healing to happen layer by layer. They have to let all their darkness, fears and shadows rise up to be removed. The more you clear yourself in this way, the more you can become a channel for divine love and light to perform miracles through you. Please remember also that God's miracle workers are not asked to become martyrs. They are simply asked to learn their lessons with joy, and to trust in an invisible power that will never fail them.

Becoming a shining example for others to follow

This godless, fearful, tired world desperately needs God's teachers and healers. Everyone dwelling on earth at this time needs miracles to happen.

People urgently need to see someone living in unshakable peace and love. When they are ready to awake, the very presence of someone dwelling in love will trigger their soul deep within them and their life will change.

So the greatest service you can perform for the world is to commit yourself heart and soul to your own healing and awakening. The more you heal yourself, the more your very presence can naturally assist others to heal. The more you find true liberation from all your self-imposed suffering, the more you become a shining example of Radiant Spiritual Warriorship for others to follow.

Your awakening will become a beacon of light in a world that is still so dark. Your awakening will bless not only those who physically connect up to you, and use you as an inspiration and as a guide for their own awakening journey, but generations long past and generations yet to come. This is God's Will for you and all His beloved children. You can delay your awakening indefinitely, but the journey's end is never in any doubt, and one day, whether in this lifetime or a future lifetime, you will graduate from the paths of awakening, healing, empowerment and surrender to become a radiant beacon of light and hope for all the world and for all who suffer here.

Exercise

Sorting out the essential from the non-essential

Sit quietly and ask your intuitive heart, ' Have I fulfilled my life's purpose yet or am I just wasting time?

Now really use the power of your mind to imagine that you only have three days left to live, and ask yourself:
Whom do I still need to forgive?
Whom do I have to ask for forgiveness?
Whom do I need to tell that I love them?
What grievances do I still need to let go of?
What dreams have I not yet fulfilled?

Don't wait to do all that you still need to do this lifetime. Pack as much as you can into the next three days. Act as though they really were all the time you had left on this earth. Go beyond your mundane daily concerns and commit yourself wholeheartedly to extending love and light unconditionally out into the world around you.

Jane's Story: Part 15

I have certainly not yet graduated as a Radiant Warrior. After an amazing initial spiritual opening in 1998, and a blissful spiritual honeymoon period that lasted for almost four years, I have been very gradually awakening just a little bit more each year for several years now. During this time, I have undoubtedly experienced a few moments of pure enlightened 'being-ness,' but I know that I still have a very long way to go before these moments become a more or less permanent feature of my consciousness. I have also healed quite a few very dark shadows within my psyche, but I know there is still plenty more inner-darkness for me to heal and release to the light.

As the years have sped by, I have gradually moved from playing the role of spiritual student to sometimes playing the role of spiritual teacher. Observing this gradual transition, I am amazed and extremely grateful for the inner strength and empowerment that has been bestowed on me, and I regularly pray that I may resist my ego's persistent attempts to sabotage any genuine spiritual progress that I may make. I am also incredibly grateful to absolutely everyone in my life who has supported me and pushed me forwards on my incredible journey this lifetime, particularly my parents, my spiritual teachers and my close spiritual friends.

Whilst attempting to give priority to following my spiritual path every day of my life, I find that I still enjoy many 'normal' activities such as sharing a good meal with friends, reading a novel or watching a 'girlie' movie with Gloria. But by far and away the most fulfilling activity in my life at the moment is giving talks and workshops on *A Course in Miracles*. I have always enjoyed teaching and lecturing, but the love, light and joy that I have experienced whilst sharing some insights into *A Course in Miracles* is way beyond anything that this world could ever have to offer.

When I first began to give public talks on *A Course in Miracles* I relied quite heavily on my own intellect and prepared copious notes to guide me whilst speaking. More recently however I have been able to get my lower mind out of the way for a while, and just allow a much higher intelligence to use my brain and voice to teach through me. It is impossible to describe this experience. All I can tell you is that when I feel as though I am being used in this way, it makes every challenge on the path totally worthwhile. It is literally out of this world.

I do not really want to bring my story to any definite conclusion here. I sincerely hope that I have many years of physical life left to allow me to progress further down the Radiant Warrior Path. Meanwhile I would just like to thank you so much for reading my story to date. I hope and pray that it may have assisted you just a little on your own unique and miraculous spiritual journey. Please never, never give up hope that one-day you will return home to the infinite love, peace and joy that are your natural birthright. As a fellow traveller on the Radiant Warrior Path, I salute your courage and your commitment, and I send you all my love and best wishes for a very safe, joyful and fulfilling journey home.

Another dream . . . .

Ever since I dreamt about the loving young couple who were taken to the Radiant Kingdom to receive mystical teachings from the great light-being Zun-Ji, I have been holding another dream deep in my heart. Throughout all the challenges and distractions of the last ten years, I have never for one moment let this dream fade.

In my new dream, I am standing on the top of the Radiant Mountain, but I am not alone. Hundreds of advanced Radiant Warriors are standing there with me in a circle of bright light filled with love and peace. As we gaze down the mountain towards the valley, we see thousands upon thousands of laughing, joyful people beginning to climb the mountain path. Some are very young and bound up the path with great ease and vitality. Others are much older and a little frail, but they too are steadily climbing the path with a bright smile on their faces. Every now and then the young ones at the front run back down the path to help those at the back.

As I look down on this amazing sight, my eyes are filled with tears and my heart overflows with gratitude. I am so grateful to all the pioneers on this path whose courage, dedication, generosity, love and compassion have enabled them to climb to the very top of the Radiant Mountain. I am also eternally grateful to all the ascended masters and light-beings from the Radiant Kingdom who have tirelessly assisted humankind to reach this miraculous point of evolution and collective awakening. I know that our seemingly endless detour into fear and suffering is almost at an end. We are all nearly ready to make the journey back home to love.

And so we reach the end of this amazing journey together. I sincerely dedicate all the teachings in this book to your spiritual progress. May we join together, you and I, hand in hand and heart to heart, on the peak of the Radiant Mountain. Let us now rejoice together that the truth is available to us right here and now. Let us celebrate the fact that the means for removing all our self-imposed obstacles to knowing this truth have already been given to us. Let us commit ourselves, heart and soul to seeking for this truth with all our might, and let us promise one another that, once we have found it, we will share it selflessly, and extend it without limit until it bathes the entire universe in its love and its light.

Jason Chan's Courses, Retreats, and Merchandise

Jason Chan runs courses in Infinite Tai Chi, Infinite Chi Yoga and Ling Chi Healing in the UK and Ireland. Additionally, he runs several spiritual retreats each year in the UK, Ireland, Europe and Thailand. For further information and to order the merchandise below, please visit his website at www.lightfoundation.com

Book by Jason Chan

Seven Principles for Radiant Living
In the search for understanding and enlightenment in regard to the secrets of greater harmony in our lives and the world, we are drawn toward those teachings that convey the sometimes deep but simple beauty of ancient wisdom. Presented here are seven principles based on this timeless wisdom.

DVDs featuring Jason Chan

Infinite Tai Chi for Beginners
This DVD is suitable for people of all ages and levels of fitness. After an initial warm up routine, Jason Chan will lead you through three stages of the Infinite Tai Chi long form. Practising Infinite Tai Chi daily will revitalise your physical body, calm your mind and restore your spirit.

Infinite Tai Chi for Health
Jason Chan shows how you can regain physical, emotional and mental well-being in just 20 minutes each day using controlled breathing and simple, flowing body movements of the Infinite Tai Chi short form. The multi-screen camera work enables you to see Jason's movements from a range of angles so that you can follow him with ease and precision.

Infinite Chi Kung for Health
Infinite Chi Kung is a slow but dynamic sequence of controlled breathing and body movements designed to

assist you to cultivate radiant energy, physical strength and peace of mind. The more you practise Infinite Chi Kung, the more you will return to your natural state of being and unleash your infinite potential. Featured on this DVD are two Infinite Chi Kung exercises: The Golden Sun and Spirals in the Air.

Infinite Tai Chi

Beginning with just ten minutes of gentle practice of Infinite Tai Chi a day you could regain the power to tell your body how it feels. Infinite Tai Chi is a wholesome discipline for perfect harmony in life. Jason Chan takes you step by step through the form and the techniques of breathing and elemental movement.

Audio CDs featuring Jason Chan

Infinite Meditation

A sacred gift offered to those committed to pursuing their unique spiritual path. Jason Chan takes you through the sequence of his Infinite Meditation allowing you to tune your mind in, open your open your heart, and connect with the divine light.

Seven Stages to Spiritual Enlightenment

Eventually the whole of mankind will achieve enlightenment. These insights are shared to re-ignite the spirit of Truth. Jason Chan will take you through the seven stages to spiritual enlightenment beginning with a burning desire and culminating in divine integration..

Whole Life Journey for Abundance

Through many years of devotion to his personal inner spiritual journey, Jason reveals the wisdom, joy, love and peace Life waits to share with us.

ISBN 1425137482